SOUTH ASIAN WRITERS, LATIN AMERICAN LITERATURE, AND THE RISE OF GLOBAL ENGLISH

Ever since T. B. Macaulay leveled the accusation in 1835 that "a single shelf of a good European library was worth the whole native literature of India," South Asian literature has served as the imagined battleground between local linguistic multiplicity and a rapidly globalizing English. This book traces an unexpected journey to Latin America for South Asian literature in English. The cohort of authors that moved between these regions include Latin-American Nobel laureates Pablo Neruda and Octavio Paz; Booker Prize notables Salman Rushdie, Anita Desai, Mohammed Hanif, and Mohsin Hamid; and foundational literary and cultural figures such as Geeta Kapur, Jagdish Swaminathan, and Arvind Krishna Mehrotra. In their explorations of this new geographic connection, Roanne L. Kantor claims that they formed the vanguard of a new, multilingual world-literary order. Their encounters with Latin America fundamentally shaped the way in which literature written in English from South Asia exploded into popularity from the 1980s until the mid-2000s, enabling its global visibility.

ROANNE L. KANTOR is Assistant Professor of English at Stanford University. She has published in *Comparative Literature*; *Interventions*; *South Asia*; *Global South Studies*; *Comparative Studies of South Asia, Africa, and the Middle East*; and *Transmodernity*. Her translation of Juan José Saer's *La mayor* won the 2009 Susan Sontag Prize.

CAMBRIDGE STUDIES IN WORLD LITERATURE

Editors
Debjani Ganguly, University of Virginia
Francesca Orsini, SOAS University of London

World literature is a vital part of twenty-first-century critical studies. Globalization and unprecedented levels of connectivity through communication technologies force literary scholars to rethink the scale of literary production and their own critical practices. As an exciting field that engages seriously with the place and function of literary studies in our global era, the study of world literature requires new approaches. Cambridge Studies in World Literature is founded on the assumption that world literature is not all literatures of the world nor a canonical set of globally successful literary works. The series will highlight scholarship on literary works that focus on the logics of circulation drawn from multiple literary cultures and technologies of the textual. While not rejecting the nation as a site of analysis, the series will offer insights into new cartographies – the hemispheric, the oceanic, the transregional, the archipelagic, the multilingual local – that better reflect the multiscalar and spatially dispersed nature of literary production. It will highlight the creative coexistence, flashpoints, and intersections of language worlds from both the Global South and the Global North, as well as multiworld models of literary production and literary criticism that these have generated. It will push against existing historical, methodological, and cartographic boundaries and showcase humanistic and literary endeavors in the face of world-scale environmental and humanitarian catastrophes.

In This Series

Sarah Quesada
The Afro-Caribbean Heritage in Latinx Literature

Levi Thompson
Re-Orienting Modernism: Mapping a Modernist Geography Across Arabic and Persian Poetry

SOUTH ASIAN WRITERS, LATIN AMERICAN LITERATURE, AND THE RISE OF GLOBAL ENGLISH

ROANNE L. KANTOR

Stanford University

Shaftesbury Road, Cambridge CB2 8EA, United Kingdom

One Liberty Plaza, 20th Floor, New York, NY 10006, USA

477 Williamstown Road, Port Melbourne, VIC 3207, Australia

314–321, 3rd Floor, Plot 3, Splendor Forum, Jasola District Centre, New Delhi – 110025, India

103 Penang Road, #05–06/07, Visioncrest Commercial, Singapore 238467

Cambridge University Press is part of Cambridge University Press & Assessment, a department of the University of Cambridge.

We share the University's mission to contribute to society through the pursuit of education, learning and research at the highest international levels of excellence.

www.cambridge.org
Information on this title: www.cambridge.org/9781009018449

DOI: 10.1017/9781009039727

© Roanne Kantor 2022

This publication is in copyright. Subject to statutory exception and to the provisions of relevant collective licensing agreements, no reproduction of any part may take place without the written permission of Cambridge University Press & Assessment.

First published 2022
First paperback edition 2025

A catalogue record for this publication is available from the British Library

Library of Congress Cataloging-in-Publication data
NAMES: Kantor, Roanne L., author.
TITLE: South Asian writers, Latin American literature, and the rise of global English / Roanne L. Kantor, Stanford University.
DESCRIPTION: Cambridge ; New York, NY : Cambridge University Press, 2022. | Series: Cambridge studies in world literature | Includes bibliographical references and index.
IDENTIFIERS: LCCN 2021039880 (print) | LCCN 2021039881 (ebook) | ISBN 9781316510797 (hardback) | ISBN 9781009039727 (ebook)
SUBJECTS: LCSH: South Asian literature (English) – History and criticism. | South Asian literature (English) – Latin American influences. | English language – Foreign countries. | BISAC: LITERARY CRITICISM / General | LCGFT: Literary criticism.
CLASSIFICATION: LCC PR9570.S64 K36 2022 (print) | LCC PR9570.S64 (ebook) | DDC 820.9/954–dc23
LC record available at https://lccn.loc.gov/2021039880
LC ebook record available at https://lccn.loc.gov/2021039881

ISBN 978-1-316-51079-7 Hardback
ISBN 978-1-009-01844-9 Paperback

Cambridge University Press & Assessment has no responsibility for the persistence or accuracy of URLs for external or third-party internet websites referred to in this publication and does not guarantee that any content on such websites is, or will remain, accurate or appropriate.

To Hayden and Emmanuelle

Contents

List of Figures	*page* viii
Acknowledgments	ix
Introduction	1
1 Transmigrant: Neruda's Rebirth as the Soul of World Literature	31
2 Stranger: Paz's Peregrinations through Indian Poetry	57
3 Displacee: The Andalusian Allegory and Dreams of a Shared Past	88
4 Pilgrim: Journeys to the Roots of Magical Realism	113
5 Revenant: Dictator Fiction and Mobile Modernist Form	144
Epilogue	178
Notes	189
References	205
Index	225

Figures

1.1 Vivan Sundaram, "Portrait of Pablo Neruda," from *page* 36
    The Heights of Macchu Picchu (1972).
2.1 Vinod Ray Patel, "Portrait of Jorge Luis Borges," *Vrishchik*   77
    2–3, no. 12–1 (October/November 1971) (Patel 1971).
5.1 Cell 13 from Mohsin Hamid's "The (Former) General in His   159
    Labyrinth" (Hamid 2008).
5.2 "Map of Story" from planning documents for "The (Former)   160
    General in His Labyrinth" (Hamid 2010, 321).

Acknowledgments

The bibliography is a canon; the acknowledgments are its countershelf. The former inevitably includes some baggage we would rather leave behind. The latter frames the field as we would like it to be, a collection of supportive, chosen affiliations. In naming it, perhaps, we hasten that field's coming.

First I owe thanks to Cambridge University Press, my editor Ray Ryan, and the series editors Debjani Ganguly and Francesca Orsini. Their feedback, as well as that of the anonymous reviewers, greatly strengthened the arguments of the book. They understood this vision and shared their enthusiasm. I am thrilled to be part of this series. Thanks also to the Cambridge University Press production team: Edgar Mendez, Liz Davey, Gayathri Tamilselvan, and most especially Wade Guyitt for his thorough and thoughtful edits of this text.

Several institutions supported this research. My journey began at UCLA, where Ross Sheidler and Kathleen Komar introduced me to something called Comparative Literature and suggested I might want to keep going. The late, great Michael Henry Heim welcomed me to the world of literary translation – the world in which the authors in this book encountered and imagined one another. More than anyone else, he shaped me into a sensitive reader and grounded my understanding of translation not as a theoretical game but as a real labor, one undertaken out of love. That commitment was cemented when I was entrusted to translate the Argentinian writer Juan José Saer's *La mayor* (*The One Before*) by the prize committee at the Susan Sontag Foundation. David Reiff, Anne Jump, Susan Bernofsky, and Johanna McKeon supported that work. Rebecca Lippman tested every sentence of that translation with me. Fundación TyPa, Fundación PROA, and Open Letter Press helped bring it to fruition.

The University of Texas at Austin supported this research during graduate school. César Salgado, who shares with me a soft spot for *El mono gramático*, guided the first draft of these pages. Without his emphatic support, my very vague hunch about this book would have withered on the vine. This book is the "looking-glass twin" of the dissertation I wrote for him: "in many ways opposite and yet apparently identical." Many other faculty members in Austin mentored and supported me, including Elizabeth Richmond-Garza, Rupert Snell, Héctor Domínguez-Ruvalcaba, and Karen Grumberg. The office manager for the Program in Comparative Literature, Billy Fatzinger, kept us all afloat and added a bit of joy to every visit to the program office. Snehal Shingavi provided a model for studying literature written in English, something I did not yet imagine I was doing in graduate school. He helped me figure out how a comparatist finds her way into an English department. Syed Akbar Hyder prompted me to study Urdu and handed me the endlessly productive "Safarnāmāh-e Kyūbā." He also introduced me to Ellie Strand, Sara Grewal, Daniel Majchrowicz, and Anand Taneja, friends and scholars who have been essential in shaping the approach to Urdu in this book. Laura Brueck and Naminata Diabate have gone above and beyond as alumni mentors and role models. I owe so much to the group of graduate students with whom I studied, most of all Frank Strong, who showed me the ropes, Dusty Hixenbaugh and Katie Logan, who ran the course with me, and Hannah Alpert Abrams, for whom I was supposed to pave the way, though she just as often returned the favor. Michael Reyes and Amrita Mishra, who came after, have kept faith with what is best about literary study at Texas.

This project was also shaped by Cornell University and friends in Ithaca, which hosted me for almost a decade of visits while my husband was a graduate student and then postdoctoral fellow. Many friends shaped our time both there and in India, especially Anaar Desai-Stephens, Andrew Amstutz, Carter Higgins, Yasmine Singh, and Brinda Kumar. Many sweet memories and deep insights alike have come in conversation with you. Many of my best ideas came outdoors with our biking buddies Alicia Swords, Tim Shenk, Janice Gallagher, and her house full of writers. Visiting fellows at the Society for the Humanities brightened my time at Cornell, especially Ayelet Ben-Yishai and Rahul Mukherjee, with whom I had so much fun searching for the lost 1970s. I was also delighted and inspired by the postdocs who stayed on as professors, Naminata, Jenny Goldstein, and Matt Velasco. The South Asia Program hosted a 2017 invited talk about the South Asian "boom," which forms some of the background of this book. The faculty at Cornell has always astonished me with their generosity and collective brainpower. I learned so much from

Durba Ghosh and Bronwen Blesdoe, among many others. I have been humbled by the ongoing support of Debra Ann Castillo, who blows me away with her energy and collaborative spirit. She always knew there was something to this idea, and without her I would have never found it.

In Boston, my time teaching at Brandeis University, Boston University, and Harvard University shaped this book. Ulka Anjaria and Faith Smith gave me my first opportunity as a visiting professor in the Department of English at Brandeis. Many other faculty members welcomed me there, including Harleen Singh, Caren Irr, and Greg Childs. My time at Brandeis ushered me into a vibrant intellectual community in the Commonwealth of Massachusetts. Among its many luminaries, I owe special thanks to Isabel Gómez, Renee Hudson, Benjamin Siegel, Caterina Scaramelli, Kareem Khubchandani, Marina Bilbija, Aslı Zengin, Kate Nash, Kathleen Vandenberg, Stephanie Byttebier, Octavio González, Susan Ellison, and Liza Oliver.

At the Department of Comparative Literature at Harvard, Karen Thornber, Saul Zaritt, and Mariano Siskind were among the generous faculty who went out of their way to welcome me during my two-year post. It was that community that showed me how to think about world literature through fresh eyes. Karen, in addition to her inspiring commitment to deeply researched, multilingual, and historically grounded literary scholarship, went out of her way to help me get my sea legs on Quincy Street. Mariano wrote about magical realism with such fierce elegance and reminded me about that Chile section in *The Reluctant Fundamentalist*. Ateya Khorakiwalla and Anna Wilson shared with me the most intellectually productive space at Harvard: the MAC pool. Vivian Huang, Cécile Guédon, Lisa Gulesarian, and René Carrasco kept me company as part of the invisible edifice of lecturers without whom the Barker Center would cease to function. Ernest Mitchell, a true Harvard institution, embodied commitment to our students and their writing. He is also the most wonderful interlocutor on the topic of twentieth-century writers and their transnational inspirations. I appreciated the terrific undergraduate students who tested out this research with me: Kierin Kresevic Salazar, Hamna Nazir, José Coronado Flores, Iris Feldman, and Lucas Cuatrecasas, among many others.

This book was rewritten at Stanford University as a member of the Department of English. Gavin Jones, Paula Moya, Michaela Bronstein, Vaughn Rasberry, and Alex Woloch read a large volume of writing, saw something worthy in this idea, and asked penetrating questions that shaped its development. Ato Quayson read the entire manuscript and made a number of sharp critical comments. Ramón Saldívar, Michele Elam, Shelley Fisher Fishkin, Peggy Phelan, Elaine Treharne, Patricia Parker, Margaret Cohen, Nancy Rutenberg, Mark McGurl, Nick Jenkins, Blair Hoxby, Roland Green, Alice Staveley, Blakey Vermule, and Terry Castle have all provided mentorship and guidance on the long road to publication. John Bender is a model of energetic engagement and an unparalleled resource for institutional memory. Mark Greif and Mark Algee-Hewitt have been not only incredibly supportive colleagues but also welcoming neighbors. The two of them, along with Michaela, Tom Owens, and Esther Yu, have shared the task of navigating new faculty life here and made it a pleasure. Usha Iyer and Marci Kwon in the Department of Art and Art History offered me key insights about the visual arts discussed in this book. None of this would function without the hard work of the English department's dedicated office staff, Maritza Colon, Vivian Beebe Sana, Patrick Heyer, and Priscilla Catbagan. Academics tend to hide away in our offices – our staff encourage us out into the corridors and provide the social glue that makes Margaret Jacks Hall come alive. So many students have shaped my thinking for this project, but not least graduate students Radhika Koul, Alberto Quintero, Mai Wang, Helena Hu, Luke Williams, Alex Sherman, Emma Brush, Chiara Giovanni, and Chloe MacKinnon. So many insights that appear here were tested out in my class on the Indian novel, with its brilliant undergraduates, including Maddie Sunmi Kim, Ryan Sud, Nibha Akireddy, and Karunya Bhramasandra, among others. Much of the archival research in this book was made possible through generous funding from the Department of English, the Hellman Foundation, and the Department of Human Biology. The Stanford Humanities Center hosted an invaluable manuscript workshop organized by Kelda Jameson. I am deeply grateful to Ulka, Anjali Nerlekar, Sandra Berman, and Héctor Hoyos for their incredible generosity, insightfulness, and encouragement as readers. The book in your hands was deeply shaped by you.

Several libraries, collections, and archivists molded this project. As a graduate student, I profited from my proximity to the incredible Harry Ransom Center. I had no idea when I dropped by on a whim during my first year of graduate school that archival research would become such a key part of this project. I also benefited greatly from spending time at the Bombay Poets Archive at Cornell. In addition, this project was enriched by finds from the Widener Library at Harvard and the Bancroft Library at the University of California, Berkeley. This book was transformed by access to the collections of little magazines in the British Library and the companionship of so many other researchers in the Oriental and African reading room – especially Liza, Katie, and Fatima Burney. The Tinker Foundation funded my research in Chile, where I owe thanks to the Biblioteca Nacional and the Fundación Pablo Neruda, and their affiliates Javier Ormeño Bustos and Dario Oses Moya. Some of the most important meetings and finds happened in India. My former boss B. N. Varma at Primus Books tried his best to make me a precise reader and gave me a firsthand look into Indian publishing. The teachers at the American Institute of Indian Studies in Jaipur encouraged my explorations in Hindi. Rashmi Sadana wrote the most insightful book on that subject, *English Heart, Hindi Heartland*. She has always been generous with her advice, including the providential suggestion that I hang out at the Sahitya Akademi to "see what happens." Vibha Maurya is one of those who has long worked on a project like the one in this book. She was so generous with her time and resources regarding Neruda. Subhro Bandopadhyay built his own version of the countershelf at the Instituto Cervantes.

Workshops and conferences provided the space to hone these arguments. These were also places where many publications and many friendships were born. The 2015 Yale South Asia Workshop put together an unparalleled group where I met Madhumita Lahiri, Chris Moffatt, Katy Hardy, and Ethiraj Gabriel Dattatreyan, all of whom have had a hand in the direction of this project. Madhumita and I also collaborated on two other gatherings, a seminar at ACLA in 2016 and a preconference at Madison that fall. It has been a pleasure to think through the conundrum of the Global Anglophone with her. Magalí Armillas-Tiseyra invited me to work through ideas related to this project as part of the CLCS Global South at MLA in 2018. Her scholarship on dictator fiction has been foundational for this book. Susan Wadley has been organizing the Madison "Dissertation to Book" Workshop for years, which helped me measure my dissertation against more mature projects of many scholars who are now also friends. Fatima brought me to SOAS for a talk in 2017 and encouraged me to attend the 2019 Postcolonial Print Workshop organized by Francesca. Literally all of the presentations were brilliant, but this book has been particularly shaped by Neelam Srivastava, Duncan Yoon, Hala Halim, Laetitia Zecchini, Venkat Mani, Ruvani Ranasinha, Shital Pravinchandra, and Paulo Horta. Anjali, who built the Bombay Poets Archive, wrote the book on it and then suggested that, perhaps, I should make a serious search for the lost 1970s inside. This swept away the book I had been planning and set the foundations for this one to rise in its place.

Ragini Srinivasan had the idea to craft an intellectual community out of a cohort of job seekers. This is the group who have seen more of this book than almost anyone: Nasia Anam, Monika Bhagat Kennedy, Akshya Saxena, and our more recent addition, Kalyan Nadiminti. Nasia also facilitated friendships with Fatima, Isabel, Renee, Marina, and later Duncan and Yu-ting Huang. I'm awed by their collective brainpower. Fellow travelers like Daniel Elam and Paul Nadal, who didn't even know me when they offered a keen editorial eye but have since become friends. This whole cohort of scholars came of age in the "meantime" between economic emergencies. Along with those crises came a set of terms including "the Global Anglophone" and all of their many conditions. We did not choose them, but we did not shrink from them either.

My search has been buoyed by others looking for the countershelf, who inspired me to keep going. My deep thanks to Subhro, Vivan Sundaram, Taimiya Zaman, A. K. Mehrotra, and Karan Mahajan, who spoke to me directly about their brilliant work. Atreyee Gupta, Bhavya Tiwari, Gayatri Gopinath, Vibha, Shital, and Deb are all investigating literary and artistic connections between these two regions. They are, collectively, "another hand, unknown to you," one that reached out to me and to this project. There is so much yet to be done, and I can't wait to see how they will do it.

I owe the deepest debt of thanks to my family. My parents Susan Sharp and Glenda Sharp and my little sister Azure Sharp never, ever doubted. My twin sister Sonja Sharp began pushing me in the womb and never, ever stopped! She has talked through every notion that ever had to do with this book, while her husband Tal Sholklapper and her son Ram Sholklapper provided joyful breaks in between. My grandmother Gladys Kruger mailed me books by the boxful. I attribute my early interest in the world of letters to her. My aunt Karen Kruger pushed me out the door and into the world. She and my cousins Clare Kruger, Noah Pen-Kruger, Aaron Pen-Kruger, and Elijah Pen-Kruger created a home away from home for me growing up. My Connecticut family, David Kruger, Riva Lewinter, Ben Kruger, Joel Kruger, and Sophie Kruger, made me welcome all the years I visited and lived on the East Coast. My family by marriage, Patricia Kantor, Alan Kantor, and Danielle Kantor, welcomed me with open arms. I have been tinkering with this idea the whole decade we have known each other, and their support has meant the world to me. Their extended family, the New York and San Francisco Kolnicks, the Boston Kerbels, and the London Kantors, likewise have done so much to support me and this research over the years. There are also friends who have become like family: the Scanlons, the Brownsteins, the Leaffers, and the Azads.

My husband, Hayden Kantor, has thought with me about this project more than anyone. This book and its author would have been adrift without him. Hayden read every word of every draft multiple times. If you object to a line in this book, I likely kept it against his objections; if you like something, you can be sure he has approved it. This book is dedicated to you, my most careful and constant reader, and to the other collaborative project that we recently brought to fruition: our daughter Emmanuelle.

Introduction

> As the evening rolled on, [Faiz] and Neruda recited to one another. The translators did their bit and translated from Spanish into English and Urdu into English but as the night wore on both poets dispensed with the translators. [Faiz] was reciting to Neruda in Urdu and he was reciting to [Faiz] in Spanish and I think both of them understood one another perfectly.
>
> (Hashmi, Hashmi, and Razvi 2011)

One night in 1962, the renowned Pakistani poet Faiz Ahmed Faiz found himself in an impromptu transnational *mushāʿirah*, or poetry recitation, with the Chilean poet and future Nobel Prize laureate Pablo Neruda. According to a recollection of the event by Faiz's daughters, the exchange produced an almost mystical form of "perfect understanding."[1]

Forty years later, the renowned Pakistani novelist Mohsin Hamid would have his own encounter with Neruda, this time through a visit to the dead poet's home in Valparaíso, Chile. It is this imagined confrontation that frames the personal crisis and political awakening of his protagonist, Changez, at the climax of Hamid's novel *The Reluctant Fundamentalist* (2006). Like Faiz's dream of perfect understanding, Hamid uses Neruda's ghostly presence to offer a glimpse of an alternative vision of world literature that could have connected places like Pakistan and Chile outside the mediation of English or the economic interests of its empires. It is a vision that is fulfilled by Hamid's intertextual gesture, even as it is seemingly betrayed by the language of its composition.

This book traces an unexpected journey to Latin America, a journey through which we can understand the multilingual world that both haunts and continues to shape South Asian literature in English. The cohort of authors that moved between these regions includes Latin American Nobel laureates Pablo Neruda and Octavio Paz. They are joined by Booker Prize notables Salman Rushdie, Anita Desai, Mohammed Hanif, and Mohsin

Hamid. These globally familiar names accompany a host of literary and cultural figures who range from foundational writers of the 1960s like Geeta Kapur and Zulfikar Ghosh to up-and-coming authors like Tanuj Solanki. In their explorations of this historically unprecedented geographic connection, these authors formed the vanguard of what they dreamed might be a new world-literary order. And they remain haunted by that multilingual dream even when writing in a language, English, whose global spread threatens to eradicate it.

The study of "global" literature written in English is haunted in turn, rooted in a long-standing relationship to Latin America that it does not acknowledge, one that binds it indelibly to literary traditions outside itself and its carefully cultivated coterie of linguistic others. Personal relationships and later intertextual exchanges fueled by the Latin American "boom" of the 1960s–70s did more than enable a series of essential – and understudied – stylistic developments in South Asian fiction. They also set the template for the emergence of South Asian fiction as a market phenomenon from the 1980s onward, enabling it to enjoy pride of place as a premier literature of the new global order (Kantor 2018).

This was the era when South Asian Anglophone fiction gained institutional power as the primary regional exemplar for variously constructed literary spaces: the Commonwealth, then the postcolonial world, and now, possibly, the Anglophone globe. These are the major geographic-cum-conceptual categories through which literature from the Global South is legitimized in institutions of the Global North. Ironically, it was at this very moment of ascendance that such academic frameworks progressively excluded Latin America and Hispanophone literature from concepts of a shared literary world, consolidating their boundaries as de facto English-exclusive categories.

And yet, even as this institutional understanding of South Asian literature was growing in force, South Asian authors themselves were constructing a "countershelf" of Latin American literature. This reference "shelf" of model authors, ideal texts, and shared styles functioned as a strategy to break away from the inherited, overdetermined significance of writing in English and to build a world-literary fantasy of solidarity to stand in its place. Spanning novel, essay, and memoir, poetry and prose, these fantasies sometimes took the form of ersatz personal genealogies, ones that frequently imagined reincarnation as a technology of connection across space and time. More often, they invoked a kind of psychic connection created at the moment of Columbus' original mistake: the transposition of the "East Indies" onto the West. They also adapted a long-standing interest in al-Andalus to link the conquests of Latin America and South Asia conceptually through medieval Spain. And they came together around the unique capacity of narrative form – whether modernist or magically real – to represent shared legacies of colonial oppression. Rushdie puts it just this way, describing the space that brings together South Asian and Latin American writing "bounded by frontiers which are neither political nor linguistic but imaginative" (Rushdie 1992, 69).

In different ways, all of these fantasies encode wonder at the world's unexpectedness, along with a form of equality that does not erase multiplicity. They rely on the world's vastness – both spatially and temporally – to retain a capacity for newness, making associations that did not exist, that could not have been imagined, until they appeared. Here, specifically literary aesthetics of wonder – expressed in terms like *a'jūbe, extrañeza,* and *asombro* – act as a category of practice that can counter the dull cultural flattening of the "globe" that the rise of the Anglophone seems to presage. The related idea of "unexpectedness" offers a category of analysis that scholarship can take up from these authors, allowing us to grasp patterns of association these authors created and argued for, ones poorly anticipated by existing frameworks for the study of planet-wide circulatory theories.

The countershelf fantasy is fundamentally one of reading – often, as we shall see, literally situated on a bookshelf. Yet it also operates like a mirror with two distinct but related facets. For Faiz, Latin America is a looking glass, a location of immediate, unexpected self-recognition. For Hamid, it is a rearview mirror, one that enables a backward gaze onto the past as both a site of nostalgic identification and a possible model for the future. These relational fantasies endure across decades of literary production, even as more overtly political categories of association – Third World, postcolonial, Global South – have waxed and waned. And it was by embracing the fantasy of the countershelf, imagining themselves not as a minor subset of a British or South Asian canon but as equal contributors to this worldly tradition, that South Asian authors made the unexpected journey to the very heart of "Global English."

"The World as India": Locating the Stalemate between World Literature and Global English

Shortly before her death in 2005, Susan Sontag delivered a lecture affirming the value of world literature in translation, an essay she titled "The World as India" (Sontag 2007). It now appears as the herald for the posthumous translation fellowship funded by her estate. For her, the

Indian subcontinent is, at once, home to a spectacular proliferation of literary languages and the vanguard of English-speaking as a global phenomenon. Lament over the effects of the latter is expressed here, as in so much cultural criticism of that era, through the concept-metaphor of the call center worker (Srinivasan 2018a). India thus locates the essay's conflict between a multilingual, egalitarian sphere facilitated by translation and the looming threat of a hierarchized, technologized Anglophone globe.

Opening with Sontag – who was by no means an expert in South Asian or postcolonial literature – captures the two major critical anxieties this monograph seeks to address. The first is that multilingual world literature and what we now call Global Anglophone literature are and always have been enemies, foils, and fierce combatants in a winner-take-all contest for the planet. Second, but related, South Asia is the key battleground for this contest, being the location of both an exemplary multilingualism and a particular historical, geopolitical, and economic vulnerability to English.[2] To understand the appeal of the countershelf, it is first necessary to account for this long-standing stalemate, which South Asian authors are using Latin American literature to "counter."

South Asia has played this tense dual role of multilingual hotbed and Anglophone vanguard since the colonial era. Perhaps predictably, no document of the era more clearly articulates that tension than T. B. Macaulay's "Minute on Indian Education" in 1835. Almost any writing about South Asian literature in English begins with a ritual invocation of the Macaulay Minute (Bhabha 1984; Mukherjee 2000; Bahri 2003). Macaulay's memorandum to the British Council of India on the subject of Indian education is the document that undergirded the decision to fund English-medium instruction, and defund education in other languages, in colonial India. Though the decision itself was much more complex, the Macaulay Minute has come to stand metonymically for the whole ideological apparatus of English education and, through it, for the logic of British colonization as such (Bhabha 1984; Vishwanathan 1989; Spivak 1999). As Venkat Mani argues, Macaulay's statement essentially inaugurates the Anglophone–World polemic that Sontag and so many others will continually reanimate thereafter (Mani 2017, 58–62).

Beyond its standing as a legal document, references to the Minute endure because of the specific rhetorical flourishes through which Macaulay justifies his position, rhetorics our fields are still working to counter. In the document's second-most infamous phrase, he justifies the defunding of Sanskrit and Arabic scholarship in favor in English by stating baldly that "a single shelf of a good European library was worth the whole native literature of India and Arabia" (Macaulay 1835).

This spectre of the "single, good shelf" is one that arguably haunts traditional understandings of world literature as much as the postcolonial context in which it is more often invoked. Indeed, so much scholarship in these fields hinges on a particular imagined location in which readers encounter texts. Emily Apter imagines world literature as a sort of museum shaped by decontextualizing and appropriative acts of curation (Apter 2013). Both Gayatri Spivak and Gauri Vishwanathan understand it as the university classroom, implicating education in the process of indoctrination (Viswanathan 1989; Spivak 2005). Aamir Mufti, Priya Joshi, and Venkat Mani construe it as a library defined by uneven forms of circulation and state sponsorship (Joshi 2002; Mufti 2016; Mani 2017). Several scholars invoke an airport kiosk as a metaphor for world literature's rootless cosmopolitan elitism paired with its middlebrow aesthetics (Watroba 2018). More recent South Asian criticism invokes instead the pavement bookseller as an object lesson in the inequalities of linguistic and educational access that underlie literary production in the Global South (Narayanan 2012; Sadana 2012).

It should call our attention that all of these bookshelves of world-literary contestation are institutional, shaped by either the market or the state. As Pheng Cheah astutely notes, "recent theories of world literature ... define the world in terms of the circulation of commodities, that is, as the expression, field, and product of transnational market exchange" (Cheah 2016, 6). This observation about "recent theories" holds just as true for studies of globally circulating literature originally written in English. Economic and political concepts predominate both fields: world systems theory, or evolutionary theory, combined and uneven development, or even Orientalism (Moretti 2000; Casanova 2004; WReC 2015; Mufti 2016). In addition to the market, scholars have also preferred circulatory systems that track neatly onto histories of domination (postcolonial studies) or geographic contiguity (area studies and the "oceanic turn"). Even the turn toward digitally mediated "distant reading," as Lauren Klein argues, likewise runs into the problem of "scale," in which the preference for large volumes of texts is inadequately attentive to "the subject positions that are too easily (if at times unwittingly) occluded when taking a distant view" (Klein 2018).

These models leave little space to explore how world literature can operate in the way Sontag describes, as a location of positive affiliation and growing worldly consciousness for her own development as a writer.

Instead, the focus on institutional circulation produces a bifurcated agential model in which authors, especially those from the Global South, are cast as cynically omnipotent market masterminds, while at the same time, and with no apparent irony, utterly helpless victims of various systems that deliver a certain kind of literature to their doorstep and force them to recapitulate it (Jameson 1986; Brennan 1989; Lazarus 2011). Increasingly, these authors are charged with eagerly hastening an era of predictable, eminently digestible, and stylistically moribund "global lowbrow" (n+1 2013; Fisk 2018; Watroba 2018).[3]

Resistance to these systems can only be imagined as, on the one hand, a strategic essentialism and exoticism, a kind of ironic knowingness about one's capitulation to global forces, or, on the other, an intransigent refusal of circulation through incommensurability and untranslatability (Huggan 2001; Brouillette 2007; Melas 2007; Spivak 2009; Apter 2013; Chakravorty 2014). Any kind of relationality encoded in such gestures is profoundly hierarchical and negative – to do with the refusal of relations between North and South. Responsive to the historical violence of comparison, they emphasize difference without leaving space for the way authors themselves thought and wrote in comparative terms.

The turn toward incommensurability preserves a particular type of "innocence" of Global South writers from capital in its social, political, and economic forms. This innocence safeguards the author's worthiness for scholars in the Global North. But it also preordains the powerlessness of these literatures on the world stage, functioning, as Miriam Ticktin explains, "only insofar as it is a space of freedom from desire, will, or agency" (Ticktin 2017, 579). As Gloria Fisk argues, such an attachment to innocence in world-literary studies might also be read through Pierre Bourdieu's analysis of the literary field, in which authors' legible desire for, will to, or agency around success operates inversely to their perceived deservingness of it (Fisk 2018). This makes it all but impossible to theorize gestures of South–South solidarity as something more than symbolic, as actually significant forces in literary history.

A quite similar set of unsatisfying binaries arise in the study of writing from the Global South originally produced in English. They, too, radiate out from the Macaulay Minute. Its most infamous and frequently cited lines have come to dominate the discussion of English as a literary language in South Asia, the ones in which the spread of English is the means to create "a class of persons Indian in blood and colour, but English in tastes, in opinions, in morals and in intellect" (Macaulay 1835). English, then, is no mere language in Macaulay's figuration. It is a vector that deforms the whole embodied experience, the very self of South Asian subjects, bending it to the will of colonial domination (Bhabha 1984; Mukherjee 2000; Bahri 2003). This transformation, moreover, was to be affected by an education in English literature, directly implicating both object and discipline in the program of colonization (Viswanathan 1989). This document, this phrase, is the traumatic origin of South Asian Anglophone literature – perhaps all Anglophone literature, since policies enacted first in India became standard across the empire (Gikandi 2014). How could any author hope to redeem the practice of writing in English from such an origin?

Simon Gikandi summarizes the common answer for postcolonial studies. He summarizes the common polemic in which writers "have limited options: they could master English and use it to create a literature of their own, or they could make an epistemic break with the language and turn to the mother tongue as a place of reconciliation" (Gikandi 2014, 11). The binary opposition of this answer elides the many colonial and postcolonial writers who wrote in multiple languages without experiencing it as particularly fraught or traumatic. To put it more pointedly, this framing reinforces a narrative convenient to the Anglophone center of postcolonial studies, one in which sticking with the "mother tongue" guarantees the innocent intransigence that means that literature will circulate only locally, leaving English as the single, naturalized pathway into the globe.

Pervasive in scholarship of the Anglophone globe is the idea that, if one chooses English, either one may unproblematically adopt British literary influence or one may use English to "write back" to Empire (Ashcroft, Griffiths, and Tiffin 2002). Scholars of English literature often cue this choice through the Shakespearean metaphor of Ariel and Caliban, where the latter's English becomes a resistant tool against its erstwhile master: "You taught me language; and my profit on't / Is I know how to curse" (*The Tempest*, 1.2.437–438). This dyad of colonial selfhood is so self-evidently "English-y" that we might forget it doesn't come from English at all: it was actually first pioneered at the turn of the twentieth century by an Uruguayan writer named José Enrique Rodó (Rodó [1900] 1988).[4]

It is now commonplace to observe how the "obsolete postcolonial and ironically acutely Eurocentric cliché of 'writing back' to the West" maintains English (especially British literature) at the center of an ostensibly decolonized literary project (Zecchini 2014, 17; Yoon 2015, 245). But there are problems, too, in upholding "local," "mother tongue," or "vernacular" languages – often referred to as *bhasha*s in South Asianist scholarship – as the sole safeguard of postcolonial authenticity. First, this position reifies a Eurocentric language ideology of the "mother tongue" that did not historically exist in places like South Asia (Yildiz 2013; Orsini 2015; Mufti 2016). More troublingly, it paints postcolonial scholarship into a corner from which the only convincing avenue to rehabilitate Anglophone writing is to claim that it never really was written in English but is always already translated – perhaps "born translated" – from the author's authentic mother tongue.[5] This figuration, one ironically presented as resistant to Anglophone domination, can conceive of no cosmopolitan, "foreign" languages but only admits other languages as "vernaculars" already familiar to the author – a construction thoroughly critiqued by Mufti (Mufti 2016). These languages and their literatures end up fulfilling an imagined relationship of subservience, the local insiders that foil English's pervasive and exclusive rights to the outside, the "globe."

These patterns reappear in the common histories of South Asian literature in English. They are cast either as a set of multilingual and cosmopolitan relationships geographically limited to the subcontinent or as an English-mediated entrée onto the world. The latter is shaped by relationships of contest against, collaboration with, and ultimately capitulation to the former colonizing power.[6] Despite their differences, both start with the Indian novelist Mulk Raj Anand, and both end with Rushdie.

This first set of narratives about Anand emphasize his identity as, to playfully tweak Orsini's term, a "multilingual local": someone who enacts a kind of cosmopolitanism through their facility with the multiple languages, registers, and cultural contexts of a single region (Orsini 2015). Let us borrow Orsini's apt phrasing and declare this the "local" narrative. Often in tandem with authors like Ahmed Ali and Raja Rao, such narratives recall Anand's intimate association with the multilingual collective the All India Progressive Writers Association, his and others' facility with other languages of India, and his relationship to the struggle for Indian Independence. These stories use Mulk Raj Anand as an exemplar for the transformation of Anglophone literature from niche to mainstream, prefiguring the much more forceful emergence of the Anglophone novel in the 1980s and the political rise of English in India in the 1990s. They also call on Anand to parallel the larger story of English in India in this period, which found its footing as a language of administration, education, and business – a "global" language, in short – unexpectedly, almost by accident, emerging as a stopgap to fill political vacuums left by fierce contests between (in the case of India) Hindi and South Indian Dravidian languages.

Ruvani Ranasinha tells a different story about Anand, one that routes through London. Let's call this the "abroad" narrative.[7] Beginning with Anand's memoir *Conversations in Bloomsbury* (1981), Ranasinha traces

Anand's personal relationships with literary figures – especially E. M. Forster – as well as the way his writing was received and marketed in the United Kingdom (Ranasinha 2007). She emphasizes the difficulty that Anand had in finding a robust British readership and his compromises with the exoticizing desires of the publishing establishment that had no idea how to market his writing (Ranasinha 2007). This sets up a contrast with later chapters where, she claims, the emergence of first V. S. Naipaul and later Rushdie paved the way for an entirely new reception of writing by authors of South Asian origin (Ranasinha 2007).

Both narratives about Mulk Raj Anand do important work to push back against the assumption that Anglophone writing is only a few decades old, coinciding tidily with the massive uptick in attention that such writing has garnered since the 1980s, centered around the figure of Rushdie. For the sake of simplicity, let us say that Rushdie's publication of and Man Booker Prize for *Midnight's Children* (1981) was the transformative moment for South Asian Anglophone writing. Consider, for example, the way that title has been played upon in the apt description of Indian literary historiography divided into "before" and "after" midnight (Joshi 2002) or contests between Anglophone and *bhasha* writing, described respectively as midnight's "children" and "orphans" (Shankar 2012). Even now, scores of scholarly articles and monographs center on this author and novel, all seeming to validate Neil Lazarus' infamous quip that "there is in a strict sense only one author in the postcolonial literary canon. That author is Salman Rushdie" (Lazarus quoted in Sorensen 2010, 11).

Still, while asserting a continuity between Anand's moment and ours, these narratives actually reveal a curious rupture. Both at home and abroad, South Asian Anglophone literature was a struggling, puny thing. Until, suddenly, it wasn't. Rushdie's string of successes over the course of the 1980s presaged a larger South Asian "boom," starting with Vikram Seth's record-breaking advance for *A Suitable Boy* (1994), hitting an early peak with Arundhati Roy's record-shattering payment and Booker Prize win for *The God of Small Things* (1998), and waning after twin literary events – the Booker Prize for *The White Tiger* and the Best Picture Oscar for *Slumdog Millionaire* (based on the 2006 novel *Q&A*) – a decade later in 2008 (Kantor 2018). Foundational critic Meenakshi Mukherjee poses a question that no later scholar has sufficiently answered: "Why are we suddenly witnessing a total reversal at the end of the 20th century when an unmistakable and ebullient proliferation of fiction in English written by both resident and non-resident Indians has become a globally recognised and consequently a nationally highlighted phenomenon" (Mukherjee 2000, 13)?

Following a pattern set by Mukherjee, both local and abroad historiographies jump abruptly from the very full archive of the 1930s–50s to the dramatic rupture of 1981 and everything that came after. Each essentially brushes aside the 1960s and 1970s as if they don't matter.[8] This critical feint on the matter of literary historiography becomes more baffling still when we consider the essential role that Indian literature in English played in the establishment of a narrative about postcolonial literature. The startling shift in reception for South Asian Anglophone writing – beginning in the 1980s, coming into full bloom in the 1990s and early 2000s, and slowly withering over the last ten to fifteen years – traces roughly the same timeline that marks the rise, dominance, and quiescence of postcolonial studies. The problem of the missing midcentury in India is now a problem for the periodicity of the entire project of narrating "global" writing in English, one that endures even as the specific power of postcolonial studies has declined.

In truth, the event that unites South Asian writing from the 1950s with South Asian writing in the 1980s happened neither locally nor in some narrowly defined Anglophone "abroad." It originated, instead, in Latin America, in the "boom" of Hispanophone writing in the 1960s and its worldwide proliferation in English during the 1970s. While the most obvious utility of "boom" literature to South Asian authors was as a pathway out of the contest between Anglophone literature and its "vernacular" foil, Latin American writing of this period also offered a model for moving beyond the increasingly orthodox social realism of the Independence-era progressive writers, without abandoning politics altogether. The turn to Latin America extends well beyond the development of so-called postcolonial magical realism – the only part of this transnational exchange to have ever garnered critical attention. Instead, it concerns a pervasive development of stylistic and thematic approaches adapted from "boom" superstars like Gabriel García Márquez, Mario Vargas Llosa, and Julio Cortázar, as well as earlier canonical figures like Alejo Carpentier, Jorge Luis Borges, César Vallejo, Neruda, and Paz. At the level of style, topic, and perhaps especially persona, these writers provided a blueprint for writing about issues common to the Global South, including models for negotiating how those areas would become legible to readers in the Global North.

To understand the particular appeal of Latin American literature for these authors requires a return to the rhetoric of Macaulay's second-most-infamous phrase, in the endless polemic it forces between "the native literatures of India" and the "good shelf" of writing in the colonizer's tongue. Nearly 200 years later, the same dyad plays out in Sontag's India-focused lament for world literature and in dozens of scholarly monographs about postcolonial writing in English. After the rupture of colonization, there is no going back to a pure version of "native literature." Nor can one unproblematically bury oneself in the "European library" Macaulay endorses. Instead, again and again, South Asian authors have navigated toward a third option. They invented a countershelf.

The Countershelf

The countershelf is a collection of texts, authors, and locations of world literature through which writers in the Global South identify against the Anglophone globe in which they are simultaneously compelled to circulate.[9] While its primary metaphor is the bookshelf, the countershelf encompasses a diverse array of gestures that includes all four categories of world-literary "contact" described by Karen Thornber. These are solitary "readerly contact" with texts outside one's home culture; interpersonal "writerly contact" with foreign authors; the kind of "textual contact" that structures new writing based on inheritances of style; and "linguistic contact," in which the political meaning of a globally hegemonic language, English, is reinterpreted through its indebtedness to relatively less powerful tongues like Spanish and Urdu (Thornber 2009, 2).

Like the concept of a "counterpublic" from which it takes its name, the countershelf uses literature to enact a minoritized discursive space, one irreducible to – though not untouched by – either the economy or the state (Fraser 1990). As Nancy Fraser and, later, Michael Warner have argued, counterpublics are not automatically constituted out of minoritized communities – in this case, Anglophone authors from the formerly colonized world (Fraser 1990; Warner 2002). Nor does a counterpublic take particular positions – Third Worldism, let's say – as ideologically pregiven. By the same token, Karima Laachir, Sara Marzagora, and Francesca Orsini remind us "the world" of world literature "is not a given, but is produced by different, embodied and located actors," a perspective they explicitly contrast with the systematized theories of world circulation described earlier (Laachir, Marzagora, and Orsini 2018, 294).

In this sense, the countershelf is more closely aligned with a concept like the Global South. Unlike the postcolonial world, which is defined externally by the historical fact of having been colonized by Europe, many theorizations of the Global South emphasize a form of consciousness, a "mutual recognition of shared circumstances by those groups that are disadvantageously positioned within the capitalist world system" (Armillas-Tiseyra 2019, 6).[10] Central to the concept of a countershelf, then, is an author's active choice to affiliate to another part of the world, the dynamic range of meanings that can be ascribed to that choice, and the ability of one participant to disagree with others about what fits on the shelf and how to interpret it.

This ideological flexibility allows the countershelf to extend beyond a particular moment or movement. As we shall see, Neruda's popularity held steady, even as the communist internationalism that attracted South Asian authors of the 1950s and 1960s became anathema to certain passionate adherents of later generations. In the 1990s, the scholarly community progressively lost faith in the radical potential of magical realism as an authentic Third Worldist form, but García Márquez's modernism remained appealing to South Asian authors well into the 2000s. The politics of the countershelf emerge not uniformly but through the constellation of these very different uses that rely, paradoxically, on the same attachments, the same core imaginary.

"No single text can create a public" like the one the countershelf enacts (Warner 2002, 62). For this reason, the itinerary of a single author or work is insufficient to grasp it, though much scholarship on world literature has proceeded in that mode. Instead, the shelf must meet the threshold of "significance," in the way Laachir, Marzagora, and Orsini have described: "trajectories and imaginaries that are *recurrent* and/or that *matter* to actors and texts" (Laachir, Marzagora, and Orsini 2018, 294, emphasis original). The countershelf is *recurrent* in a sense that aligns with the literary "contact nebulae" explored by Thornber – it occurs not author-to-author or text-to-text but tradition-to-tradition (Thornber 2009).[11] South Asian authors almost always drew on what they considered a Latin American tradition constituting several authors, or at the very least several texts that made up the career arc of a single author. Likewise, the countershelf *matters* because it acts as an enduring discourse of affiliation and resistance that helped many differently situated authors negotiate their own positions within the tradition of South Asian literature and the field of world literature. As the site of that negotiation, the gesture toward Latin America seems to have offered, almost despite itself, a major pathway to the commercialization of South Asian writing in English (Kantor 2018).

We might think about the countershelf in the idiom through which Paz once described his time in India: "frank realism allied with delirious fantasy" (Paz 1998, 32–33). What would it mean to follow Paz's lead and let frank realism and delirious fantasy act as "allies," in which neither reveals the insufficiency of the other? Following Warner's description of counterpublics, the relationships established on the countershelf are "imaginary, which is not to say unreal. . . . Their imaginary character is never merely a matter of private fantasy" (Warner 2002, 55). The exploration of a countershelf can reveal shared imaginaries that undergird certain practices of reading and writing but must also follow through the real conditions that enable those readings and the real effects they produce in the field.

For South Asian authors, the basic contours of countershelf fantasy were these: Latin American writing achieved world circulation outside of English and the political and economic structures that sustain it. That tradition, moreover, developed a set of representational modes that were particularly appropriate to the experiences they shared with authors from South Asia. Finally, the health and survival of multilingual local writing was inextricably bound up with the survival of such a sphere at the level of the world. As such, the consumption of Hispanophone writing – albeit in English translation – can be part of the project of constructing a truly multilingual literary world, even for authors who themselves write in English.

It must be underscored that these fantasies do not accord with a more scholarly approach to Latin American literature.[12] They consistently underestimate the Eurocentrism of authors like Carpentier and especially Borges, while at the same time participating in some of the exoticizing "Occidentalist" projections that made their literatures marketable in English. Even so, countershelf fantasies are still operative, even today, among South Asian authors, and their operation has created its own set of realities in South Asian literature.

A Countershelf Is Contrary

It doesn't take much to build a countershelf. It can be as simple as a list of books. Partway through his 2011 essay, "Seven Places in My Heart," the Pakistani novelist Mohammed Hanif recalls living in "a dead poet's house," a "world of wonder" that consisted of:

> Nothing but books. Many-times thumbed books, read with love, passages underlined, reactions noted, little slips of paper with cross-references inserted, obscure words circled and explained. Here, your housemates are Borges, Calvino, and Muhammad Khalid Akhtar. You have always read books, but you've never really learned to read like this. Here, each book you pick up comes with the gentle guidance of your late landlord, Sagheer Malal. He tutors you from beyond, he teaches you the bleeding obvious, you can't write if you don't know how to read. (Hanif 2011)

But if the concept requires "nothing but books," not just any books will do. It's notable that, on the countershelf for this Anglophone novelist, nobody is composing in English. The three authors are exemplary in their linguistic and generic diversity: a homegrown Urdu poet, a European essayist and novelist, and a short-story writer from Argentina.

In one sense, the sheer diversity of genres represented here and in other countershelf gestures belies the common critical assertion that novels are the privileged site of Worldly or Global circulation. And yet, there seems to be a kind of longing that registers in the repeated turn to other genres – poetry above all – a suggestion that these forms encode a kind of literary resistance to the novel's hegemony. Poetry, because of its investment in form, because of its special attention to language, because of metrical and rhyme schema too fragile to be easily transported, has long been understood to be untranslatable. To invoke the old chestnut by Robert Frost, poetry is defined by its loss in translation. This is precisely why the iconic countershelf fantasy of world literature – mystical mutual intelligibility – usually emerges around poetry rather than prose. For equal and opposite reasons, conceptions of the Global Anglophone have tended to coalesce around the novel – a single, robustly mobile form, whose linguistic specifications are, well, less specific.

Such contrarianism is the first and most important element of the countershelf. As much as the gesture toward Latin American literature is positive and affiliative, its primary meaning emerges in the negative, the way it allows a particular English-language writer to stand against the dominant codes of the Anglophone sphere. It is the rhetoric through which, for instance, Rushdie aligns with "literature, in many languages ... [of] the less powerful, or the powerless" to insist in 1983 that the Anglophone-exclusive category of Commonwealth Literature "Does Not Exist" (Rushdie 1992, 61–70). Its key gestures insist that English writing emerges out of what is *not* English and that novels emerge out of what are *not* novels. In line with Madhumita Lahiri's rehabilitation of the Global Anglophone through Rabindranath Tagore, authors sought a "use of English to build an emphatically non-Eurocentric internationalism" (Lahiri 2020, 26). They turned to Hispanophone literature in translation to argue that literary diversity can be preserved in forms that initially seem inimical to it.

A Countershelf Is Curated

Nor is the shelf inert, pregiven. Instead, it requires a particular type of relationship, Hanif's concept of the "gentle guidance" of a local mentor, or the discrimination of an individual taste. This echoes Walter Benjamin's

"Unpacking my Library" (1931), which celebrates the individual collector as an agentive creator of literary meaning, and how the books arrive on the shelf is sometimes more important than what they say (Benjamin 1968). In "Seven Places in My Heart," world literature passes through the quite literally deforming hands of local writers – ones that thumb, underline, and circle (Hanif 2011). Hanif here seems to offer a pretty tidy illustration of Damrosch's model of elliptical circulation, through which literature arising in one region is productively deformed as it moves into receiving traditions (Damrosch 2003).

Discussions of curation in a world-literary context tend to emphasize collections put together by experts – hence the appearance of the state library, the national museum, and the official syllabus as primary sites of its imagining. In this vein, the Anglophone novelist Amitav Ghosh describes his initial disillusionment in "The Testimony of My Grandfather's Bookcase" (1998) when he comes to discover that his forebearer's seemingly eclectic multilingual literary collection was, in fact, curated by another actor – the Nobel Prize.

Yet Ghosh goes on to reveal something unexpected. "This idea [of world literature] may well have had its birth in Europe but I suspect it met with a much more enthusiastic reception outside" (Ghosh 1998). Here he echoes Priya Joshi's insights about the "centripetal" force exerted by Indian readers on British literature (Joshi 2002, 11). Books do indeed often circulate from North to South, or reach various Souths only through translators and publishers in the North. But the meaning of those books is not shelf-stable. It changes in reception. The concept of the countershelf is a way of marking that reception as a significant force in world literature. Without losing sight of the role institutions have in curating a canon, it is this sense of personal attachment, of agency, that sets the countershelf apart.

That Hanif's and Ghosh's libraries are each filtered through a mentor – a relative, a friend, a local literary luminary – instead conveys the kind of affinities we often feel instinctively, as passionate lay-readers of literature. As Gayatri Gopinath argues, such collections recast curation not as a capitulation to global arbiters of taste but as the material trace of an affective relationship (Gopinath 2018). She quotes Erica Lehrer and Cynthia Milton's linking of curation with the affective stance of caring: "not only as selection, design, and interpretation, but as care-taking – a kind of intimate, intersubjective, interrelational obligation" (Lehrer and Milton quoted in Gopinath 2018, 4).

Often this intimacy is a kind of memorialization. Hanif's landlord and Ghosh's grandfather are dead. In the same way, many authors signal their investment in the countershelf by offering up their own writing as a crypt for texts that have gone missing or were intentionally destroyed: an absent volume of Neruda's poetry, the charred remains of a García Márquez novel, or the millions of volumes symbolically burned in the conquest of Granada. For other authors, encryption is a stylistic choice through which to manage the publicness of their writing in English – its potential to be discovered by potential new "friends" or encountered by unfriendly "strangers." They use a curated reference to Latin American predecessors as a kind of secret language that only others immersed in the countershelf tradition will be able to decode, or they borrow certain elusive styles that allow the description of current crises to hide in plain sight.

Anglophone Kashmiri poet Agha Shahid Ali plays up these curatorial aspects in his own very literal countershelf gesture. He offers a looking-glass image of a shelf that blurs the lines between literary and personal genealogies and casts it as a space of mourning for a former home that political violence in Kashmir has transformed into a ruin: "by Ritos and Rilke and Cavafy and Lorca and Iqbal and Amichai and Paz, my parents are beautiful in their wedding brocades, so startlingly young" (Ali 2000, 47).

A Countershelf Is Circulated

In order for the countershelf to register the "writerly contacts" it facilitates among South Asian authors, the texts themselves have to get around. This means accounting for the manner of their circulation – the "how" of world literature – but also its motivation – the "why." Recounting his relationship with the Anglophone and Marathi poet Arun Kolatkar, the equally multilingual writer Arvind Krishna Mehrotra paints him as a kind of mobile bookshelf. "I never saw him reach out for a book, but whenever he spoke about one, whether it was a Latin American novel, *The Tale of the Genji*, or a Sanskrit *bhand*, it was as though he had it open in front of him" (Mehrotra 2014, 100). Like the dead poet of Hanif's recollections, Kolatkar serves his fellow writers by acting as a local curator for world literature, incorporating it seamlessly into a repertoire that remains ready to hand. "He bought books, read them, and passed them on to his friends," Mehrotra recalls (Mehrotra 2014, 100). "This is how I acquired my copy of [García] Márquez's *Love in the Time of Cholera*, which he had bought in hardback as soon as it became available at Strand Book Stall" (Mehrotra 2014, 100).

Here, as in the passages from Hanif and Ali, the names of authors, specific texts, or even a placeholder like "a Latin American novel" suggest the physical presence of books on a shelf. Reading that Kolatkar purchased García Márquez's 1985 novel "as soon as it became available" in Bombay underscores a basic problem for the study ahead: how did Latin American literature, translated into English, end up on shelves in the subcontinent? To answer this question means addressing the discontinuity between the relatively minor global status of both South Asian and Latin American letters in the early 1960s and their "post-boom" stature today. The question of "how" would have been relatively simple to answer in the mid-1980s, when García Márquez was a Nobel laureate writing books that were translated and then traveled almost as soon as they were composed. The question would have been significantly more complex in the mid-1960s, when García Márquez, Kolatkar, and Mehrotra were all obscure writers composing in and about the Global South. This question requires an engagement with the kind of literary-sociological studies that predominate in the field. A study of the countershelf cannot be innocent of the economic and geopolitical motivators for literary circulation, even when its fantasized aspect runs contrary to those powers. It must, in Paz's words, be allied with such studies.

But these names and dates alone do not tell us why South Asian authors built out a library of Latin American texts. In a later poem, "Borges" (1998), Mehrotra clarifies how the inheritance of the countershelf operates in his own writing:

> A borrowed voice sets the true one
> Free: lead me who am no more
> Than De Quincy's Malay, a speechless shadow in a world
> Of sound, to the labyrinth of the earthly
> Library, perfect me in your work   (Mehrotra 1998, 3)

In this poem, Mehrotra asks Borges for "a borrowed voice" that leads to his "true one." This is a gesture that can effectively counter the silencing of Asian subjects – "De Quincy's Malay" – in British Orientalist fantasy. As we will see in Chapter 2, Mehrotra explicitly imagined Latin American literature as a rearview mirror, "a model from which we ought to learn" (Mehrotra 1969).

For Mehrotra, Borges can also act as a model for the critical apparatus around South Asian Anglophone literature. "The example of Borges is enough to show that the Indian English poem needs to be read in a radically different way: not as a delectable slice of reality which the critic applies to his nose, but as a place, a construct, housing two or more ways of seeing" (Mehrotra 2014, 170–171). For Mehrotra, the fact that Latin

American literature was able to circulate as an aesthetic innovator – a "way of seeing," rather than a merely sociological "slice of reality" – paves the way for South Asian writing to undergo a similar shift in reception as it circulates in the Global North.

Of all the writers who appear on the countershelf, Borges is perhaps the most revealing for thinking about circulation. He has traveled further than anyone, all the way into literary theory. A number of critical fields use Borges as a deracinated "global" supplier of clever, enigmatic epigraphs, the most famous instance of which is probably Michel Foucault's citation of "El idioma analítico de John Wilkins" (1951) in *The Order of Things* (1966), a reading critiqued in Jerónimo Arellano (Arellano 2010). The references to Borges by Mehrotra, Hanif, and many others in this book prompt us in the opposite direction from Foucault. They seek not the abstractions of theory but the specificity of storytelling. Following John Beverley, Borges drives us to ask "would it be possible to have a work of 'theory' that would be composed entirely of stories?" (Beverley 1999, 34–35). In honor of the shelf metaphor at its heart, the work ahead builds out from a large archive of exemplary texts. In teasing out their implicit theories of world consciousness, such an analysis engages what Octavio González calls "immanent" close reading (González 2020, 43). It honors authors' own categories as part of the critical engagement of their work, even when – perhaps especially when – such concepts operate as "misfits" within a dominant critical paradigm (González 2020, 51).

A Countershelf Is Contested

South Asian authors' overriding attachment to Latin American literature is a "misfit" within Anglophone literary studies. But that affiliation can also create dissent among its own ranks. If a countershelf is actively curated and circulated by various individuals, it follows that each of those individuals might construct their shelf differently and to a different purpose. Like counterpublics, then, countershelves are not so much a stable canon or fixed ideology as a dynamic location for debate. While the primary "contrary" energy of the countershelf is directed outward, toward the overdetermined meaning of English speaking, its "contestedness" operates internally. Thus, writers whose work is diametrically opposed in both political and aesthetic terms nevertheless draw on a shared vocabulary of the countershelf, even occasionally the same poem by the same author – as we will see in Chapter 1 with Neruda's "Alturas de Macchu Picchu" ("The Heights of Macchu Picchu") (1949).

Tracing these fantasies, there is a striking contrast between the authorial passion for the countershelf and the scholarly aversion to genealogies of this type. The paranoid gaze passes over the descriptor "influenced" and reads instead the judgment "derivative." In part, this traces the rise and fall of a specifically Bloomian mode of "influence studies" and the kind of combative Freudian relationships it seemed to require (Lawrence 2018, 9). Yet a recent spate of writing about genealogical ties between stalwarts of the Euro-American canon and authors in the Global South has seemed to signal a shifted interest, this time in less anxious forms of affiliation (Walkowitz 2006; Friedman 2015; Bronstein 2018; Lawrence 2018). In the South Asian context, however, this anxiety is also perhaps one more legacy of the Macaulay Minute, what Parama Roy calls the "imagined origin" for the "preoccupation with originality and secondariness" in South Asian literary study (Roy 1998, 72). The countershelf suggests, instead, that an idea of adaptation, even of mimicry, need not only be a threatening contest between colonizer and colonized. It can also be theorized as a mode of identification between writers in the formerly colonized world.

Another aspect of this resistance has to do with the perception that the literatures of Latin America and South Asia can have no organic relationship, that they only come together at the convenience of the scholar in the Global North under the aegis of unsustainably capacious geopolitical concepts like the postcolonial world, Third World, and Global South.

Take, for example, Aijaiz Ahmad's "Jameson's Rhetoric of Otherness and the 'National Allegory'" (1987), a scathing rebuttal to Fredric Jameson's infamous article "Third World Literature in the Age of Multinational Capital" (1986). In his article, Ahmad polemicized against the category of "Third World literature" as a coherent comparative term. "Peru and India," Ahmad writes, "simply do not have a common history of the sort that Germany and France, or Britain and the United States, have; not even the 'experience of colonialism and imperialism' has been in specific ways the same or similar" (Ahmad 1987, 10).

In this passage, Ahmad's pairing of "Peru and India" stands in for all possible Global South associations. The pair's very unexpectedness operates rhetorically to demonstrate how ridiculous it is to seek to unite such obviously foreign locales under a single banner. Moreover, Ahmad insists that "the kinds of circuits that bind the cultural complexes of advanced capitalist countries simply do not exist" among these other regions (Ahmad 1987, 11). Between history and culture, there is no exchange that would justify the inclusion of Latin America and South Asia in a single literary category.

And yet, a few pages on, Ahmad suddenly contradicts this assertion. Refuting the claim that the texts Jameson identifies as Third World cannot be canonical, he challenges the standards by which Jameson assesses canon. "Neruda, Vallejo, Octavio Paz, Borges, Fuentes, [García] Márquez et al. (i.e., quite a few writers of Latin American origin) are considered by the American academy as major figures in modern literature" (Ahmad 1987, 16–17). If that were not proof enough, he continues:

> Salman Rushdie's *Midnight's Children* was awarded the most prestigious literary award in England, and *Shame* was immediately reviewed as a major novel . . . . The blurbs on the Vintage paperback edition of *Shame* . . . compare him with Swift, Voltaire, Stern, Kafka, Grass, Kundera and [García] Márquez. What else is canonization? (Ahmad 1987, 88)

It is a countershelf of Latin American literature – a list of personae so instantly recognizable that only poor Paz requires a first name – through which Ahmad initially demonstrates, contra Jameson, that Third World texts can indeed achieve canonization. In doing so, Ahmad uses Latin American authors to pave the way for his more sustained intervention around Rushdie. Rushdie's canonization, too, requires a countershelf, this one more cosmopolitan but still primarily non-Anglophone. And, of course, this shelf also includes García Márquez. Ahmad narrates this argument as if the relationship between the two shelves were incidental. It isn't.

Ahmad rushes unconsciously up to the precipice of his own argument. It would take only one more step to tumble into the conclusion that relationships among certain Third World literatures "simply do ~~not~~ exist." He is on the cusp of the insight that canonization of Latin American literature in the middle of the twentieth century was constitutively related to the canonization of South Asian Anglophone literature at its end. That, indeed, it was not only Ahmed as a critic who had access to such a Latin American countershelf. His fellow South Asian writers were reading it, citing it, and using it, just as he was, to launch their own claims over a global literary order.

"Common History": Misfit Concepts of World Time

Contra Ahmad, the absence of "common history" does not necessarily suggest that these literatures do not belong together. Instead, it may speak to a real, enduring mismatch between global history and global *literary* history, one that belies the intimate association of those fields in orthodox postcolonial criticism. The countershelf has been introduced as a place, a field of debate that offers an alternative to the many other spatial relationships imagined by various global and worldly literary orders. But, as Cheah, Debjani Ganguly, and other recent theorists emphasize, the construction of a literary world also implicates history and time (Cheah 2016; Ganguly 2016). The shift from space to time carries with it, for both, an orientation away from purely material critiques of globally circulating literature as a manifestation of markets and political orders. It prompts us, instead, to ask how a literary tradition imagines the world, otherwise.

Yet when it comes to the larger argument about "cultural complexes" and the "experience of colonialism and imperialism," Latin America and South Asia did indeed operate in radically different ways, making the scholarly imputation of "common history" a troubling thing. To a significant degree, these conflicts over whose history would be salient for the field served to bracket off Latin American literature from that of the postcolonial world. The more recent embrace of the Global Anglophone makes the exclusion of Latin American literature explicit on linguistic terms. At the same time, it threatens to do away with the concept of history altogether, quietly sweeping aside the unsightly events through which English became "global" in the first place. The way both categories have failed to account for the commitments of the countershelf suggests an enduring "misfit" between scholarly paradigms and their object of study. The first part of this section addresses these discontinuities in greater detail.

As we have seen, the primary purpose of the countershelf is to imagine a literary world that hangs together "contrary" to the ordering of an Anglophone Globe. Behind theories of relatedness in the present, South Asian authors have made various historiographic claims about the time and manner of a relationship with Latin America to justify their turn to the countershelf. These register in the frequent mirrorwork images of reflection and recognition that appear all over their archive. The figure of the looking glass suggests contemporaneity, a model in which Latin American and South Asian artists stand united against the assertion of their regions' belatedness or peripherality on the world stage. The rearview mirror, on the other hand, is an image of retrospection, in which the past of one location can offer a template for the present of the other. Both frameworks also imply a type of futurity, a theory about how the future emerges from these images of past and present (Ganguly 2016). The second part of the section examines South Asian gestures toward Cuba that imply arguments about time: its place in the origins of modernity and the establishment of a "psychic connection" of colonial domination; its central agency in a Cold War paradigm linking literary circulation with geopolitics; its abjected role in a unipolar world order in the present; and its imaginative freedom from these histories in the untimeliness of utopian thinking.

The Shrinking Postcolonial World, the Engulfing Anglophone Globe

Postcolonial studies was the organizing banner under which many of the South Asian authors in this volume were long promoted and investigated. The focus on temporality is front and center in its very name – the tension between the forward-looking "post" and a deep rooting in a prior historical period, the "colonial" (Hall 1996). Yet Latin America's experience of colonialism was quite different from that of former British colonies, while India was, here as elsewhere, the jewel in the crown.

Even as postcolonial theory ascended in the academy, its adherents and opponents echoed Ahmad in the anxiety that the category was too big to function coherently. In the deep past, scholarship fractured around the relationship of colonization to the inauguration of modernity – whether it should begin with the resource extraction at the conquest of the New World, with the opening of the transatlantic slave trade, or with the concomitant access to Indian riches and the beginning of industrial capitalism in northern Europe (Loomba 1998; Coronil 2008). Another fissure appeared around the temporality and manner of decolonization, nominally achieved in Latin America almost a century before Asia or Africa, but only in very partial terms (Hall 1996, 245). These debates resurface in Chapter 3. Likewise, questions arose around which twentieth-century associations of solidarity would be the best template for the geography of the postcolonial world. Should it be the Asia–Africa model imagined at the 1954 Bandung Conference, which pioneered the idea of a "Third World" united beyond and against the domination of the First (the USA and allies) and Second (the USSR and allies)? Or should it rather be the 1966 Tricontinental conference in Cuba, which included Latin America and also suggested associations with oppressed racial communities within the First World (Young 2016; Mahler 2018)? Chapters 4 and 5 take up debates around the political meaning of literary styles transacted through these circuits. One very common response to these debates, however, has been a winnowing of the territory that constitutes the postcolonial. And, for reasons Chapter 3 explores in greater depth, Latin America was the region most likely to be left out.

Still, the broader exclusion of Latin American experience might not have mattered to the narration of *literary* traditions, were it not for the deep materialist strain in postcolonial criticism that poses political and literary history as functionally identical. As Ganguly argues, the most prominent analytic use of "world" literature in postcolonial studies has been understood, following Edward Said, "to situate [a text] as a product of its material allegiances and historical affiliations" (Ganguly 2016, 20). This perspective is key for reassessing an existing canon, recovering the traces of colonial power in texts whose overriding concerns seem essentially domestic (Said 1993). But it offers little purchase into the project of world-making as a creative endeavor that engages the concept of canon from a position to the South.

Here again, Paz is instructive, insisting on the integration of realism and fantasy into the concept of literary history. Texts must be apprehended as material objects with literal circuits, but they are also just as much shared imaginaries, what Ganguly calls "the work of the human in making worlds through language" (Ganguly 2016, 20). When enough authors insist upon a literary tradition connecting "India and Peru," their repeated references make that world "through language," even as the circulation of texts forms new "material allegiances." The absence of a prior "common history" connecting those locations ceases to matter very much. As Kumkum Sangari has argued in her pathbreaking essay connecting magical realism in these two regions, the tradition creates new connections of its own (Sangari 1987).

Most of the authors in this book self-consciously building those circuits were writing from the 1970s through the 1990s – the heyday of postcolonial studies. Most of them are quite canonical: either regional exemplars, in cases like Zulfikar Ghose and Geeta Kapur, or international heavyweights, like Ali and Rushdie. As Chapters 4 and 5 argue, this relationship holds the roots of two major stylistic trends around which postcolonial literature effectively gelled as a literary concept – magical realism and revenant modernism. Why has it remained practically invisible to the field?

In the face of this history, it is tempting to suggest that seemingly legitimate concerns about historical coherence provided convenient cover for a deeper commitment: the desire to maintain postcolonial studies as an English-exclusive category by shrinking its operative territory until it matched the Commonwealth. Such commitments effectively protect a version of literary history in which contemporary Anglophone literature emerged solely from acts of "writing back" to the Anglophone center and authenticating returns to safely homebound linguistic (m)others.

Ironically, South Asian Anglophone authors have been used as the vanguard of this argument, the sharpest point on the slim end of the wedge. Their stratospheric global rise has helped to justify a decisive disciplinary shift toward a wholly and unapologetically Anglophone cartography.

In this context, the newly ascendant category of the Global Anglophone is not a betrayal of postcolonial studies but merely the fulfillment of its longtime trajectory, bringing its true linguistic commitments right to the surface. The Global Anglophone's appealingly transparent nomenclature presents the whole category as a fait accompli. All the agonized debates of the 1980s and 1990s over where to place the historical and geographic boundaries of the postcolonial world puff away like so much smoke.[13]

But if the term "Global Anglophone" makes itself immune to historiography, there is still a kind of futurity lurking there. "Global" does not modify "Anglophone" by acting as a euphemism for "not United States, not United Kingdom," though that is how it has found its way into our lexicon as a market term (Anam 2019; Lahiri 2020). Nor does "Anglophone" modify "Global" by delimiting its coverage area to "the parts of the globe where English is spoken" – the functional meaning of "the postcolonial world," itself a renomination of "the Commonwealth" (DeWispelare 2017; Srinivasan 2018b; Anam 2019). "The Anglophone" does not limit the globe at all. Instead, it prefigures and wills into existence the world as "the globe, where English is spoken."

Cuba as the Face in the Mirror

When the South Asian authors in this book created out of whole cloth an unprecedented, unexpected connection to Latin American literature, they, too, willed a new world into existence. Contrary to the exclusionary futurity of "the globe, where English is spoken," they created a version of history in which a Global Anglophone tradition developed out of an unexpected journey through multilingual world literature, in which these fields, as opposed to being bitter enemies, become one and the same.

That journey through Latin American literature brought writers to new imagined locations, from the Peruvian highlands to the Chilean coast, from the Amazonian interior to the deserts of Mexico – even notionally related cities in southern Spain! Each location carries with it a different vision of the world, its history, and the relationships that sustain it.

But it is Cuba, more than any other place, that crystallizes the imaginaries of time through which South Asian authors willed themselves into a shared world with Latin America. These histories echo but do not quite overlap with the histories of colonization and decolonization, of Cold War polarization and capitalist global domination that shape the fields described earlier.

For certain South Asian authors, Cuba is an invitation to consider the longue durée of a fantasized relationship between these two regions. It stands for the "discovery" of the New World, Columbus's looking glass in which the Caribbean is mistaken for India. It is this event, which inaugurates the age of colonization, that will ultimately impact both areas, creating for the first time a single, interconnected, maritime planet. Ghose takes up this history in "Arrival in India" (1998) by sending his hapless Morisco stowaway on a sea voyage from Spain to India by the untested western route. These meditations on shared "experiences of colonialism and imperialism" emerge around the appearance of baroque aesthetics in Mexican and Indian poetry in Chapter 2 and in narratives about the multivalent meanings of 1492 described in Chapter 3.

Closer to the current moment, Cuba emerged as a premier site from which to imagine the possibilities and threats of the Cold War. In *The White Tiger*, for example, Adiga ironically invokes "this man called Castro who threw the rich out of his country and freed his people" as a rearview mirror, a model for his class-warrior protagonist and would-be strongman Balram Halwai (Adiga 2008, 79). Chapter 1 engages the endurance of these and other Cold War imaginaries through the figure of Pablo Neruda.

In the present, Cuba enters the imaginary in a text like Kamala Shamsie's *Burnt Shadows* (2009) as Guantánamo, the location of indefinite detention of South Asian suspects in the War on Terror. These conflicts have transformed US engagements with Pakistan and the global experience of Muslim identity in a way that clearly impacted the rise in popularity of Pakistani Anglophone literature in the new millennium (Gamal 2013; Mufti 2016, 173–178). Their echoes are felt in the turn to Latin American dictator fiction and modernist narrative style as a rearview model for South Asian authors in Chapter 5.

And sometimes Cuba is simply an escape: a place, sometimes explicitly imagined through Thomas More's *Utopia* (1516), without location in space or time – a place held apart from the violent political orders of the globe (Quintero-Herencia 2002; Tietchen 2010). Early on in Hamid's *Exit West* (2017), his protagonists Nadia and Saeed imagine traveling as tourists to the Chilean desert and the Cuban seaside. For Nadia, Cuba is simply the place of "music and beautiful old buildings and the sea" (Hamid 2017, 24). Her desire to travel there as a tourist ironically inverts her eventual forced migration to escape political violence. But in this earlier moment, when both she and her lover share a fantasy of Latin America, their world is evanescently "tinged with wonder" (Hamid 2017, 25). And at the end of the novel, the unexpected return to these landscapes signals the perseverance of utopian hope. The political power of fantasy is explored in Chapter 4, around the hotly debated concept of magical realism. But fantasy and wonder also appear throughout the book as a whole. In all of these cases, and often in very unexpected ways, imaginative connections with Latin America help authors contextualize seemingly new or geographically isolated circumstances into a vision of a shared world.

South Asian authors did more than just imagine Cuba – they also traveled there. In 1973, ten years after his meeting with Neruda in the USSR, Faiz embarked on a two-week tour of post-revolutionary Cuba, the basis for his "Safarnāmāh-e Kyūbā" ["Cuban Travelogue"] (1973). The piece offers Cuba as a rearview mirror, in which everything from land redistribution to anticorruption efforts to education reform and a history of successful defiance of the United States can act as a model for the future of Pakistan under the socialist-leaning Zulfikar Ali Bhutto.

Yet within the overtly political travelogue, Faiz draws on a very literary form of wonder in order to negotiate unexpected terrain. After comparing the lyrics of a Cuban *bolero* to the equivalent sentiment in an Urdu couplet, or *shi'r*, Faiz writes, "On hearing this [the *bolero* or *shi'r*] the sound of 'encore'; and *'wāh-wāh'* can be heard . . . . Here, at every moment and at every step, one finds such *wonders*" (Faiz 1973, emphasis added).[14] He then offers several examples of everyday "wonders" of the revolution as a series of poetic paradoxes, inviting his readers to make sense of Cuba as they would a *ghazal*, a loosely related series of couplets. Poetry thus acts as a vehicle through which political futurity can be appealingly expressed.

Almost twenty years later, Mohammad Hanif would repeat Faiz's journey in his travelogue "Viva Havana!" (1992). Among many everyday images of the revolution, we see again the *bolero* singer, the spirit of Cuban cultural life who stands in for the role of the poet in Pakistan. This time, however, he is plotting to move to Florida. Cuba is now a looking glass for Pakistani political dysfunction: crowded Cuban busses "induc[e] near nostalgia in me for the KTC busses back home," Hanif tells his hosts in "broken Spanish" (Hanif 1992, 157). The two countries come to be comparable for Hamid because they inhabit related positions in a unipolar, post–Cold War world order, one now mediated by miserable public transportation.

Both countries, moreover, exemplify a relationship between literary expression and geopolitics. It was the artistic proxy war ignited by the

Cuban revolution that helped "put Latin America on the world's literary map" in the 1960s, as Hanif tells us (Hanif 1992, 158). Most of the Latin American authors on the countershelf emerged or came into greater prominence during the "boom," generally understood to open around 1958 and end between 1971 and 1973 (Rama 2005; Larsen 2011; Cohn 2012; Iber 2015). "[Vargas] Llosa, Fuentes, [García] Márquez – worked in Cuba during the initial days of the revolution and have acknowledgedly been inspired by it" (Hanif 1992, 158).

Similar concerns about Pakistan and the War on Terror would help propel Hanif's own career as a novelist in the 2000s. His 2008 debut, *A Case of Exploding Mangoes*, addresses these concerns obliquely, through an allegorical narrative about the Soviet-Afghan war of the 1980s. In the telling of that story, Hanif is "acknowledgedly inspired" by Latin American narratives of Caribbean dictatorship in the early twentieth century, produced by the same "boom" superstars he names. The novel's three temporal levels – post-9/11, late Cold War, and turn-of-the-century – themselves imply a strange, recursive mirror game of experience, in which time moves forward without ever really moving on.

When Hanif references the "world's literary map," he reminds us, once again, that his affiliation with Latin American authors is always mediated by English translation. This returns us to the central anxiety expressed by Sontag about an increasingly monolingual world. The specter of that future is a real threat, one that threads South Asian Anglophone writing with profound ambivalence.

Yet, within this anxiety is the assumption that all writing in English equally hastens the coming of that future. It assumes that, when Faiz hails the audience for his travelogue as "us," this "we" (*hum log*) is virtually guaranteed to refer to a regionally bounded audience – an audience composed of readers very like the author. Hanif's English "we" is perceived to do the opposite. Existing theorizations of Global Anglophone writing assumes that writing in English determines in advance the audience to which authors speak, the collectives to which they may belong (Sadana 2012; Chakravorty 2014; Anjaria 2019). It assumes Hanif is doomed to speak only to a readerly "we" in the Global North.

But look again: "Viva Havana!" is both imagined as and published for an explicitly Pakistani we. It is not even really "we" – it is a "*nosotros*" delivered in "broken Spanish." R. Radhakrishnan takes from Derrida the idea of an "as yet to be determined we" that is willed into existence by the act of comparison (Radhakrishnan 2009, 9). The pursuit of this "we" has sent South Asian writers on several unexpected routes on the journey into Global English.

An Unexpected Journey: The Plan of the Book

This unexpected journey beckons many different kinds of traveler. Each chapter condenses a different imaginary of connection – the delirious fantasy of their symbolic cargo, as well as the frank realism of their literal routes.

Chapter 1, "Transmigrant: Neruda's Rebirth as the Soul of World Literature," illustrates the major claims of the countershelf through one of its most frequent occupants, Pablo Neruda. Yet his iconic appearance operates quite differently from that of later Latin American authors, who act primarily as stylistic models. Instead, it is Neruda himself who lives on, reincarnated as a "transmigrant" who acts as a site of internal contestation between projects that are stylistically, even generically, quite distinct. After his Nobel Prize and untimely death in the early 1970s, the painter Vivan Sundaram, poets including Agha Shahid Ali, Marie Cruz Gabriel, and Sirsir Kumar Das, and prose writers like Mohsin Hamid and Ravish Kumar all reincarnated Neruda's persona as a way of thinking about a very different types of worldly affiliation, as well as the contest between aesthetic and political commitment through which their own creative endeavors might become global. Their perception of Neruda's conflictual commitments emerges out of the real arc of his poetic career. These prompt a reconsideration of one of the most politically and aesthetically discordant – and yet essential – moments of Neruda's oeuvre: his reincarnation-themed poetry of the first volume of *Residencia en la tierra* – written while Neruda worked as a consular functionary in British India from 1927 to 1929.

Chapter 2, "Stranger: Paz's Peregrinations through Indian Poetry," turns to the curatorial role of authors on the countershelf, tracing the impact of Paz's sojourn as the Mexican ambassador to India (1962–8) on a cohort of Indian poets and artists in the little magazine scene of the 1960s and 1970s, including Mehrotra, Kapur, and Jagdish Swaminathan. While Neruda often formed the image of the countershelf for South Asian authors, Paz was the nearly invisible engine through which that imaginary consolidated. Paz's sensibility of "strangerhood" is a framework that guided both his observations of India and the way he represented his experiences there. It reflected Paz's growing interest in the baroque, a form that emerged to aestheticize the rapidly and radically changing concept of the world in the era of colonial expansion. This same strategy was taken up by several creators of Indian little magazines, among whom Paz helped to establish a very particular idea of world-literary friendship.

This distinct version of world literature proposes, in place of an increasingly unified and easily digestible singular style, a series of intentionally disorienting enigmas. Though both route through Latin American literature of the 1960s, the Indian poetry of the 1970s was setting a very different course for global English, one that the rise of the novelists in the 1980s dramatically interrupted and then, essentially, cut off.

Chapter 3, "Displacee: The Andalusian Allegory and Dreams of a Shared Past," shows how the countershelf can offer a "contrary" theory of global modernity hinged around the totemic date of 1492 – simultaneously the fall of Muslim Spain and the violent opening of the "New World." Approaching the quincentenary of these twinned traumas, novelists of the 1980s and 1990s linked them conceptually through a renovation of what had been a common theme in South Asian writing for more than a century: the Andalusian allegory. Gestures that "displace" waves of trauma in the subcontinent onto medieval Spain can be traced through Urdu writing including Hali, Abdul l'Halim Sharar, and especially Mohammad Iqbal's poetry from Spain. At the end of the twentieth century, Rushdie, Intizar Husain, Tariq Ali, and Ghose creatively recapitulate these same affiliative projects, as did authors from the Americas, Paz and V. S. Naipaul. And yet, it was this same anxiety about comparable histories of colonization, in the very same moment of the 1990s, through which Latin America was pushed beyond the boundaries of the "postcolonial world." The layered historical fictions of this chapter suggest a need to reevaluate postcolonial historiography on its own grounds.

Chapters 4 and 5 address the question of circulation on the countershelf through the adaptation of literary styles. Chapter 4, "Pilgrim: Journeys to the Roots of Magical Realism," considers the "globalization" of magical realism in the 1980s and its relationship to the consolidation of postcolonial literary studies in the same moment. Even as Latin America was being progressively marginalized in favor of taxonomic accounts of magical realism, Rushdie and other South Asian authors became "pilgrims." They use textual journeys to Latin America to declare the centrality of that tradition to their own forays into literary magic. Based on their understanding of the form in the writing of Carpentier, García Márquez, and others, Rushdie and Ghose both pose Latin America as a funhouse mirror that reflects back a hyperbolically distorted but ultimately referential image of postcolonial political life. Ghose is joined by Desai in his approach to Latin America as a concave mirror, one that allows both to invert the implied political meaning of institutional affiliation in "America" by redirecting their attachment to the continent southward.

Finally, Sunny Singh interrogates the postcolonial critical desire for magical realism to act as a transparent window onto traditions of home, framing it instead as a looking glass, where difference, even inversion, is no barrier to identification.

However, an overidentification of Latin American midcentury writing with magical realism has obscured the many other stylistic and thematic genealogies that link South Asian Anglophone writing to the countershelf. Chapter 5, "Revenant: Dictator Fiction and Mobile Modernist Form," traces the reappearance of key features of literary modernism in South Asian dictator fiction, especially *A Case of Exploding Mangoes* (2009) by Mohammad Hanif. The case of Hanif reveals that several techniques credited to Anglo-American modernists became "revenants" in South Asia not through their automatic connection to a shared language, nor through the ironizing gesture of "writing back," but instead through an affiliative movement toward an unacknowledged middle generation in Latin America. Hanif, joined by Rushdie and Hamid, portray the specter of political violence in Pakistan by adapting some of the most recognizable traits that "boom" superstars García Márquez and Vargas Llosa developed out of their own readings of the North American modernist William Faulkner. Modernist narrative complexity has often been cast as apolitical or even reactionary. In contrast, South Asian authors suggest that such styles undo the easy certainties the dictator offers and use language to challenge him on the grounds of the literal power to "dictate." At the same time, Hanif and others use revenant structures to manage the "overheard" quality of writing in English – that is, as a way of addressing two totally distinct audiences at once.

Finally, the Epilogue weaves together disparate strands of resistant, worldly thinking under the aegis of Latin America. The scholar Taymiya Zaman uses Cortázar and Borges to decolonize the writing of history. The novelist Karan Mahajan references Bolaño to demand that American readers approach his version of India on its own terms. And two writers – the despondent Tanuj Solanki and the hopeful Mohsin Hamid – invoke the countershelf at the end of the world.

CHAPTER 1

Transmigrant
Neruda's Rebirth as the Soul of World Literature

> When the relations of my legs get mixed up with each other
> When my words become a dove cooing in an arching tree
> I have some questions for the Neruda sitting on my headboard
> (Syed n.d.)[1]

These are the final lines of a short poem "Sheher Badr" ("City in Exile") by the Pakistani playwright, television writer, and occasional poet Asghar Nadeem Syed. The poem up to this point has followed a parade of surreal, shape-shifting things whose appearance echoes one of Pablo Neruda's most iconic poetic styles: the object-list.[2] These objects are not selected at random, mere imitations of an ersatz Nerudian style. Instead, images like anthropomorphized legs are direct citations of the first volume of *Residencia en la tierra* (*Residence on Earth*) (1933) – in this case, the poem "Ritual de mis piernas" ("Ritual of My Legs"). The dove – here the *kabutar*, there the *paloma* – was a particular favorite in this series, one of several objects Neruda repeats half a dozen times.

Though he extended it further in his later works, Neruda's habit of listing objects was one he initially developed in *Residencia*, the first volume of which he began writing in 1925 and completed in the early 1930s (Loyola 2006). Longing for a way to reach the world beyond Chile and struggling to make a living despite the success of his early poems, Neruda joined the diplomatic corps. In his early assignments between 1927 and 1929, he languished as a low-level consular official representing Chilean guano interests in what were then various peripheries of British India – postings in Burma and Ceylon, as well as stints in several cities in India (Neruda n. d.). Despite his unhappiness and the utterly banal nature of his official labor, the move to Asia also inaugurated one of the most stylistically innovative moments of Neruda's career. Travels through various parts of South Asia inspired the key innovations of the first volume of *Residencia*. This series, in turn, precipitated his standing as a writer of world literature,

31

"not simply as another good poet, but as the major new poet of the Spanish language," to borrow René de Costa's tidy summation (de Costa 1979).

Yet the Neruda of the South Asian sojourn, the Neruda whose poetry Syed cites, is emphatically not the Neruda who himself becomes an object at the end of "Sheher Badr." That image is based on a later moment in Neruda's career, a moment in which he violently rejected his own poetic project in *Residencia* in order to embody a particular ideal of politically engaged, culturally authentic, and world-famous authorship. In the words of one *New York Times* critic, the iconic Neruda resembles nothing so much as "a happily retired banker, what with those immobile features broken only by heavy-lidded eyes that penetrate everybody and everything" (Coleman 1972). It is this figure that Faiz encountered in Sochi in 1962, and it is in this guise that the figure of Neruda appears, over and over, in the South Asian writing traced in this book. Without a doubt, Neruda is the most prominently "cited" Latin American author on the countershelf.[3]

For all his popularity, however, by the end of his life "Neruda [had] few 'followers' stylistically" (Coleman 1972). That makes his iconic appearance quite different from that of later Latin American authors, who act primarily as stylistic models. Instead, it is Neruda himself who lives on in projects that are stylistically, even generically, quite distinct.

What to make of this contradictory invocation, the uneasy relationship between the real Neruda and his various South Asian incarnations? This chapter takes up the poet and his iconic reappearance as an ideal figure through which to trace all four key elements of the countershelf. First, like other references to Latin American literature in this book, the gesture toward Neruda suggests a set of worldly affiliations posed intentionally against the "expected" trajectories for South Asian writing. It proposes instead a scenario in which poetry can be a legitimate predecessor for prose, just as Spanish can be a legitimate predecessor for English. When creators like M. C. Gabriel, Agha Shahid Ali, and Vivan Sundaram address a readerly "you" in the Americas, Neruda is the idiom through which that invocation is translated. Second, Neruda's own global peregrinations have much to say about circulation, both the material pathways for mid-century writing and its producers, as well as the fantasized attachment those movements produced. Yet the particular contexts in which Neruda's persona is reanimated do not merely affirm the power of circulatory agents like the Nobel. Instead, he often reappears as part of a scene of curatorial connection – enabling Zulfikar Ghose's authorial stand-in to make friends with Latin America's foremost realist novelist, or offering the common ground between Mohsin Hamid's protagonist and the Chilean literary editor whose small press he threatens to dismantle.

Most significantly, however, these contradictory invocations of Neruda's persona suggest how the countershelf can act as a space of contestation. So, for example, when one of the ill-starred lovers in Ravish Kumar's Hindi short-story collection *Ishq mein Shahar Hona* (*A City Happens in Love*) (2015) identifies himself as "Your Pablo, the poet Pablo," his beloved scolds him for placing demands on her "in Neruda's name" (Kumar 2018, 84–85).[4] For Kumar, "in the test between politics and love," only Neruda could play both sides, while his lovers, mere mortals, must ultimately choose one or the other (Kumar 2018, 87).[5] Kumar here joins the many other South Asian authors who make demands "in Neruda's name." Many assert different, mutually incompatible political and aesthetic commitments, few of which align tidily with the overdetermined political affiliations suggested by the postcolonial world and other scholarly geographies.

These movements across fantasy and reality, space and time reshape Neruda into a "transmigrant." *Transmigration* is a relatively archaic English term for the movement of a single soul among otherwise unrelated bodies. At a literal level, Neruda's poetic development in the 1920s is the result of migration – geographic and aesthetic movements impelled by a desire to belong elsewhere. The poetry of *Residencia I* likewise operated according to a logic of transmigration. Clarence Finlayson describes it as a project of "mutual and profound correspondence ... between the self and the non-self" – an incipient social consciousness based on the empathetic embodiment of otherness (Finlayson 1969, 378).[6] Neruda used Buddhist- and Hindu-informed ideas about reincarnation as technologies of affiliation in the early *Residencia* period. While critiques of these spiritualist gestures among Western writers are rife, Leela Gandhi has drawn attention to the way that interests in reincarnation are a primary vehicle for what she calls "affective cosmopolitanism": "the ethico-political practice of a desiring self inexorably drawn toward difference" (Gandhi 2006, 17). It is the moments of measured optimism and gestures of hesitant connectivity – his gestures of transmigrant affiliation – that connect Neruda's surrealist *Residencia* poetry with his later writing and with the writing of his South Asian admirers.

The reception of Neruda among South Asian authors, and their particular sensitivity to the transmigrant energy of his writing, prompts a reconsideration of this early collection. As Michaela Bronstein argues, when later writers invoke literary predecessors "out of context," scholarship has a duty to take seriously what elements of an earlier text and writer made such uses available to the future. For that reason, the chapter begins by tracing both conflicts and underlying continuities in Neruda's iconic reappearance, before seeking the roots of those elements in his own writing.

The perception about Neruda's dual, sometimes conflictual commitments "in the test between politics and love" emerges out of the real arc of his poetic career, as well as the distinct manner and motivation through which that career filtered to South Asian authors in translation. A collected volume of Neruda's poetry was first translated into English by Ángel Flores in 1946 and circulated in India very soon thereafter (Armenti 2015; Vibha Maurya, personal communication, January 29, 2019). As an American-sponsored project, this translation put the greatest emphasis on Neruda's reputation as a surrealist (including only poetry from the first *Residencia* onward). However, Ilya Ehrenburg had already translated Neruda's early political poetry into Russian six years prior, the event that would define Neruda as both poet and persona in the Soviet sphere and its transnational networks for decades to come (Djagalov 2020). According to Subhro Bandyopadhyay, early *bhasha* translations of Neruda, though mostly produced from English models, likewise emphasized his communist affiliations. Neruda was therefore a well-known poet in India by 1950, when he returned to the subcontinent for a brief tour (Das 2001; Satyarthi 2006).[7]

By this time, Neruda had completed two of his best-known volumes of poetry: the earlier love verses in *Veinte poemas de amor y una canción desesperada* (*Twenty Love Poems and a Song of Despair*) (1924), and the more serious "surrealist" verse of the first two *Residencia* volumes. Then, as a result of his experiences in the Spanish Civil War, Neruda had rejected those earlier styles and announced a turn to politically engaged poetry in *España en el corazón* (*Spain in Our Hearts*) (1936) (Santí 1982). This rejection also contributed to the assertion that the early *Residencia* is purely apolitical – a charge addressed in the second half of this chapter. Though that volume was originally published separately, it now is generally included as part of the full, three-volume *Residencia* series, putting it cheek by jowl with the very writing it repudiates.

Neruda spent the 1940s becoming increasingly involved in communist political causes. When Chile made a sudden rightward shift to align with the United States in 1948, the government stripped Neruda of his diplomatic immunity and issued an order for his arrest. Rather than submit, Neruda went into hiding – he was, effectively, under house arrest – where he remained until he could be smuggled across the border to Argentina in

1949 (Varas 2003). It was in this atmosphere of desperate conditions and hair's-breadth escapes that Neruda completed his magnum opus, an epic poem about the history and fate of the Americas, *Canto general* (*General Song*) (1949). That volume, and the idea of Neruda as the embodiment of the Americas, continues to be the most frequently referenced on the countershelf for South Asian authors, even as their specific political context has been left behind.

Toward the end of his life, in 1971, Neruda won the Nobel Prize for Literature. His South Asian reception in the wake of that award in some ways reversed the turn he had made in 1936. He was no longer only a communist poet but once again a "world" poet. Only in this moment did Neruda's image consolidate as the winner of "the test between politics and love" – a poet whose political commitments and global fame did not dilute the technical mastery or authentic feeling of his writing.

For these reasons, most South Asian references to Neruda do not operate like Syed's mentioned earlier. They are not so much intertextual – not echoes back to specific poems about legs and birds – but iconic. They imagine encounters with various versions of the "headboard-sitting Neruda" to whom the poet might merely gesture or might ask "some questions." Yet if Neruda is an object on the headboard, it is not precisely clear what kind. Is he a figurine, some serene secular Buddha, wise, fat, and happy? Is he a book of poetry, as he would be in a more traditional countershelf gesture? Or is he an image?

Perhaps this image?

"The Neruda Sitting on My Headboard": South Asian Objectifications of Neruda

"Neruda, A Mere Word": Sundaram's Transmigrant Portraits

In 1968, the Indian artist Vivan Sundaram and his wife, the art critic Geeta Kapur, attended a speech by Pablo Neruda. Sundaram was on the cusp of giving up art in favor of a full-time career in politics. But by 1971 his political career was proving more of a struggle than he had imagined. When a friend urged him to return to art, the recent Nobel Prize brought Neruda back to mind and gave Sundaram a place to start.

For him, as for Kumar and so many others, Neruda represented a way to harmonize political commitment with the "sonorous and expansive" sensuality of his poetry (Vivan Sundaram, personal communication, January 20, 2019). The resulting pen and ink series, *The Heights of*

Figure 1.1 Vivan Sundaram, "Portrait of Pablo Neruda," from *The Heights of Macchu Picchu* (1972).

Macchu Picchu (1972), includes three portraits of Neruda (see Figure 1.1) as part of a larger meditation on his poetic cycle *Alturas de Macchu Picchu*, published as part of *Canto general*. For Sundaram, the specific tenor of Neruda's politics was still quite important in a way that later writers would minimize or dismiss outright – the series also contains a portrait of Karl Marx. Yet he shares with other South Asian scribblers the vision of Neruda that the poet himself projects in this series – the embodied representative of the Americas as a singular political unit, one moving toward a future free from imperial domination.

Sundaram also shares a particularly readerly orientation to the poem. "There is a particular image proposed by the text, and so they have a fairly close association. If you read the poem and see the images, they are like illustrations" (Vivan Sundaram, personal communication, January 20, 2019). Thus, according to their creator, the drawings represent a kind of close reading, an insistent literalism in which the poet's words completely determine what is on the page. Sundaram did not even consult visual references to Macchu Picchu! The landscape that results, then, is a vivid example of the project that Aijaz Ahmad brushes off as a joke in the Introduction to this book: a fantasy of political solidarity between Peru and India (Ahmad 1987).

And yet, there is something resolutely non-literal about the illustrations, too. While the major image in each picture clearly follows Neruda's text, on closer inspection these seemingly coherent forms dissolve into minute patterns of stonework, textiles, vegetation, and human bodies. These details suggest the line in which Neruda commands the buried laborers at Macchu Picchu to "tell me everything, tell chain by chain, / link by link, and step by step" (Neruda quoted in Sahni 1974).[8]

In the way they merge into larger figures, especially human faces and hands, these details suggest Sundaram's underlying sensitivity to the transmigrant logic of *Alturas de Macchu Picchu*. That is, Neruda's concept of political witnessing is not primarily visual or vocal but embodied, pulling subjectivities from the past into the present of his figure. Lines where Neruda promises to "speak through your [dead] mouth" or commands "give me your hand out of the depths" – the subject of two other ink drawings – invoke Finlayson's description of "the self in the non-self."

Sundaram's portrait of Neruda as figurehead, as transmigrant witness, gained additional power as it circulated in literary venues. The same year he composed the *Machu Picchu* series, Sundaram published the portrait seen in Figure 1.1 in the arts and literature magazine *Vrishchik*. It immediately preceded the first installment of Kapur's essay *In Quest of Identity* (1973), discussed in Chapter 2, which likewise offers Latin American literature as a mirror for the politics of Indian art.

Sundaram's portrait then gained new life as Neruda's ghost. It appears as the iconic image of the poet on the cover of a 1974 special issue of *Lotus*

India marking the one-year anniversary of Neruda's death on the heels of Pinochet's coup. Edited by the Hindi novelist Bhisham Sahni, the magazine was a subsidiary of the Soviet-sponsored *Lotus: Journal of Afro-Asian writings*, one of the major vehicles for South–South internationalism in the mid-twentieth century. It thus upholds Neruda's older fame as a specifically communist author, while also helping to shape his future as a world-literary icon. A Hindi-language poet named Harsh wrote:

> Neruda, a mere word
> . . .
> A word that has joined
> men of different races
> of different lands
> of different colours
> of different creeds
> into one fraternity   (Harsh quoted in Sahni 1974)

The Indian Anglophone poet M. C. Gabriel wrote a tribute to Neruda directly addressing the people of Chile:

> but when they come, as sure they will,
> deafening their despair in a frenzied cry
> "Your Pablo Neruda is dead"
> do not believe them   (Gabriel 1973)[9]

Gabriel appears to inaugurate a transmigrant trope that will become commonplace in treatments of Neruda for subsequent generations, where the author's spirit is not eradicated by death but liberated by it:

> Let's not pretend
> he can be dead
> like any of us.
> Instead
> now that he is loose
> watch him come
> through every door
> of every home   (Gabriel 1973)

The Continent Vanishes: Agha Shahid Ali's Visions of Chile

Over the course of the 1970s and 1980s, Neruda's countershelf identity shifted away from politics and toward geography. In precisely the way Sundaram imagines, the Latin American landscape coheres in and makes sense for South Asian authors through Neruda's person. So, for example, an encounter with Neruda frames, quite literally, Salman Rushdie's first view of Nicaragua in his travelogue *The Jaguar Smile* (1987). Looking out his airplane window onto the Central American landscape below, Rushdie cites Neruda's *Canto general*: "Your eyes in Nicaragua / touch me, call me, grip me, / ... O, long-suffering peoples, O, slender waist of tears" (Rushdie 2008, 15–16). The same claim interests the Pakistani novelist Zulfikar Ghose, who opens the second section of his semi-autobiographical novel, *The Triple Mirror of the Self* (1992), "on a certain spot" in Peru where "Pablo Neruda ... had stood and found himself overcome by a premonition of his great poem," "Alturas de Machu Picchu" (Ghose 1992, 102). This location acts as the meeting point for his authorial stand-in and the Latin American novelist who will articulate Ghose's own commitment to the countershelf, discussed in Chapter 4.

Both Rushdie and Ghosh replicate Sundaram's approach to the production of *The Heights of Machu Picchu* in that they take Latin American literature as the primary or even the sole authority for constructing their own portraits of Latin America. But they are further united against Sundaram and earlier writers in their open antipathy to the poet's communism.

For Rushdie, who comes to Nicaragua to explore the impact of the Sandinista revolution, the communist leanings of the revolution are alternately jokingly minimized – as when Rushdie facetiously redeploys the communist phrase "triumph of the revolution" (usually used in reference to Cuba) to describe Indian Independence – or raised as a spectral threat to specifically writerly "freedoms" that were a chief concern of anti-communist liberalism in the Cold War (Brennan 1989; Brouillette 2007; Iber 2015). Ghose goes further still. While South Asian authors tended to celebrate Neruda for winning the "contest between love and politics," Ghose finds the opposite. Complaining about the contested nature of his own deployment of Neruda, he wrote to his friend Thomas Berger:

> My crime, it seems, is that I use the work of the great communist Pablo Neruda for the title of the novel [*A New History of Torments*] and its two parts – defiling, apparently, the memory of the sacred socialist by producing what the reviewer calls a "lurid extravaganza." As far as I'm concerned, Neruda will live on as a great poet, and his political affiliations will soon be forgotten or considered naïve. (Ghose 1982b)

The phrases "great communist" and "sacred socialist" jump out like zombies, dripping acid sarcasm. How different from the earlier writers' reverence for Neruda's politics. Different, too, from the phrase "great poet," which Ghose seems to mean sincerely, the part of Neruda that will "live on" as his politics rot away and are "forgotten." These figures of the poet, arguments over which aspects of his creation and persona should be sacralized, really might be read through the supernatural: a mummified politics grasping at life as opposed to an aesthetic practice primed for fresh birth.

At the same time Ghose and Rushdie were writing about Latin America in the 1980s and early 1990s, the Kashmiri poet Agha Shahid Ali also began a decade-long mediation on Neruda. Like them, his writing focuses mostly on the poet's artistic persona rather than the specificity of his politics. And yet, like Mohammed Hanif's writing in "Viva Havana!," Ali's poetry is haunted, sometimes quite concretely, by the memory of a socialist future which more recent events have radically foreclosed.

Ali expresses these spectral politics through an unusual degree of sensitivity to the embodied, transmigrant qualities of Neruda's oeuvre. It likewise reflects Ali's own investment in the practice of citation as a type of "queer curation," one that emphasizes personal relationships and willed affiliations to other literary traditions over "natural" flows of either genetic or literary inheritance (Betts 2017; Moscaliuc 2017; Gopinath 2018). These queer readerly genealogies and their physical, transmigrant incorporation come to the fore in a diptych from the middle of *The Half-Inch Himalayas* (1987): "Vacating an Apartment" and "The Previous Occupant."

In the first poem, Ali imagines a heterosexual couple that moves into his old flat, progressively erasing the traces of his queer body with their heteronormative, reproductive futurity. When placed beside it, the second poem, originally published in 1981, counters "Vacating an Apartment" with a queer form of inhabitation, a transmigrant form of identification, in which Ali opens up his own body to "the previous occupant," a man who has been killed by political violence in Chile. The poem opens:

> There's enough missing
> for me to know him. On the empty shelves,
> absent books gather dust: Neruda. Cavafy.
> I know he knew their poetry, by heart
> the lines I love   (Ali 2009, 63)

Here we see a clear image of the countershelf as a collaborative space, one that emerges out of encounters with foreign authors that are also mediated by literary predecessors at home. For the physical bookshelves discussed by Hanif, Ghosh, and Mehrotra in the Introduction, the countershelf exists as matter, holding the traces of a prior reader that thumbs, circles, and underlines. It is by following these physical pathways that the new occupant can be guided into the mental habits of the one before. Ali proposes something different: the ability to see what is not there anymore, to reconstitute a life from what are not even remains. Rather than the physical residue of the book (poetry as a written trace), Ali focuses on recitation (poetry as embodiment). Ali reminds us that poetry – quite unlike prose – is something we share by holding it in the mouth, swallowing it down, and keeping it "by" the heart. By opening on Neruda as a shared enunciative act, Ali introduces the logic of introjection that progressively overtakes the other Chilean at the heart of the poem, a man who has been "disappeared" in the political violence then engulfing the Southern Cone.

The poem continues by deepening the association between voice, identity, and introjection. "No detergent will rub his voice from the air / though he has disappeared in some country / as far as Chile" (Ali 2009, 64). The idea of language as an embodied trace recalls, again, Macaulay's most infamous phrase, in which English is an oral vector for embodied colonization (Bhabha 1984; Bahri 2017). Some of Ali's earliest published poetry makes this relation explicit, conflating eating and speaking as a way of working through his relationship to the English language.[10] But the borrowed and rearticulated words of recitation, when resituated on the anti-Anglophone countershelf, also call up the opposite: the persistent fantasy of world-literary collaboration, where poetry is always spoken person-to-person, and language can be infinitely varied and yet pose no barrier to "perfect understanding."

Ali gradually adds a visual dimension to "The Previous Occupant" in order to draw out one of the most common motifs through which South Asian authors understand their relationship to Latin America: the looking glass.

> Though he is blinded in some prison,
> though he is dying in some country
> as far as Chile,
> no spray will get inside the mirror
> from where his brown eyes ... stare   (Ali 2009, 65)

Having come to recognize himself in the Chilean, in the final lines Ali offers up his body (and his poem) as a crypt in which to safeguard the absent one. "Now that he's found me / my body casts his shadow everywhere. / He'll never, never move out of here" (Ali 2009, 65). Here he invites a kind of haunting that is also a return to flesh, a reincarnation – a transmigration. The images of one's body willingly bearing another's reflection, casting another's shadow, offers yet another image of the countershelf – a willed, nongenealogical association from which another may be recognized, preserved, and carried forward. Neruda is not precisely the subject here, but there is little doubt, as the opening suggests, that Ali's identification with Chile is shot through with an idea of the poet.

These themes come further into focus in the poem "I See Chile in My Rearview Mirror" from Ali's subsequent collection, *A Nostalgist's Map of America* (1991). The poem's conceit is that, as the speaker drives north toward Utah, he looks southward and sees the hemisphere's inverted image in his rearview mirror. From the perspective of the early 1990s, Ali gazes on a continent riven by civil war (Peru and Colombia) and dictatorship (Brazil, Argentina, Uruguay, and especially Chile). Mirroring operates as an inversion in a very literal sense – the speaker is driving through a summer landscape while looking at late fall or early winter in South America. At the same time, the poem's focus on dictatorial violence constitutes the dark reflection of earlier expansionism in the American West (Gopinath 2018).

As the poem progresses, Ali's attention comes to settle on a single figure – a witness to the concentration camp set up at the Estadio Nacional in Santiago, Chile, from September to November 1973.[11] "He's taken there / those about to die are looking at him, / his eyes a ledger of the disappeared" (Ali 2009, 162). It is easy to imagine this figure as the same disappeared Chilean in "Previous Occupant." Yet this section of the poem was written much earlier than the rest, first published as "A Dream of Buenos Aires" in 1984! Certainly, the central ideas of the poem might operate just as easily in Argentina, which was also controlled by a dictatorship that habitually "disappeared" political dissidents in the same period. Why, then, change the location to Chile, and why add to that autonomous work these other reflections about driving through the United States?

Neruda suggests an answer. By adding the motif of the rearview mirror, Ali holds together two continents otherwise separated by language and riven by political violence. He thus writes his own contribution to the project made famous in South Asia through Neruda's *Canto general*, of willing a hemispheric Américas into being. In this light, Ali's everyman at the Estadio Nacional also takes on new meaning. As a "ledger of the disappeared," he redeploys the witnessing function that Neruda employs throughout *Canto general*, one that has important, unacknowledged precursors in *Residencia I*. Ali seems to sense the same transmigrant energy that informed

Sundaram's visual recapitulation of "Alturas de Macchu Picchu," the way that Neruda claims this witnessing role by recruiting other souls into his very body. "Rush into my veins and to my mouth," Neruda commands at the end of the poem (Neruda quoted in Sahni 1974, 39). "Speak through my words and in my blood" (Neruda quoted in Sahni 1974, 39). Through this transmigrant act, the poet shelters and reanimates those killed by political violence, precisely what Ali aims to do in his own poems.

But in 1991, Ali evokes silence instead of sound. A glass-bounded vision of the mirror overtakes and holds back the introjection promised by speech. Seeming to invoke Neruda via Chile, Ali also names the violence during which he died. That same dictatorial wave foreclosed Neruda's vision for Chile and for the Americas. For Ali too, the dream of *Canto general*, of inter-American solidarity, of continental identification, shatters. The final line is unequivocal: "The continent vanishes" (Ali 2009, 162).

"The Home of Neruda Did Not Feel Removed from Lahore": Hamid's Neruda Kitsch

By the turn of the new century, Neruda's image had changed again. Rather than a witness to the violent political landscape of Latin America suggested by *Canto general*, Neruda was now the composer of *Odas elementales* (*Odes to Common Things*) (1954). So while Neruda's South Asian reception has long had this objectifying quality, this most recent turn to objectification helps illuminate the commoditization of literature in a newly unipolar, increasingly capitalized world.

The Pakistani novelist Mohsin Hamid stages an encounter with Neruda as part of an extended set piece about his protagonist's visit to Valparaíso, Chile, at the climax of *The Reluctant Fundamentalist* (2006). The novel tells the story of a young Pakistani financial analyst working in the United States who goes through a series of personal crises that ultimately prompt him to abandon his aspiration to assimilate in America and return to his family home in Lahore. It has most prominently been read as a meditation on identity and the expansion of the security state in the wake of 9/11. In this reading, Changez's personal crisis originates in his inappropriate, bemused reaction to watching the Twin Towers fall.[12]

A second line of interpretation points to the fact that Changez does not immediately abandon his job after 9/11, but only does so in response to an extended trip to evaluate the finances of a publishing company based in Valparaíso. Changez's role in this project will ultimately justify shutting down the unprofitable literary wing of the company so that it can be sold to a larger conglomerate. Critical readings that focus on the episode in Chile have tended to emphasize Changez's growing understanding of, and disgust with, the depredations of global capital and his role in perpetuating it (Gamal 2013). Yet *The Reluctant Fundamentalist* also can be read as a more specific critique, one focused on the capitalization of world literature. In this reading, South Asian Anglophone literature operates as a "janissary" – that is, a mercenary against one's own kind, the metaphor through which Changez ultimately comes to understand his own role in global finance.

These anxieties about world literature and the market are primarily articulated through a conversation between Changez, his American boss Jim, and the Chilean literary editor Juan Bautista:

> "What do you know of books?" [Juan Bautista] asked us. "I specialize in the media industry," Jim replied. "I've valued a dozen publishers over two decades." "That is finance," Juan Bautista retorted. "I asked you what you knew of books." "My father's uncle was a poet," I found myself saying. "He was well known in the Punjab. Books are loved in my family." (Hamid 2013, 141–142)

When Bautista later shares with Changez a copy of his great-uncle's Punjabi poetry translated into Spanish by his publishing house, he offers Hamid's protagonist a fleeting glimpse of the countershelf, an alternative version of world literature that celebrates its roots outside of English. It is a version of world literature that Hamid suggests both Changez and, by extension, he as author have been conscripted to destroy.

But why should an allegorical crisis about the role of South Asian literature in the world market take hold of the novel's protagonist in Chile, of all places? The suggestively named Juan Bautista might just as easily have been an editor in the Philippines, where one of Changez's earlier consulting projects takes place. It is Bautista's association with Neruda, as literary figurehead, which provides the answer.

Neruda himself is long dead. Unlike poetry or magical realism, the conventions of a realist novel do not allow Hamid to reincarnate him. But the soul of Neruda has "gotten loose" and remains available through the aura of his house, now a *casa-museo* (museum), La Sebastiana. During his visit, Hamid reflects neither on Neruda's politics in life, nor on the coup that came just at its end. Unlike South Asian predecessors Gabriel or Ali, he does not register the state-sponsored violence to which La Sebastiana had borne witness: ransacked and left to molder along with

Neruda's other houses after the 1973 coup. A different book might have reflected on the coincidence of dates – 9/11 – in both that coup and the recent American terrorist attacks that set Changez on the path back to Pakistan. A different book might have even suggested parallels between the US government's geopolitical interest in that coup (preventing the spread of communism) and its current presence in Pakistan (preventing the spread of fundamentalist Islam). Perhaps another reading would attempt to recover these parallels, as Albert Braz does (Braz 2015).

The only historical critique that rises to the surface of the text has to do with Valparaíso's role as a port of strategic importance to nineteenth-century British trade, linking contemporary global capital with its predecessor in the colonial era. Unbeknownst to Hamid, it was precisely this circulation that brought Neruda from Chile into the wider world, emerging from this very port to his first role as a representative of the Chilean government to British India.

But these traces, too, are left in the substrate of the text. Instead, for Hamid, the stuff of Neruda's legacy is, quite literally, his stuff. The *casa-museo* preserves his style – though tables and chairs, rather than meter and metaphor. Wandering its kitschy, colorful rooms, Hamid muses that "the home of Neruda did not feel as removed from Lahore as it actually was; ... in spirit it seemed only an imaginary caravan away from my city" (Hamid 2013, 167). Like his predecessors, Hamid imagines that Latin America might act as a transmigrant looking glass, revealing a deeper association in which whole cities and whole groups of people recognize their relatedness through a mystically mediated caravan. Indeed, this recognition is quite concrete: at one point, Hamid's protagonist actually observes himself through one of Neruda's funhouse mirrors.

Hamid and other South Asian authors are hardly alone in their pretension to "objectify" Neruda in this way. Indeed, the whole logic of the *casa-museo*, and much of the scholarship on Neruda, is built on the purported legibility of his stuff. At its best, Neruda's objects can offer South Asian authors imaginative links to a literary relation. But the physical detritus of the poet, as well as its absence, has also made a world of trouble for scholars as they try to account for Neruda's own, more complicated relationship to the subcontinent.

In the aftermath of Pinochet's coup, Neruda's three homes in Chile were symbolically gutted or left in various degrees of disarray (González 1985). They remained in that condition until the middle of the 1990s, when a Spanish telephone company funded their refurbishment and opening to the public as *casa-museo*s (Echenique Guzman 1990a). As restoration began in the early 1990s, a great deal of attention and correspondence centered on preserving, repairing, repainting, polishing, and otherwise restoring objects to their original luster. In the fall of 1990, the architects suggested removing and evaluating all of Neruda's possessions from the three homes (Echenique Guzman 1990a). In the process it became clear that certain objects were missing or were so broken or decayed that they could not be preserved.

In the wake of this discovery arose a kind of ad hoc heuristic in which certain types of objects merited the status of "artifacts" of Neruda's life, while others were merely "things" or "stuff" (Echenique Guzman 1990b).[13] The latter need not be preserved but could be discreetly discarded and replaced. Though the designers did their best to reproduce the three houses through mid-century photos and an extensive, room-by-room inventory, they also needed to make up for some of what had been damaged or lost (Echenique Guzman 1990a; Javier Ormeño Bustos and Dario Oses Moya, personal communication, July 29, 2013). The Santiago home, La Chascona, had been raided and flooded, while La Isla Negra was boarded up and under seal, and thus relatively preserved, though in poor condition (González 1985). The curators occasionally reshuffled "artifacts" between the homes (Javier Ormeño Bustos and Dario Oses Moya, personal communication, July 29, 2013). There were also known pockets of Neruda objects that had been lost in previous eras, for example a carefully photographed collection of masks acquired during his time in Asia that was then left behind in Spain. In these cases, the Foundation occasionally purchased new items with a "Neruda-like" feel (Javier Ormeño Bustos and Dario Oses Moya, personal communication, July 29, 2013).[14]

In no way do these adaptations to circumstance make the *casa-museo*s "inauthentic." They are all of a piece with the restoration and curatorial work that makes any object from the past available for interpretation in the present. Yet this particular restoration process reflects and deepens an existing assumption, particularly prevalent in Neruda criticism, that his objects can lead to a direct, unproblematic knowledge of the poet's experience. It is through Neruda, as object, that Ali comes to know the former occupant of his flats. And it is the idea of Neruda as a collection of objects that undergirds Sundaram's portraits. Moreover, when Hamid calls Neruda into presence through his tchotchkes, he is doing no more or less than the organizing principle of the *casa-museo* demands: literally insisting that the careful arrangement of Neruda's things, in the words of one of the project's architects, "truly evoke the presence of The Poet in Valparaíso" (Echenique Guzman 1990b).[15]

While the unconscious link between a person and his or her things might be true for any *casa-museo*, it takes on new resonance for Neruda, the poet of object-lists and an inveterate collector of stuff. "Well known is Neruda's passion for collecting all manner of things," opens *Las Casas y Cosas de Pablo Neruda* (*The Houses and Things of Pablo Neruda*) (2010), one of the coffee-table volumes of the type available for purchase at La Chascona (Vial and Alemparte 2010).[16] "This book of photographs reveals the magical relationship between the objects chosen by the Nobel Laureate and the spaces he created for them in each of his *casa-museos*" (Vial and Alemparte 2010).[17] While Neruda scholarship might not so openly avow its belief in the "magical" power of Neruda's objects to explain Neruda's poetry, it often depends on a very full archive of fairly random objects that are understood to transparently corroborate and deepen the story of Neruda's life and work. In addition to the mountains of Neruda's stuff arranged in the *casa-museo*s, the Colleción Neruda at the Universidad de Chile holds his entire personal library. The archive also holds a collection of 7,000 shells. Because they are tangible – preservable and preserved – even the shells find their way into authoritative reconstructions of Neruda's early career (Kantor 2014).

Neruda's Asian Residence: Recovering Solidarity in *Residencia I*

"No Positive Meaning to Cover the Void": Archival Absence in Neruda Scholarship

What is the result of this attachment to objects in a moment of Neruda's life when the archive disappears? From the first years of his Asian residence, almost no "artifacts" have been preserved in the way they were for almost every other period. There are a few pockets of correspondence – with a lover, a sister, a friend – but there are also vast expanses of silence. The official paper trail is even scanter: infrequent invoices for shipments of nitrate or tea, announcements of appointments, vacations, and transfers (Neruda n.d.). Neruda tantalizes future generations of scholars with one letter about a brownie Kodak camera (Neruda 1978, 38). Alas, no photos of his time in Burma survive. The very lack of historical detritus has made it easy for generations of scholars to ignore or misinterpret the impact of Neruda's Asian residence on *Residencia I*.[18]

Certain critics respond to this absence of "stuff" by suggesting that Asia itself was an empty place. For these scholars, Burma, India, and Sri Lanka are states without qualities, a blank canvas of total isolation in which

Neruda perfected the "self-absorbed" stance of the early *Residencia* poems. The stylistic and ethical fractures of *Residencia I* thus emerge as a symptom of the physical displacement the author experienced in Asia during the early years of his consular work for the Chilean government. Marjorie Agosín writes that "the solitude projected in his poetry is the product of all his feelings of alienation in a foreign land" (Agosín 1986, 39). Yurkievich concurs that *Residencia I* "can be considered a gestation provoked by particular personal experiences, by an alienating posting in the Orient" (Yurkievich 1971, 207).[19] Bluntly put, Neruda's experience in British India, whatever it was, powerfully impacted the trajectory of his writing and career.

So what was that experience? "Solitude," "alienation," "isolation," and their aesthetic products, "hermeticism" and "self-absorption," are omnipresent in critical descriptions of the living conditions that produced *Residencia I*. To be more precise, these descriptors are the only ones many critics use to address the Asian context, at all. Such is the insistence on Asia's blankness, it is as if Neruda had endured a prison sentence in solitary confinement instead of being sent abroad. There is a pronounced reluctance to explore the influence of Asia, an insistence that it was unimportant as a place unto itself, such that Yurkievich can write without qualification that in Burma "the poet finds no footholds, neither cultural nor social nor historical, no positive meaning to cover the void" (Yurkievich 1971, 207).[20] Inés María Cardone is even more blunt: "His poetry in the Orient reflects solitude and nothing more" (Cardone 2003, 90).[21]

Unsatisfied with this approach, a second critical stream has turned to another type of object to fill in the gaps of Neruda's time in Asia: books. These scholars construct a version of the *Residencia* period out of the picturesque landscape of so many French and English Orientalist novels. In this paradigm, Neruda might as well never have experienced Asia firsthand, since it accords exactly with what he or his critics had already read in Rudyard Kipling, Pierre Loti, Arthur Rimbaud, Leonard Woolf, T. S. Eliot, and, most importantly, George Orwell.[22] Neruda biographers Loyola, Volodia Teitelboim, and Adam Feinstein all spend considerable space tracing the poet's English reading list in the *Residencia I* years (Feinstein 2004; Teitelboim 2004; Loyola 2006). This includes attempts to recreate the contents of a literal library, the personal collection of a well-known Ceylon intellectual and artist Lionel Wendt, from whom Neruda apparently borrowed books. They then attach any specific Asian referent to that list.[23] In this way, Neruda scholars raise the specter of their own bookshelf, one that oddly yet exactly recapitulates Macaulay's assertion that "a single shelf of good European literature" can stand in for Asia (Macaulay 1835).

This vision of Neruda's time in Asia as an Orientalist fantasy persists in no small part because books are objects, durable and reproducible, and thus an easily accessible reference for a moment when other forms of evidence are fragile, lost, or absent altogether. By allowing these texts to have the last word on Neruda's Asian experience, however, scholars are reauthorizing the Orientalist assumption that Asia can only be experienced through the prism of literature – or that such texts constitute the ultimate authority about how Asia really is.

"An Established and Assured and Ardent Witness": First Glimmers of Connection

Fault for the relative lack of attention to the Asian context does not lie with scholars alone. It also comes from Neruda himself. In his *Memorias* (*Memoirs*), composed at the end of his life and published posthumously in 1974, Neruda seems unequivocal: "I have read some essays about my poetry which suggest that my stay in the Far East has influenced certain aspects of my work, especially *Residence on Earth* . . . . This claim of influence strikes me as mistaken" (Neruda 2000, 85).[24] Yet it becomes clear as one continues reading that Neruda has not positioned himself against the concept of any Asian influence whatsoever. Instead, he defends himself against a kind of Asian influence particular to the era in which the memoirs (and not the poems themselves) were written. When Neruda inveighs specifically against "Western vagabonds, not to mention residents of both North and South America . . . speaking only of Dharma and Yoga," he is writing in an age when interest in South Asia revolved almost exclusively around this kind of spiritual tourism (Neruda 2000, 85).[25]

Such an enchantment with the East, which Neruda reports having abandoned as early as 1927, remained unattractive to him later in life (Loyola 2006, 304, 307). Instead, he retroactively defines his own understanding of Asia as "a great, wretched human family, without any space in my mind for its gods or their rites" (Neruda 2000, 85).[26] He thus reduces the cultural difference between himself and the Asian population he encountered in the 1920s to a matter of religion – a form of false consciousness that Marxism casts off to reveal an underlying unity. Although such a characterization fits neatly into Neruda's Marxist political leanings at the time of writing the *Memorias*, it is not, in fact, appropriate to his attitude in the 1920s. Both Neruda and his critics have tended to imply that the process of moving from enchantment to disenchantment involves the peeling back of illusion to reveal the sordid reality beneath. This line of thinking suggests that *Residencia I*, which was infamously isolating and which Neruda would later condemn as "soaked in atrocious pessimism and anguish," was ideally situated to observe the truth about its Asian milieu (Neruda quoted in Rodríguez Monegal 1988, 13).[27] Certain scholars, like Teitelboim, even credit this pessimism as proof of Neruda's clarity of vision and incipient Marxist leanings (Teitelboim 2004).

Instead, it is the moments of measured optimism and gestures of hesitant connectivity – his gestures of transmigrant affiliation – that connect Neruda's surrealist *Residencia* poetry with his later writing and with the writing of his South Asian admirers. A fresh examination of *Residencia* demonstrates Asia was a vibrant environment eliciting a strong reaction from Neruda. His reaction to Asia is far more complex than mere self-absorption: Asia was not incidental but intrinsic to the development of a symbolic system and a mode of burgeoning social commentary that distinguishes the *Residencia* series from Neruda's other styles. *Residencia I*, moreover, is not as purely self-obsessed as it has been portrayed but also contains the germ of social consciousness that bore fruit a decade later in Spain.

Writing from Ceylon, Neruda described *Residencia* to a friend as "something very uniform, like a single object begun over and over again, like elaborated eternally without success" (Neruda 2008, 55).[28] This unity through repetition suggests an experience of reincarnation, one that is clarified in several subsequent poems. Although Neruda always stands firm in his antipathy to these religious philosophies, antipathy is not the same, in his case, as ignorance. We know that Neruda was familiar with the life and philosophy of the Buddha from one of his letters to Héctor Eandi in which he encloses a photograph of the "strange hungry Buddha, after those six years of senseless deprivation" (Neruda 2008, 35, 40).[29] The cycles described in many of the poems, then, may be read as reflecting *samsara* (cycles of rebirth), from which Buddhists and Hindus endeavor to escape into *moksha* (release or nirvana), or at least the Asian landscape in which such beliefs would tend to thrive.

In at least one poem, "Significa sombras" ("It Means Shadows"), the concept *samsara* is absolutely clear: it is unquestionably the cycle of reincarnation that places the angel wings on Neruda's speaker such that the path toward death is not the length of a single lifetime but rather "a violent flight begun many days and months and centuries ago" (Neruda

2004, 93–93).³⁰ If Buddhist practice is meant to liberate humans from this cycle, Neruda wants nothing to do with it:

> Ah, let what I am go on existing and ceasing to exist,
> and let my obedience be ordered with such iron conditions
> that the tremor of deaths and of births will not trouble
> the deep place that I wish to keep for myself forever.
>
> Let what I am, then, be in some place and in every time,
> An established and assured and ardent witness,
> Carefully destroying himself and preserving himself incessantly
> Clearly insistent upon his original duty. (Neruda 2004, 92–93)³¹

Posed in the form of a prayer in the subjunctive tense, the poem asks perversely for the opposite of what a Buddhist cosmology might offer: rather than a desire to be released into nirvana, the poet a wish to continue in an endless cycle of deaths and rebirths eternally attached to his ego. At the same time, the idea of infinite transmigration, without release, can act as a technology through which genetically and culturally unrelated people may be seen as united. This is, it appears, the first moment where Neruda calls upon the theme of transmigrant testimony: the "established and assured and ardent witness," who will reappear with greater force in *Canto general*. It is through a specifically embodied imaginary of witnessing as reincarnation that Neruda finally invites the builders of Machu Picchu to "speak through my words and in my blood."

During the first *Residencia*, Neruda also pioneered the poppy as a symbol through which to imagine a shared incarnation in singular flesh. Practices associated with the poppy – as the base crop of opium – both enable the poet's prophetic vision and condition his inclusion in an incipient cross-cultural collective.³² These are especially clear in his poem "Colección nocturna."

According to the work of Loyola, most of Neruda's *Residencia* poems can be dated with significant precision (Loyola 2006). For him, the poem that opens Neruda's time in Asia is "Colección nocturna," written, he claims, on the boat between Singapore, the first stop on Neruda's Asian tour, and Burma, his first diplomatic post. This would make it one of the first handful of poems in the *Residencia* series. But "Colección nocturna" was also one of the last poems to be completed in the first *Residencia*, and Loyola concedes it was most likely edited at the same time Neruda was writing "Significa sombras" (Loyola 2006, 429). Such a temporal layering would also suggest the possibility of an experiential layering of early and late experiences in the British Raj.

Loyola links "Colección nocturna" to Neruda's experience of insomnia during the ocean journey to Burma that the poet recounts in one of his contemporary essays for *La Nación*, "El sueño de la tripulación" ["The Crew's Dream"] (Loyola 2006, 306). "El sueño de la tripulación" contains Neruda's observation of the ship's crew as they sleep, "each one wrapped in his own dream, as much as in his own clothing" (Neruda 1999, 337).[33] Here sleep is associated with isolation and the failure to connect, a feature that is underscored by ethnic and regional differences among the sailors: "the blacks from Martinique," "the arabs," "the chinese," "the hindus" (Neruda 1999, 337–338).[34] Even in the supposedly shared activity of sleeping, members of the crew are held apart by the strange habits – for example, covering their eyes, facing Mecca – just as their "style of dressing" distinguishes them during the day (Neruda 1999, 337–338).[35] Thus, although images of sleepers and references to a marine environment in "Colección nocturna" do echo "El sueño de la tripulación," an additional element is needed to explain how the theme of separation in the essay is abandoned in favor of a theme of connectedness.

Opium is that element. Neruda's memoirs include a rich description of opium dens and their inhabitants as well as descriptions of Neruda's two confessed experiences with the drug. Beyond these, he claimed, "I never returned to the opium dens" heavily implying that Neruda never smoked opium again (Neruda 2000, 89–90).[36] Yet in the very act of seeming to confess everything, Neruda likely concealed a significant amount. His correspondence with Eandi suggests a different relationship to opium than the one he represented in the *Memorias*. At the bottom of a letter dated January 1929, Neruda's traveling companion Álvaro Hinojosa wrote a postscript indicating, "Pablo sleeps, smokes an opium pipe, and only wakes up to take care of official duties" (Neruda 2008, 45).[37]

The first four stanzas of "Collección nocturna" comprise an initial appraisal of the "angel of sleep": "he is the wind that shakes the months," "perfumed with sharp fruits," "wine of a confused color," and "a dusty passing of bellowing cows" (Neruda 2004, 45).[38] These three characterizations are all reflected in Neruda's description of opium smoke from the *Memorias*. Like the angel's sour smell, opium's odor is described as being "*extremely repulsive and powerful*," "*obscure*," and "*milky*" (Neruda 2000, 89, emphasis original).[39] His "substance" and "prophetic food," as well as later reference to his "those bland fruits from the sky," all seem to suggest a comestible substance associated with an altered state of consciousness beyond mere sleep (Neruda 2004, 26, 28).[40] More concretely, this substance comes to the speaker in a "black basket," evoking the particular physicality of opium, which is generally a dark brown or black resin transported in large, dark casing (Neruda 2004, 26).[41] The image of "immense black grapes, swollen" in stanza ten reinforces this idea: a large dark shell that holds an even darker seed (Neruda 2004, 30).[42] The physiological effects of opium smoking also appear, as when the angel "gallops in the breath and his step is kisslike," which indicates the duality of smoking as both nauseating and enticing, just as Neruda later described it (Neruda 2004, 26).[43]

In the second section of the poem, the speaker makes a nocturnal journey through an unnamed city accompanied by a group of dreamers, whom he calls the angel's "warriors" (Neruda 2004, 28).[44] The sleepers in "Colección nocturna" are no ordinary dreamers like those in "El sueño de la tripulación" but very obviously recognizable according to the descriptions of opium eaters in Neruda's *Memorias*.

> I often recognize his warriors
> His rooms corroded by the air, his dimensions,
> And his need for space so violent,
> That he comes down to my heart to seek it
> ...
> I hear the dream of old companions and beloved women,
> Dreams whose pulsings shatter me:
> I tread in silence on their ruglike substance,
> Their poppy light I bit deliriously.   (Neruda 2004, 28)[45]

In the passage where he describes them, we can see an atmosphere that reminds of the desperate, depressing environs of the opium den. The angel's "violent need" that penetrates the speaker's heart is a clear analogue for addiction, rather than mere somnolence. The focus on dreaming, especially shared dreaming, is likewise an obvious opium trope, confirmed when Neruda's speaker begins to share the dream at the very moment when he consumes the "poppy light" and enters its "delirium."

Having consumed the poppy, Neruda begins to speak in plural. What this seems to indicate is that opium can act not only as a cure for insomnia but as a tool of connection that breaks down barriers of class and ethnicity. Unlike quotidian dreaming of the sea voyage in "El sueño de la tripulación," in which the cosmopolitan potential of the ship is undercut by each dreamer's isolation into stereotype, the poppy light seems to both emanate from and provide a link to other participants in the dream.

After their first appearance in the opium-inflected "Colección nocturna," poppies recur over a dozen times in poems written between 1927 and 1935. Although rarely as easily identifiable with the experience of taking opium, poppies often retain features of both enlightenment and death.

Hinojosa's annotation to Neruda's correspondence makes it clear that Neruda was using opium on a daily basis as a means of withdrawing from a world he found uncomfortable and alienating. Yet at the same time his portrayal of opium, both in "Colección nocturna" and in his *Memorias*, reveals its latent potential to encourage empathetic connection and social consciousness, directly counteracting those feelings of estrangement. Neruda ultimately felt that this form of empathy was neither direct nor potent enough for the political project of his later years, but that does not mean that it can be as neatly bracketed from those later projects as his more mature poetry would have us believe.

But if scholars have been insufficiently attentive to this burgeoning social awareness, if they have construed *Residencia I* as an outlier in the larger oeuvre, they have again taken their cue from Neruda himself. In *España en el corazón* Neruda made a definitive break from the aesthetics of his earlier work. Enrico Santí points to the poem "Explico algunas cosas" ["I'm Explaining a Few Things"] from that collection as one of Neruda's best-known "conversion poems," implying the reflection on a previous mode of existence and its rejection from a point in the future when the world has become comprehensible (Santí 1982, 89).

In "Explico algunas cosas" Neruda famously rejected the matter and the mode of *Residencia* with an explicit reference to the poppy and all its symbolic cargo – including, apparently, its Asian cargo. He addresses the audience directly, breaking with the hermetic convention of the earlier *Residencia* poems, in order to predict his readers' displeasure: "You will ask: where are the lilacs? / And the metaphysical blanket of poppies?"[46] And later, "You will ask: why does your poetry / not speak to us of sleep" (Neruda 2004, 254)?[47] Both poppy-covered metaphysics and poetry of sleep, two prominent encapsulations of his former symbolic system, foreground his interest in the power of shared dreaming as a potential avenue into social awareness. Yet here they are offered as parodies of themselves, as a completely insufficient response to Franco's violence. Instead of lyric descriptions, the new Neruda makes direct demands of his audience: "Come and see the blood in the streets" (Neruda 2004, 260)[48]

"Another Hand Unknown to You": Transmigrant Aesthetics Live On

The Indian literary scholar Sirsir Kumar Das recounts his engagement with Neruda in his meditation on comparative literature, *Indian Ode to the West Wind* (2001). For the most part, the chapter "Pablo Neruda: The People's

Poet" tells the familiar, pre-1971 story about Neruda as an exemplary communist poet – the history this chapter has attempted to complicate. The tidbits about the Chilean's time in India are likewise expected – the tour of India in 1928, the return as a Partisan for Peace in 1950 – all politically sanitized recollections from the poet's posthumous memoirs. When poetry is mentioned, Das skips right from the infamous "free translation of Tagore" in *Viente poemas de amor* (*Twenty Love Poems and a Song of Despair*) (1924) to the transparently political poetry of "Himno y regreso" ("Hymn and Return") (1939) (Das 2001, 160).[49] *Residencia I*, the poetry Neruda was writing in South Asia, makes no appearance at all.

And yet, the themes born of the *Residencia* series are there, the sense of mystically mediated connection between the past, its dead, and their incarnation in the present. Das touches on just this imaginary when he says that Neruda "came to us not only in his English *incarnations* but also in translations in our own languages" (Das 2001, 161, emphasis added). He goes on to recall how he and his companions read aloud the final lines from "Un canto para Bolívar" ("A Song for Bolivar"), a poem from the third and final *Residencia* volume, in which the speaker imagines a circle of hands reaching out to grasp the dead revolutionary and take up his project in the present. "Another hand unknown to you / Comes also, Bolívar, to clasp yours" (Das 2001, 161). These hands, for Neruda, come from all over the world, not just in the present but from the dead. These gestures demonstrate that the turn from the metaphysical meditations of *Residencia I* to the political imaginaries that followed in *España en el corazón* and *Canto general* is not only a rejection, as Neruda and so many of his critics have claimed. These moments in Neruda's career are also related through the continuity of transmigrant imaginaries of global relation.

"When we used to read these lines aloud," Das writes in reference to "Un canto para Bolívar," "did we not also say to the poet 'another hand unknown to you / comes also, Neruda, to clasp yours'" (Das 2001, 162)? Is this not precisely the gesture Sundaram makes when he remediates Neruda's command to "give me your hand out of the depths"?

There is no version of Neruda's life that settles *Residencia I* comfortably into the weave of what came after. No retelling that can obscure the unevenness of his intense ambivalence and unhappiness in South Asia with the adulation of his later South Asian readers. If this chapter has tried to make sense of the parallel lives of the poet and his persona in the weft of world literature, it is not with the aim of erasing this era's more troubling aspects.

Instead, it is to suggest that Neruda and his South Asian readers sometimes find strange harmonies, indeed that South Asian rereadings, even misreadings, of Neruda reveal resonances that Latin Americanist criticism has sometimes overlooked. We saw this on the matter of objects: the way Neruda's *Residencia*-era interest in animating the inanimate, in uncovering the secret life of things, lends special force to his own later objectification as a literary figurehead. In the same way, the theme of reincarnation and collective dreaming undergirds both his own poetic practice in *Residencia I* and his utility for later generations of South Asian poets. When Ali invites a nameless Chilean to cast a shadow from the poet's own body, he seems to echo Neruda's own pessimistic prayer to "go on existing and ceasing to exist." And when Gabriel insists that death has set Neruda "loose" so that he can "come / through every door," she answers Neruda's desire to be "an established and assured and ardent witness / Carefully destroying himself and preserving himself incessantly." These poems share an imaginary of reincarnation and its fragile optimism about the capacity to will oneself into relation. This type of mystical futurity endures as the tie that binds Neruda with readers and writers in South Asia, while the horizon of possibility for the explicitly political imaginaries of his later poetry have been increasingly eclipsed. Out of the *Residencia* series as a whole, it was this particular poem, "Significa sombras," that Neruda most violently rejected in his political turn. And yet it is this prophecy – to "be in some place and in every time" – that, out of all of them, has most certainly come true.

CHAPTER 2

Stranger
Paz's Peregrinations through Indian Poetry

> My experience of India has been that of ... *a total stranger*. Not hostility (that is Spaniards and Mexicans) nor indifference (in the manner of the English) but rather ... I don't know how to put it. Coexistence – promiscuity, the feeling of being surrounded by a human vegetation that does not know you and that you will never know.
>
> (Paz 2008, 26, emphasis added)[1]

In 1968, this is how Octavio Paz described his experience as the Mexican ambassador to India, a position he held from 1962 until 1968. The word he uses, "extrañeza," appears again and again in his writing about the subcontinent, and carries a few different meanings. One is simply strange, even disorienting or estranging, here probably drawing on Paz's familiarity with the Russian formalist characteristic of *ostranenie*, what is commonly referred to as literary defamiliarization. However, translator Benjamin Sher emphasizes the multiplicity of Viktor Shklovsky's original coinage through an equivalent neologism "enstrangement," which encodes the positivity of enchantment through its prefix, while the body of the word retains its relationship to the generally negative English term "estrangement" (Sher quoted in Shklovsky 1990, xviii–xix). Along with unpleasant disorientation, the common Spanish usage of *extrañeza*, too, suggests a potentially wonderful surprise.

As with Pablo Neruda, Paz supported himself for a long time as a diplomat, and his time in South Asia likewise coincided with one of the most stylistically experimental phases of his career. Paz, however, enjoyed his time in India quite a bit more. Visiting the Chilean's former home while on vacation in Sri Lanka, Paz remarked that it was "a paradisiacal spot" (Paz 1998, 23). He was surprised, he goes on to say, "that Pablo Neruda had lived in this exact spot thirty years before and had, according to a friend, found it abominable" (Paz 1998, 23).[2] While the Asian residence inaugurated Neruda's career abroad, for Paz it heralded an end. He famously resigned the post in protest after military police massacred a group of protesting students in Mexico City in October 1968.

If Chapter 1 worked through the paradox of Neruda's iconic standing in South Asian letters in light of his more ambivalent experience there, this chapter tackles almost the opposite problem. It is well known (in India, at least) that Paz was involved in the Indian literary scene during his tenure as ambassador. But it is much more difficult to pinpoint the nature and scope of his impact. No one writes about imaginary encounters with Paz, the way they do with Neruda. Yet the archives are full of real ones. Strange as it seems, Paz operated as a "curator" who helped to usher a generation of poets, artists, and editors toward the cultural production of Latin America. And while it is Neruda who forms the image of culturally authentic world literature for South Asian authors, Paz was a nearly invisible engine through which that imaginary consolidated.

In this way, Paz embodies the countershelf value of curation: the idea that world literature is neither consumed nor produced through impersonal forces alone but must reach individual authors through their relationships with one another. It was not merely that Paz exposed Indian writers to new traditions. Through *extrañeza*, he also proposed a way of negotiating the compromises of world circulation. *Extrañeza* functions as a type of encryption, one that divides an expanding, potentially global readership into outsiders and insiders, strangers and friends. Allusion and ludic playfulness, the willful witholding of context, propose a kind of world literature that can negotiate, though not resolve, the ambivalence between a desire for worldly affiliation and an anxiety about "selling out."

Extrañeza reflected Paz's growing interest in the baroque, a form that emerged to aestheticize the rapidly and radically changed concept of the world in the era of colonial expansion (Johnson 2010; Ramachandran 2015). *Extrañeza* and the related concept of enigma can therefore act as a conceptual throughline to link together some of the otherwise quite varied writing of this era – the more traditional poetry collection cum travelogue *Ladera este* (*The East Slope*) (published in 1969, but composed in India between 1962 and 1968), the experiments with various forms of concrete poetry in *Blanco* (*Blanco: [poems]*) (1967) and *Topoemas* (some of which were published in 1968 and the full collection in 1971), and later the collections of India-influenced essays *Corriente alterna* (*Alternating Current*) (composed 1959–61 and 1965–7, published 1967) and the generically indefinable *El mono gramático* (*The Monkey Grammarian*) (published in French in 1972, Spanish in 1974).

Extrañeza is also Paz's legacy. His presence seemed to guide a whole host of writing and editorial decisions among the Anglophone poets of the often neglected *sathottari* generation of the 1960s and 1970s. Anjali Nerlekar adapts the term *sathottari* "from a narrower avant-gardism in Marathi to a broader network of experimentations and rebellions that connect multilingual literature and art of resistance" (Nerlekar 2016). It is used here as an umbrella for the multilingual, multimodal creators of mid-century India, among whom Paz helped to establish a very particular idea of world-literary friendship. That mode, informed by *extrañeza*, proposes a kind of world-literary aesthetic that is quite distinct from what we usually imagine: in place of an increasingly unified and easily digestible singular style, a series of intentionally disorienting enigmas.

This makes Paz a kind of stranger, a wanderer whose presence forces a reevaluation of settled certainties. In one sense, as the word itself suggests, this is a reinvigoration of "en-strangement," in which literature is understood to resensitize its readership to a world taken for granted. But Paz's use of *extrañeza* goes further. It uses specific descriptive techniques to blur the line between the estranged familiar and the truly unknown, upsetting readerly expectations about both. These aesthetics, as well as Paz's persona, resonated for other writers interested in theorizing a newly expanded postcolonial world – encompassing both India and the Americas – whose contours were both familiar and wholly new.

If Paz operated aesthetically as a stranger in India, practically speaking he functioned as a friend. After a surprise meeting at his Delhi hotel in 1962, Paz agreed to write the opening essay for the catalogue of the Delhi art show put on by Gulammohammed Sheikh, Jagdish Swaminathan, and collection of young, upstart painters calling themselves Group 1890. "I spent long hours before their oils, drawings, collages, prints, sculptures; we talked, we discussed, we laughed and we remained silent. We are friends" (Paz 1963, 4). As it turned out, it would be both an introduction to and valediction of that short-lived artists crew. But Paz's "friendly" association endured, shaping the subsequent decade of work by members of the group and their contemporaries in Indian arts and letters in strange and unexpected ways.

The relationships of inspiration and connection that Paz cultivated among these artists were typical of him. As Paz scholar Isabel Gómez explained to me, Paz invested in up-and-coming writers all around the world "as a part of his conviction that there was something 'universal' in the practice of poetry that made it necessary for him to have these open channels of communication with many other poets of his time, especially those from non-European traditions" (Isabel Gómez, personal communication, January 18, 2019). The same interest in networks also informed Paz's particular genius at finding opportunities to support himself through fellowships, diplomatic postings, and academic appointments. His collected correspondence, including the letter cited earlier, is full of advice about how other authors might follow in his footsteps. Readers familiar with Roberto Bolaño's *Los detectives salvajes* (*The Savage Detectives*) (1998) will recall the way that Paz himself came to be construed as an institution in the Mexican poetry scene of the 1970s (Bolaño 1998; Boullosa 2007). This is not merely metaphorical: throughout his life, Paz displayed an almost superhuman energy for organizing movements, journals, and factions. He was a master, in other words, of those practical collectives through which institutions exert their disciplinary force.

Operating at this nexus between stranger and friend, Paz helped Indian authors consolidate the desire to circulate widely without circulating broadly. The *satthotari* poets ended up engaging in a kind of world literature that moves among friends all over the globe through networks of little magazines but is not easily available – either aesthetically or materially – for people beyond these networks. They demonstrate that not only a desire for worldliness but also a concrete form of world circulation is perfectly compatible with the desire for intransigence – what Eric Bulson calls the "fear and loathing" of global circulation among little magazine producers (Bulson 2016, 41).

It is no surprise that this particular version of world literature centers on poetry rather than prose. The imbrication of South Asian Anglophone novels with commercialism is such a truism of the field that market circulations have come to stand in metonymically for Anglophone writing as such – for worldliness as such. Many sociologically inflected theories of world literature posit that there can be no significance for world circulation outside of a capitulation to those forces.

The focus on *extrañeza*, in contrast, marks the hope that multilingual poetry could circulate totally outside the market. This is why, in the common countershelf fantasy, poetry is both the safeguard of linguistic specificity and yet also the site of "perfect understanding" between unrelated literary traditions. Behind this fantasy is a desire for "a community immediately present to itself, without difference, a community of speech where all the members are within earshot" (Derrida 1980, 136). Especially in its "crystalline" structure, this image recalls the looking glass (Derrida 1980, 119). It suggests Latin American literature as a location of uncanny mutual regard, not only as a historical model, à la Neruda, but as part of the project of becoming contemporary. Yet this idea seems to directly contradict the concept of a counterpublic essential to the countershelf, which, as Warner emphasizes, centers the expectation that one will be overheard by strangers (Warner 2002, 55–57).

Of course, it is deeply ironic that in the very scene of perfect understanding, the absence of linguistic polysemy, poetry would promptly disappear. Baroque poetry and its investment in linguistic play, in particular, could not be further from this fantasy. Paz's *extrañeza* is fundamentally about a world that has become too big to comprehend and a kind of utterance that produces this feeling, rather than makes sense of it. Concrete poetry goes further, in that it is only comprehensible to the eye and leaves orality behind entirely. In this sense, the desire for "perfect understanding" must remain necessarily unfulfilled. On the other hand, the way that this writing circulated – passed in small batches between friends – does, indeed, offer the clearest vision of an uncompromised, direct contact that is fantasized in the encounter between Mohsin Hamid's protagonist Changez and the editor Juan Bautista discussed in Chapter 1.

There thus appears an irresolvable conflict between the desire for worldwide circulation and a narrow, cultivated audience, as well as between poetry as a transparent form constructing an audience of immediate self-recognition and poetry as a baroque language game reveling in its own complexity. Yet it may be possible to untangle this apparent enigma through Erving Goffman's concept of "collusion": the idea that speakers may mark out distinct insider and outsider audiences by "using allusive words ostensibly meant for all participants, but whose additional meaning will be caught only by some" (Goffman 1981, 134). The idea of encryption, allusive language, and layered meanings can be traced back to the baroque aesthetics, and its more implicit politics, that the *sathottari*s adapt from Paz.

Even so, the very success of that collusion was also a failure for these Indian poets. The *sathottari* authors are dramatically understudied compared to the Anglophone writing on either end of their era. Successful novelists of a later generation, Jeet Thayil and Amit Chaudhuri, share an investment in renarrating the *sathottari*s into the canon – but only if they can also retain their commitment against circulation. In his introduction to Arun Kolatkar's poetry collection *Jejuri* (1976), Chaudhuri thus follows a common line of criticism pitting the *sathottari*s' achievement in Anglophone poetry against the triumph of the Anglophone novel under Salman Rushdie (Chaudhuri 2005). While Rushdie is the icon of South Asian Anglophone fiction abroad, he contends, the *sathottari*s represent what Anglophone writing could have been, what it should have been. In his novel on the Indian arts scene of the 1970s, *The Book of Chocolate Saints* (2017), Jeet Thayil puts the same polemic into the mouth of a "former professor of English literature": "Why has no one written about the Bombay poets of the 1970s . . . ? Fiction has been done to death, features and interviews and critical studies and textbooks, and not one of the novelists is worth a little finger of the poets" (Thayil 2017, 47).

In one sense, the terms of these recoveries problematically reinforce the relationship between artistic integrity, authenticity, and provincialism. They suggest that the *sathottari*'s investment in estrangement is identical to a rejection of circulation, forgetting that it emerges in conversation with an existing world-literary project.

But both Thayil and Chaudhuri are right, in a way. The circle of poets engaged by Paz represent a phantom limb in the Anglophone body. They were setting a very different course for Indian Anglophone literature, one that Rushdie and "the novelists" dramatically interrupted and then, essentially, cut off. Even though both route through Latin America, the 1970s of Indian Anglophone literature really don't lead into the 1980s. The final purpose of this chapter is to suggest why not.

"A Pilgrim's Steps Are Vagabond Music": Paz's Baroque Disorientation

Late in his life, some of Paz's India-themed writings were reissued by the imprint *Círculo de Lectores* in three volumes called "*Tres vías hacia la India*" ("Three Routes toward India"). Paz clarifies that the word *vía* has two interrelated meanings: a literal route through territory and a spiritual route outlining a journey of the soul. "In the case of my three books the two meanings are mixed: they were written along the routes of India, its geographic routes, its historical routes, those of its art and thought" (Paz 1996, 5).[3] One might assume that the rhetorical focus on "routing" would mean that these texts functioned on some sort of touring logic, guided by a movement through space. And, yes, several of his writings are anchored to real locations: Delhi, Vrindaban, Cochin, Udaipur. Still, as Paz himself does in *El mono gramático* – ostensibly based on a straightforward walk through the Galta-ji temple complex on the outskirts of Jaipur – one can wander into these poetic locations and never get out again. They are quite intentionally disorienting.[4]

Paz offers the key for understanding *extrañeza* as disorientation in the poem that opens *Ladera este*: "El balcón" ("The Balcony"), a reverie inspired by the balcony in his Delhi home. Like many poems in the collection, it consists of fairly concrete descriptions of the landscape, in this case what the poet sees of the city at night from his outdoor perch. Yet this specificity is contrasted to the speaker's attitude at the end of the poem:

> I am here
>   *I don't know* is where
> Not the earth
>   Time
> holds me in its empty hands
> [. . .]
> Far off lands
>   *a pilgrim's steps are vagabond music*
>   (Paz 1970, 21, emphasis original)[5]

This juxtaposition gives the sense that no amount of literal description will be sufficient to anchor the speaker (or his audience) in his new surroundings, these "far off lands."

Paz makes what might seem to be a relatively banal observation about foreignness, were it not for the way that he situates it against an unattributed citation: "*a pilgrim's steps are vagabond music*" ("*pasos de un peregrino son errante*"). These are the opening lines of the dedication for the pastoral poem *Las soledades* (*The Solitudes*) (1613) by the Spanish baroque poet Luis de Góngora. Errantry – "vagabond music" in Eliot Weinberger's translation – is an organizational strategy for the poem, which follows a nameless sailor shipwrecked in an unfamiliar land. In this sense, it offers a structural model for *Ladera este*, which likewise follows Paz's peregrinations around the subcontinent.

Early in his epic poem, Góngora's nameless wanderer encounters a group of shepherds – former soldiers who recount to him the violently new political order of the world from which they have voluntarily withdrawn. Inaugurated by Christopher Columbus, Vasco da Gama, and Ferdinand Magellan – whose names stand in iconically for conquest in the text – this new globe is linked by the seas, creating it, for the first time, as a single planet.[6] This general history of the spread of Iberian power both east and west narrows into the particular recollections of one of the interlocutors, a former soldier who was shipwrecked in India. And so, although no part of India was ever part of the Spanish empire, with this oblique citation Paz invites readers to think about literary predecessors for his project of linking India and Mexico in a single geopolitical matrix.

Góngora's linguistic choices, his "hyperbolic, conceited [verbal] play," reinforces these politics, offering "an ironic, self-consciously subjective response to Spanish Imperial ideology, with all its objective, verisimilar pretensions" (Johnson 2010, 162). At the same time, as Christopher Johnson argues, the rapidly expanding world inaugurated by the Spanish imperial project encourages Góngora to write in "the language of discovery" (Johnson 2010, 162, emphasis original). His linguistic playfulness evinces *asombro*, the startled wonderment that also operates at the heart of Columbus' first writings about the Americas and all of the discourses of conquest that followed. The same tension inheres in Paz's use of *extrañeza* – especially its potential association with Orientalist tropes of inscrutable otherness.[7] This tension will reappear in debates about the potential politics of magical realism, discussed in Chapter 4 and, indeed, reflects the ambivalent investment in reincarnation through which Neruda expressed his growing social consciousness in Chapter 1. One of the enduring complexities of the countershelf is South Asian authors' attraction to these ambiguously politicized literary styles as sites of solidarity and postcolonial imagining.

Errantry is also an aesthetic choice, a celebration of disorientation that allows Paz and his followers to "collude" with an insider audience even as their poetry circulates in broader networks. This, too, Paz adopts in light of Góngora. Paz clarifies what he takes from Góngora in "¿Qué Nombra La Poesía?," an essay published in *Corriente Alterna* in 1967 and later translated in 1973 as "What Is Poetry?" Paz writes: "Góngora is not obscure: he is complicated.... There are veiled mythological and historical allusions, the meaning of each phrase and even each individual word is ambiguous. But once these knotty problems and teasing enigmas have been solved, the meaning is clear" (Paz 1973a, 4).

Part of Góngora's appeal, then, is that his writing requires both extended attention and a certain cultural capital to unlock. According to Góngora himself, these choices were an intentional form of collusion, a way of sorting his readership into insiders and outsiders. "I consider this poetry to have given me honor in two ways: if understood by the learned, it has earned me authority.... Further, I have earned honor by making myself obscure to the ignorant" (Góngora quoted in Johnson 2010, 172). But there is a difference, too. While seventeenth-century baroque authors' use of enigma "encourages, or some would say forces, the reader to find the intended figurative meaning rather than accepting the apparent or literal meaning," Paz and his followers extend and invert this trope (Johnson 2010, 2). They consistently present as allusive and metaphorical images that resolve, for readers in the know, into absolutely concrete citations of Indian places and texts.

When Paz reproduces "the routes of India, its geographic routes, its historical routes, those of its art and thought," he often does so in a way that intentionally obscures exactly which route is taken – to "force ... figurative meaning" out of what is often very intentionally literal. It may be useful to conceive of this practice as a kind of ekphrasis – the translation of the visual realm into the verbal, most frequently applied to literary descriptions of works of art. As Mieke Bal explains, ekphrasis transforms the single, immediate apprehension of the visual field into a narrative, either by animating objects or dramatizing them as a scene of action (Bal 2006, 125–126). This latter practice offers tools through which both Paz and writers like Geeta Kapur associate Latin American literature with contemporary visual arts in India.

But ekphrasis does more than produce collusion between the writer and his insider audience. It also furthers Paz's desire to explore the outer limits of language in its relationship to a wider world. As Bal continues, in ekphrasis "the radical, ontological difference between visual and linguistic utterances is suspended in favor of an examination of the semiotic power of each and their relation to truthful representation" (Bal 2006, 124).

This suspension of difference between visual and verbal is precisely the grounds of concrete poetry, but is also narrativized in Paz's great poetic essay *El mono gramático*. He likens the essay – which alternates between deep meditations on space and time, unmarked citations of other texts, and extended ekphrastic descriptions of the Galta-ji complex – to "a system of mirrors that have, bit by bit, revealed another text" (Paz 1996, 45).[8] As with everything else in the poem, these mirrors are both physical and metaphysical. In Section 17, Paz describes Amer Fort's Sheesh Mahal (Mirror Palace), just visible on a hill on the opposite side of Jaipur from Galta-ji. The physical nature of mirrors – a flat surface that erroneously suggests depth – reinforces Paz's central concept of the book, "a tapestry of presences that hide no secrets. Exteriority and nothing more" (Paz 1996, 112).[9] But this statement about mirrors simultaneously refers to the legend that the titular monkey grammarian, Hanuman, wrote the original version of the *Ramayana*, for which the sage Valmiki's version is merely the flawed, human reflection. It thus emphasizes Paz's ongoing concern with the inadequacy of human language to capture human experience.

This obsession with surfaces and mirroring also manifests in Paz's experiments with concrete poetry, some of which would go on to interest the *satthotari* poets. *Blanco* explores creative use of negative space (*blanco* as white) and the possibilities of the empty page before it has been filled with text (*blanco* as blank). The subsequent *Topoemas* is even more explicitly interested in the page as a space, a topos or landscape. Nearly half of the poems in that collection are based on Indian themes.

In order to make them comprehensible, the playful word-images are explained with footnotes quite a bit longer than the poems themselves. So, for example, the poem "Monumento reversible" ("Reversible Monument"), playing a different form of mirror game and written in the shape of a reflected pyramid, is explained as alluding to "the stepped pyramids of Mesoamerica and certain temples in India" (Meyer-Minnemann 1992, 1126).[10]

Similar explanatory notes appear at the end of *Ladera este*, seeming to contradict the entire purpose of the poetry's disorienting literalism. The notes give detailed, historically and culturally situated descriptions of the same places or practices that read like any standard travelers' guide. In several cases, the description given in the notes is significantly longer than the poem it clarifies. For instance, the poem "El Mausoleo de Humayún" ("Humayun's Tomb") is a scant eight lines, 35 words:

> The debate of the wasps
> the dialectic of the monkeys
> Weavil statisticians
> is opposed
>   (tall pink flame
> made of stone and air and birds
> time in repose upon the water)
>
>   the architecture of silence.   (Paz 1996, 25)[11]

Someone familiar with this popular site in Delhi could easily measure this poem against their own experience there. The "tall pink flame / made of stone" clearly refers to the color of the sandstone edifice. Wasps, monkeys, and birds are common sights in the well-maintained gardens surrounding the tomb, on a layout that later served as the model for the Taj Mahal. This literalism was clarified in "Re-Imagining Octavio Paz," a poster exhibition at the 2019 New Delhi World Book Fair, which included a photo exhibit that showed Delhiites holding snippets of Paz's poems, resituated in the locations that inspired them. The recapitulation of "El Mausoleo de Humayún," in particular, offers a kind of concrete poetry in which the text of the first half of the poem is quite literally "opposed" by the edifice in the background whose description makes up the poem's omitted conclusion.

The endnote for "El Mausoleo de Humayún," on the other hand, is twice as long as the poem itself. As with the oblique citation of Góngora in "El balcón," it is only within this frame of reference that the politics of the poem are revealed, in this case a critique of logics of development. In the poem, Paz writes:

> Son of Babur, the conqueror of India, the emperor Humayun was the father of Akbar the Great. The family descended from Timur or Tamerlan, Marlowe's Tamburlain, Clavijo's Tamburbeque. Around Humayun's tomb are located, or were located, one of those centers of study that economists and sociologists call "development," heavily frequented by Indian functionaries and foreign "experts." (Paz 1996, 169)[12]

If the disorientation of *Las soledades* is a guiding principle for Paz at the beginning of the collection, then how might we read this belated effort at clarity and contextualization? Paz himself offers two conflicting explanations. In the reissued 1996 *Círculo de Lectores* edition, Paz says merely that "since, in some passages there appear words and allusions to persons, ideas, and things that might disorient the reader [*extrañar al lector*] unfamiliar with this region of the world, several friends have suggested that I include some notes that would clear up these obscurities" (Paz 1996, 167).[13] Paz makes it clear that editorial intervention explains the guidebook feel of the footnotes, as if it had never occurred to him that *extrañeza* was one possible result of his allusive style.

But earlier editions give quite a different sense of the purpose of the endnotes. Thirty years before, in manuscript copies of *Ladera este*, as well as earlier printings, the introduction to the notes contained a final sentence that was apparently stricken from the *Círculo de Lectores* collection: "I am afraid (I hope?) that these notes, far from dispelling the *enigmas*, will only increase them" (Paz 1970, 173, emphasis added).[14] Through the reference to "enigmas," Paz further associates his portrayal of India with the hallmarks of Góngoran style as he described them in "¿Qué Nombra La Poesía?" He admits that intentionally withholding of context in baroque ekphrasis is meant to reproduce a disconcerted feeling. Yet, he seems to suggest, the attempt at a more complete citation offered in the notes will not, fundamentally, reduce the feeling of foreignness cultivated by his style. That feeling is the point.

"I Was Longing to Meet Artists": Paz and the *Sathottaris*

> The connection [with] Octavio Paz ... happened rather *unexpectedly*. ... We discovered that Octavio Paz was staying at the Ashoka Hotel, so we decided to go and see him. Vivan Sundaram, his sister Navina and I ... knocked at his door .... You can't believe how delighted he was to see us. "I've been meeting these damn politicians and diplomats all the time!" he said to us, "I was longing to meet artists."
>
> (Sheikh quoted in Zecchini 2017a, 6, emphasis added)

In 1963, nearly a decade before Vivan Sundaram left art and then returned through a vision of Pablo Neruda, he accosted Octavio Paz in his Delhi hotel room and helped bring him into the ambit of Indian cultural life. It was an era in which the realms of art-making, criticism, poetry, prose, editing, and even publishing were not the separate, professionalized spheres they tend to be today but part of a vibrant, underground whole. This multiplicity is perhaps nowhere better expressed than in the modernist little magazines where so many artists and writers published their early work. As Nerlekar notes, "the common elements among these otherwise diverse set of little magazines" circulating in India in the 1960s and 1970s included "a broad-based interest in publishing translations from Indian regional literatures, a disregard for profit-making methods, a focus on popular life and its language, and a relatively short-lived existence" (Nerlekar 2016, 194). While the little magazines are where many of the most canonical Indian Anglophone authors (and scholars!) of this period got their start, the same features that made the genre exciting also made it difficult to trace these authors and their forms of circulations in a larger literary world.

The timeline presented in the Introduction makes it seem like the failure of South Asian Anglophone authors of the midcentury to gain widespread popularity was mostly external – to do with the disinterest of audiences both at home and abroad in the genre and language of writing they were producing. But in the case of the *sathottari* poets, this was also a matter of form – the choice to publish in little magazines and independently printed books – and, fundamentally, of attitude. Like little magazine producers in other parts of the world, the *sathottari*s were profoundly anti-commercial and deeply ambivalent about the compromises inherent in circulation as such (Zecchini 2014; Bulson 2016). As both Bulson and Nerlekar emphasize, there is something about the form of little magazines that requires a different type of reading. This manifests in individual publications, where, as Nerlekar puts it, it is necessary to read the entire "mise-en-page" (Nerlekar 2016). In other words, the work of interpretation must move away from the new critical concept of a wholly self-contained art object and apprehend how meaning emerges from the way such an object is situated against other writers, images, or distinct materials in the same publication space. In a broader sense, as Bulson argues, the scholar of little magazines must learn to read the field of magazines for the way the deployment of individual texts marks out factions, polemics, and nodes of association.

Yet, when Bulson makes these generalizations about little magazines, he tends to hold postcolonial little magazines apart. He uses examples of periodicals from West and East Africa to emphasize their much larger readerships and commercial pressures, and then makes those characteristic of the little magazine endeavor in all "postcolonial" locations. For him, the purpose of these magazines is to remix and "write back" to British modernists like T. S. Eliot and Ezra Pound (Bulson 2016). New "world form," per Bulson's title, same old story.

While, as Bulson rightly claims, "Ezra Pound is a recurring presence, popping up sometimes in the most unlikely places" in the Indian little magazine scene, in other ways this focus on Pound's early-twentieth-century contemporaries was precisely what the *sathottari*s were reacting against (Bulson 2016). They wanted to be more than "a satellite of preforties British poets," reaching instead for a kind of world-literary contemporaneity for which connections to Latin America became iconic (Chitre 1970).

On the other hand, when South–South literary connections are discussed in this period and form, it has largely been through references to the Soviet-sponsored periodical *Lotus: Afro-Asian Writings* (Yoon 2015; Halim 2017; Azeb 2019). Published in English, French, and Arabic, the journal *Lotus* and its associated literary prize were formed with the explicit purpose of fostering cross-cultural communication in the Third World. Yet there was an important structural difference between *Lotus* and the Indian little magazines: their size. *Lotus* was in no way "little" in terms of its relationship to institutional power.[15] Moreover, there simply does not seem to have been the kind of independent circulation, reception, and recapitulation of *Lotus*-based texts among the majority of *sathottari* poets in this period. Latin American literature, on the other hand, found a foothold among *sathottari* readerships despite its absence from many of the explicit Third World projects of that era.

A focus on the *sathottaris*' relationship with Anglophone sources in the Global North inevitably suggests the bipolar, call-and-response model of "writing back." Recognizing the aesthetics of *extrañeza*, in contrast, suggests an entirely different directionality: the desire to "write out." This means, at the same time and through the same aesthetics, both reaching outward toward producers in other parts of the world and creating collusive boundaries that invite attentive readers in while keeping others at arm's length. In a context where *sathottari*s feared tokenization – being adopted as Western readers' Orientalist "window-dressing" – they sought ways to manage and play with partial and uneven knowledge among their variegated readerships. Pazian techniques like baroque ekphrasis and decontextualized citations were appealing modes to do this. At the same time, for the writers and editors of these magazines, Paz was also a major force of connection. Paz and the Latin American literature he helped to promote were the conduit of powerful fantasies of equality and reciprocity, the pathway through which many Indian authors imagined coming onto a world-literary stage on their own terms.

"The Desire for Now": Little Magazines and the Project of Becoming Contemporary

All writers are also readers, as Hanif reminded us in the Introduction. The *sathottari* poets took this maxim to its extreme. Many writers of that era felt they did not have a robust Indian Anglophone tradition from which to draw. In one literary magazine of the 1970s, Anita Desai, one of the only significant Anglophone novelists to emerge from this period, called English "a language that in India has no tradition" (Desai 1978). When critiqued on this view, she insisted that "all modern trends in [poetry, drama, and narrative] have had to be imported from abroad" (Desai 1978). More recently, Arvind Krishna Mehrotra reflected that "we have been writing in English for 200 years, but in the sixties, we were not aware of this tradition .... We created our tradition from other sources, from whatever came to hand" (Mehrotra quoted in Marvel 2016). Speaking in the genealogical idiom of the countershelf, he says quite openly that they were "creating [our] own literary ancestors and a context for what [we're] doing" (Mehrotra quoted in Zecchini 2017b).

The many hats worn by *sathottari* writers seem to arise from this urgent need to create a tradition, to bring things "to hand." Driven by a desire to be in a conversation with everyone, right now, these poets worked double or even triple duty as translators, editors, and reviewers, circulating poetry in English as well as in translation. While the primary bent of their multilingualism was focused on other languages of India, they did demonstrate significant international interest.

This often came in the expected guise of engagements with writers from the United States and Britain – a mix of modernists like Ezra Pound and Beat poets like Allen Ginsberg. Yet there was new attention to writing on the other side of Partition-era borders as well. A smattering of poems came in from Pakistan, including translations of Urdu stalwarts like Faiz and Mohammad Iqbal as well as Anglophone up-and-comers like Zulfikar Ghose – who was primarily known as a poet until the late 1960s. When civil war broke out in Bangladesh in 1971, it produced a flood of solidarity gestures in these venues, including illustrations, eyewitness accounts, position statements, and protest poetry written in English or translated from Bangla and Urdu. Swaminathan even wrote a letter to Octavio Paz about the struggles of the new nation, part of which was published in Paz's literary journal *Plural* (Swaminathan 1971). Still, Latin America at first seems a minor entrant among these other engagements. Part of that perception, however, is due to an internal division among magazines.

The writers at the center of this chapter often defined their creative endeavors as contrary to institutions big and small. Magazines like *Vrishchik*, *CONTRA'66*, and *Ezra* cast themselves against "establishment-wallahs" – those who were committed to bigger names and more financially solid endeavors. These included rival editors at journals like *Poetry India* and *Quest*, whose preferences were relatively Anglophile and backward-looking. Although they exaggerated real differences in circulation size, duration, or the distinctness of their endeavors, there really was certain commercial slickness to *Quest* and *Poetry India* that other little magazines actively resisted. Bitingly satirical avant-garde poetry sits jarringly side by side with ads for men's hair dye and the Indian railways. Sometimes they squeeze closer still, advertisements camouflaging themselves as the magazine's contents. Consider this piece appearing in *Poetry India*, "If Leaves of Grass Grow Pale" (1967):

> Leaves of grass
> Grow pale,
> Good Earth
> Yields poor, –
> And if
> Virgin Soil Upturned
> Though seeketh
> But doth not find,
> Pray,
> Do not turn away
> In despair, moaning
> Cry the beloved country.
>
> Seek the FACT*
> And thou shalt find it,
> The foremost name
>
> In fertilisers,
>
> Apothecaries of the soil.
> [. . .]   *Fertilisers and Chemicals, Travancore Ltd.,
>   Udyogamandal, Kerala (FACT 1967)

An incredible reference shelf of literature – Walt Whitman's *Leaves of Grass* (United States, 1855), Pearl S. Buck's *The Good Earth* (United States, 1931), Mikhail Sholokhov's *Virgin Soil Upturned* (Russia, 1935), Alan Paton's *Cry, the Beloved Country* (South Africa, 1948) – was deployed, quite literally, to sell shit. When scholars present South Asian literature as a "dull global" form, derivative and nakedly commercial, this is precisely what they imagine (n+1 2013).

It feels too simple, but in the 1960s and 1970s it was true: the cool-looking, sexy, underground little magazines were doing the cool, sexy, underground work. They embraced the Poundian mantra that "nothing written for pay is worth printing; only what has been written against the market" (Pound quoted in Zecchini 2014, 31). There was neither space nor inclination for advertisements from chemical companies or anything else that whiffed of selling out. Mehrotra's journal *damn you*, for example, actively rejects foreign sales: "For reasons other than copyright, this edition is not for sale in the u.s.a or canada. It may, however, be smuggled in" (Mehrotra and Rai 1965). This statement enacts a political refusal of circulation in major Anglophone markets – "reasons other than copyright" – while leaving open a means of access that works through the bonds of friendship, "smuggled in" outside the law. These two desires – for anti-commercial authenticity and for worldwide access – sometimes came into conflict.

As opposed to the Eurocentric, primarily Anglophone, and quite belated reference shelf of *Quest*, many other little magazines were interested in participating in a literary world that was radically open and radically contemporary. As Nerlekar argues, the little magazines were shaped by a desire for the "now" (Nerlekar 2016, 54). By this, she means first a literary style appropriate to "seizing the fluid present" (Nerlekar 2016, 54). Zecchini makes a similar observation and allies these techniques more explicitly with *ostranenie*. She also notes how representative poetry of this period "revels in decontextualizations, in the blurring of frontiers and hierarchies" (Zecchini 2014, 56). But of course, the practice of close observation, of decontextualization, of blurring the boundaries between the real and the imagined, the physical and the textual, need not be recovered from so temporally and geographically distant a source. All of these are also features of Paz's India-based practice of baroque ekphrasis. Given their independent familiarity with the Indian landscape, the *sathottari* poets were uniquely situated to decode Paz's poetry and redeploy its styles.

Nowness also manifested as a quality of circulation, a form of worldliness that meant reading and being read by contemporaries all over the globe

(Nerlekar 2016). This is the desire for worldliness present in the list of exchanges and letters of support that formed a major portion of these magazines. Paz fulfilled these desires, too, being himself a contemporary and a foreign writer but acting, moreover, as a conduit through which Indian poets made other contemporary literary connections to Latin America.

"It's Up to You, Friends": CONTRA'66, J. Swaminathan

Little magazines in India depended on bonds of friendship in place of commercial ones to secure their circulation and even their basic financial survival. How did they conceive of those bonds in a situation of relative inequality with an established foreign writer? To put it otherwise: when Paz says in his introduction to the Group 1890 show, "we are friends," what did that friendship mean?

In addition to appearing as a contributor and reference in several little magazines, Paz also offered material support to magazines that sometimes bragged to their readers about running out of money for paper and ink for printing new issues (Mehrotra 1968). One of the Group 1890 painters, Swaminathan, edited the little magazine *CONTRA'66*, in which he is even more direct about the venture's financial precariousness. "It's up to you, friends. Despite the fence sitters and the snooty establishment-wallahs, the Contra has come into being. Keep it alive" (Swaminathan 1965). Paz was significant among those friends, having "taken out 10 subscriptions and promised all cooperation" (Swaminathan 1965).

More than that, the reading habits and editorial decisions of these venues seem to show marks of Paz's "curatorial" influence. This is particularly true of the repeated appearance in their magazines of the poet Sergio Mondragón, who had been Paz's collaborator for several years. Mondragón was also the coeditor, with Margaret Randall, of the bilingual little magazine *El corno emplumado* (*The Plumed Horn*) published out of Mexico City. Recalling their early efforts at distribution, Randall wrote:

> Soon we were receiving letters and submissions, and even a few subscriptions, from a dozen countries in Latin and North America and *even as far afield as India*! We began looking for a young poet willing to represent us in each of these places. This usually meant talking about the journal and taking it around to bookstores, suggesting how much an issue should sell for so that young poets in his or her country would be able to buy one, and sending us selections of poems. (Randall 2008, emphasis added)

As with Mehrotra's statement about being "smuggled in," Randall articulates a circulation strategy in which the magazine moves like a rumor, spreading through direct, person-to-person contact that depends on a trusted curator in each of its target locations.

Indian writers intensely desired inclusion in spaces like *El corno emplumado*, but only if they could appear as equals. In a letter to *El corno emplumado*, the Bangla poet Malay Roy Choudhury, a leader in the Hungryalist Movement associated with Paz and the Beats, and a contributor to Mehrotra's magazine *ezra*, wrote:[16]

> I presume you have also received bengali [sic] magazines and enjoyed the uncommunicability [sic] of the scripts. For me I have started picking up Spanish. I have bought me a dictionary. Ha ... ha ... I don't know whether I'll end up as a window-dressing for EL CORNO .... Gracias y un abrazo. (Chaudhury 1965)

We see here a somewhat tongue-in-cheek redeployment of the fantasy of world-literary exchange. It is certainly unexpected and multilingual, even mystically so – see "the uncommunicability of scripts" and "*un abrazo*" ("hugs"). Still, the venture's egalitarianism is in doubt, displayed in the tension between the desire for friendship in "*un abrazo*" and anxiety about being used as "window-dressing."

Editors both within India and beyond articulated their anxious desire for world-literary friendship through a single Paz poem dedicated to the editor of *CONTRA'66*, "Al pintor Swaminathan," translated into English by Swaminathan himself as "To the Painter Swaminathan" (1966).[17] Like so much of Paz's India writing, the bulk of "Al pintor Swaminathan" is a microscopically observed, decontextualized ekphrasis of Swaminathan's painting. It consists of a list of shapes that the painter produces "against the canvas, against the void / ... with a rag and a knife" (Paz 1966). The line "with a rag and a knife" acts as a refrain in the poem. The conflict between stroking and stabbing gestures implied by these implements enhances the dual sense of the preposition *contra* (against), which refers simultaneously to the spatial relationship between canvas and paint and also an antagonism between the painter and the blankness, the void of the canvas. As we have seen, this is a concept that obsessed Paz throughout his time in India. The word "Contra," of course, also appears in the title of Swaminathan's little magazine, a distillation of its attitude toward artistic and literary "establishment-wallas" of India.

As the poem moves forward, Paz turns his focus to colors:

> Springs the Mexican Red
> Turns black
> The Indian red springs
> turns black.　　　　　　　　　　　　　(Paz 1966)

This is a motif of transnational transformation that repeats in blue:

> The blue body of Kali
> the sex of La Guadalupe
> with a rag and a knife
> against the triangle
> the eye bursts　　　　　　　　　　　　(Paz 1966)

While the former image simply suggests the blending of colors inherent to Swaminathan's ragged style, or perhaps the looming threat of the "void" against which he works, the second encodes a stunning misogynistic violence. The preposition *contra* creates another slippage here: do the rag and knife work against the triangle of a woman's pubis, or is that triangle the violent agent against which the (masculine) eye explodes? The poem refuses to tell us, confirming only that "the canvas [is] a body / Dressed in its own naked *enigma*" (Paz 1966, emphasis added).

By writing his poem along the grain of the canvas, Paz seems to claim a role almost as its cocreator. Although the poem itself centers on the union of Mexican and Indian symbolic languages through the power of masculine creation over feminine emptiness, its title and circulation overwrites all of these other symbolic values under the sign of transnational, transmedial friendship. Paz's proprietary claims are then reversed while his claims of egalitarian friendship are amplified by the fact Swaminathan himself translates the poem into English. The poem came to circulate first as condensation of Paz's entire experience in India and second as the ideal of egalitarian, multilingual, and unexpected world-literary friendship as such.

Perhaps unsurprisingly, *El corno emplumado* was one of the first places where this piece was published, in 1966. There it came to stand for Paz's embeddedness in India for a hemispheric American audience. Years later, in 1973, the poem was republished in the little magazine *Dialogue India*, edited by Pritish Nandy. There it accompanied book reviews by a major cultural critic and future editor of the *Times of India*,

Sham Lal, introducing major Latin American writers to the Indian audience.

In 1975, Nandy published a book of his own poems, *Riding the Midnight River*. An epigraph introduces one of the last poems in the collection, "These Dark Roots of Death." Set off from the rest of the verse in italics and a different typeface, it reads "*el cuadro es un cuerpo / vestido solo por su enigma desnudo*" ("*the canvas* [*is*] *a body / Dressed in its own naked enigma*") (Nandy 1975). This is, of course, the final line from "Al pintor Swaminathan," which Nandy had published in *Dialogue India* two years prior. Yet here Nandy does more than evoke Paz as part of his countershelf. He uses the Paz citation in an utterly Pazian way – as a baroque citation. Why baroque? Because, like Paz's treatments of India, it is obscure, out of context, and intentionally disorienting. Cited in the original Spanish without any markers of attribution, it disposes with all of the multilingual friendliness of Swaminathan's translation. This ensures that essentially none of his audience can read it or apprehend the line's significance. One who didn't recognize the line on sight would, in the pre-internet era, have no resources to trace and decode it. Instead, taking its cue from lines themselves, Nandy's poem revels, Paz-like, in its irresolvable "enigma."

"Beyond Europe to Mexico": *Vrischik*, Kapur

If Swaminathan became a symbol of world-literary friendship, another group of friends engaged even more deeply with Paz as a cultural theorist. Just as Paz was leaving India in 1969, Swaminathan's colleague from Group 1890, Gulammohammed Sheikh, joined with the painter Bhupen Khakhar to found a little magazine of arts and literature called *Vrishchik* (*Scorpion*). Like many of its contemporaries, *Vrishchik* published a hotchpotch of materials: poetry in multiple languages, essays both personal and analytic, illustrations in a variety of media and styles, polemics sometimes in the guise of reviews, and sometimes as manifestos. As with most little magazines of the era, their commitment to multilingual writing oriented mostly toward other languages of India, in which English would function as what is often called a "link language" between literary traditions (Sadana 2012). However, gestures toward Latin America made up a large proportion of discussion about writing from outside the subcontinent.

In addition to scattered references to Pablo Neruda (discussed in Chapter 1), an entire issue was devoted to Jorge Luis Borges. It included a cover image, produced by a certain Vinod Ray Patel (see Figure 2.1), and an English-medium essay, "Of Being Somewhere Trapped: Borges in London"

Figure 2.1 Vinod Ray Patel, "Portrait of Jorge Luis Borges," *Vrishchik* 2–3, no. 12–1 (October/November 1971) (Patel 1971).

(1971) by the Hindi writer Nirmal Verma. In the essay, Verma meditates on the disconnect between the Argentinian writer's Anglophone inspiration and the exoticizing gaze of his British audience. "The questions put to him betrayed the gulf that separated him from his rapturous devotees, indeed the moment of 'connection' between the Argentine sufi and his sophisticated audience never arrived" (Verma 1971, 17). This framing first locates, in this foreign tradition, the conundrum that Bhabha named for Indian writers – that "to be Anglicized, is *emphatically* not to be English" (Bhabha 1984, 128, emphasis original). Second, in naming Borges an "Argentine sufi" and staging his own interpretation of the writer as explicitly contrary to the predominant British one, Verma suggests, once again, that Latin American writing was always already in dialogue with the subcontinent, that it truly belongs to South Asian inheritors.

In 1972–3, the last year of its run, this miscellany was accompanied by a serialized version of an MA thesis by the art critic Geeta Kapur, called "In Quest of Identity: Art and Indigenism in Post-Colonial Culture with Special Reference to Contemporary Indian Painting." The thesis functioned as a kind of manifesto for the magazine and was subsequently published as a stand-alone volume. In it, Kapur suggests how India might develop what she calls an "indigenous" art practice, one that she contrasts with the current "international" bent of the art world (Kapur 1973). For Kapur, internationalism faced westward toward Europe and the United States. And yet, somewhat surprisingly given the way that term is usually used, indigenism is not an exclusively Indian tradition. In her employment, "indigenism" is a calque from the Spanish *indigenismo*. The idea develops, to a significant extent, from her reading of the Mexican arts scene and the writing of Paz, especially his canonical 1950 essay, *El laberinto de la soledad* (*The Labyrinth of Solitude*) (Khullar 2015).

Kapur articulates in explicit, academic prose what will become more or less a consensus around what South Asian writers seek, sometimes inchoately, from Latin America: a model for how to be authentically local and worldly all at once. It's hard to overstate the degree to which Latin America, Mexico specifically, and Paz in particular form the kernel of indigeneity that Kapur wishes to project for India. The text is replete with references to painters like Diego Rivera, David Alfaro Siqueiros, and José Clemente Orozco, writers like Borges and Neruda, and earlier generations of thinkers like José Enrique Rodó and José Vasconcelos – the latter himself deeply interested in India as a model for Mexican racial identity (Torres-Rodríguez 2015). Kapur is also one of the only authors whose reference to the countershelf is formed in conversation with scholars of Latin American literature – Jean Franco acts as a key reference. Paz serves an even more central role: in addition to numerous citations throughout the text, a two-page explication of key passages in *El laberinto de la soledad* acts as a "Recapitulation" of the essay's thesis of indigeneity in art, which Kapur says she uses to bring the discussion "back to focus" (Kapur 1973, 12–13). Quite concretely, then, Paz acts as a lens through which to read the situation of contemporary art in India.

Hardly a page of Kapur's text goes by without reference to Latin America as the primary model for how a "Post-Colonial" country might develop an authentic modern art. It's notable the ease and assurance with which Kapur uses this category – still so new that it remains capitalized and hyphenated – to draw together India and Latin America in the late 1960s and early 1970s. This is a project that will become increasingly difficult as the concept and geography of the "postcolonial" ossifies in the decades to come, until it will seem astonishing that she has done it at all. Kapur also explicitly connects the foundational postcolonial reading of the Macaulay Minute to the countershelf gesture toward Latin America. It is not just Anglophone writing but, indeed, Indian painting whose path to the contemporary is marred by the Minute's most infamous phrase (Kapur 1973, 36). As Kapur explores how to get out from under this problem, she again and again turns to Latin America, and Mexico in particular, as a model, an alternative tradition that will help India move away from Europe.

Beyond the number of references to Latin America, Kapur's framing clarifies how conceptually central these models are to "In Quest of Identity." Mexico is dealt with "in some detail," she forewarns in the introduction, further suggesting that Latin America or Mexico serves as the best "example" in footnotes, summaries, and asides throughout the text (Kapur 1973, 6). In a gesture that recalls Paz's ekphrastic blending of architecture and literary citation, she claims that the visual language of modern artist M. F. Husain can be understood "by reference to an artist like Rufino Tamayo (although Husain is unlikely to have seen his work then)" (Kapur 1973, 48). Likewise, "the words of Jorge Luis Borges, the Argentinian writer, written for some quite different context, are peculiarly appropriate" to describe the use of symbolism by Swaminathan: "to reduce the lyric to its element, the metaphor" (Kapur 1973, 65). As opposed to predominant scholarly anxiety about the potential violence of comparison, Kapur insists on a comparative gesture between the two regions even though the context is "quite different" and any direct connection is "unlikely." Only in the case of the muralist Satish Gujral is the genealogy direct. He is praised for going "beyond Europe to Mexico, [to bring] back Orozco's savage expressionism" – a journey, not incidentally, partly supported by Paz (Kapur 1973, 42; Khullar 2015). Kapur's phrasing here is telling, where beyond acts both spatially (further west) but also temporally and conceptually (further ahead).

"My Heart's Theory" of Literary Circulation: ezra*, Mehrotra*

Vrischik is also one of the first places where the writers of this generation explored concrete poetry, especially Mehrotra's chapbook, first published by the magazine in 1971, *Pomes Poems Poemas* (Mehrotra 1971). At the end of the collection appears a list of citations headed by the title "Epilogues." Letitia Zecchini uses the "Epilogues" to validate Mehrotra's claim that the *sathottari*s were inventing a tradition "from whatever came to hand." In this sense, she claims, the "worlds of Bombay poetry" are also those of world literature, worlds imagined and reclaimed by "bulimic" readers of literature in translation" (Zecchini 2017b, 192).

The "Epilogues" represents neither precisely Macaulay's "good shelf" of European literature nor its anti-Anglophone countershelf. While the quotes seem to suggest some sort of genealogy for Mehrotra's work, his attitude toward them is a puzzle. Ezra Pound appears, of course: the poet who helped inspire the magazine movement in India, the namesake of one of Mehrotra's publication projects, *ezra: an imagist magazine*, and of his imprint, *ezra-fakir* (Nerlekar 2016). Paz is placed next to his old friend Andre Breton, about whom Paz had published a short piece in the first issue of *CONTRA'66* (CONTRA'66 1967).

The "Epilogues" also includes an extended rant by William Butler Yeats: "Damn Tagore .... Tagore does not know English, no Indian knows English. Nobody can write with music and style in a language not learned in childhood" (Mehrotra 1971). Yeats is generally praised as Tagore's chief promoter in English – having written the introduction to *Gitanjali*, the English-language collection upon which Tagore's Nobel win was primarily based (Lahiri 2020). Even Yeats' own Orientalist poetry has received nuanced and ultimately sympathetic treatment as an exemplar of "global" poetics (Ramazani 2020). But the inclusion of this citation can only be read as a challenge against which the poems themselves form a response – in other words, the classically postcolonial gesture of "writing back." Recall *damn you*, Mehrotra's editorial endeavors that "could be smuggled in" to friends in the United States. Mehrotra later wrote that the magazine's name was inspired by the American Beat magazine *Fuck you* (Mehrotra 2014, 60). Still, given the inclusion of the Yeats quote, it's tempting to read it, too, as a response to the arrogance of Yeats and other English-language poets: "Damn Tagore? Damn you!"

The Paz citation, on the other hand, seems to provide a justification for Mehrotra's relatively recondite literary style. "The problem of poetry's meaning becomes clear only when one observes that the meaning is not outside of the poems but within: not in what the words say, but in *what is said between them*" (Mehrotra 1971, emphasis original). It thus offers a strategy for decoding the rest of the chapbook like Paz's own citation of Góngora in *Ladera este*. And, indeed, this citation immediately precedes the moment in the essay "What Is Poetry?" in which Paz articulates his interest in Góngora.

"¿Qué Nombra La Poesía?" is the first essay in *Corriente alterna*. In the *CONTRA'66* essay, the book was described as "a miscellany of art, poetry, morals, politics, etc. to be published shortly" (CONTRA'66 1967, 3). This is true, in a way, since the collected essays were published in 1967. But they were only published at that time in Spanish. In the era before Hispanophone texts reliably entered the ranks of what Rebecca Walkowitz calls "born translated" literature, *Corriente alterna* did not appear in English translation until six years later, in 1973 (Walkowitz 2015). How, then, did an Indian writer with little to no facility in Spanish get his hands on it in 1971?

It seems that Indian poets were accessing new Latin American writing from little magazine editors in the Americas. Breton's article, for instance, had earlier appeared in *El corno*. Mehrotra first encountered Paz's "What Is Poetry?" translated by the American poet Muriel Rukeyser in the American journal of contemporary "world literature," *Mundus Artium*. There it appeared as part of a 1969 special issue on Latin American writing edited by Mondragón, immediately after pressure from the Mexican government forced the shuttering of *El corno emplumado* (Mondragón 1969).

The issue seems to have made quite an impression on Mehrotra. He hand-copied the entire entry by Paz as well as one by the Chilean poet Vicente Huidoboro. After reading it, Mehrotra wrote breathlessly to his friend and fellow poet Adil Jussawalla:

> Have done another *mukhbodh* poem and sent it to *Mundus Artium*. Very fine journal, that. Their recent Latin American fiction number is tremendous. Also Paz's great long poem *Sun Stones* [sic] in a Texas Quarterly. Will bring along a copy of it for you. Again my heart's theory, we're part of Latin America and Africa emotionally, and their literature is the one from which we ought to learn. (Mehrotra 1969)

Mehrotra's comments demonstrate, first, the relationship he imagined between the success of Latin American literature in translation from Spanish and, second, the future of his own multilingual, locally rooted poetic practice. That is, if *Mundus Artium* has shown an openness to Latin American literature, writing in particularly Indian forms might also find a place with American readers. Second, these lines show his investment in the fantasy of a sphere of literary equality in the Global South, echoing Mondragón's insistence in the introduction to the *Mundus Artium* volume that "in poetry there is no 'underdevelopment.' ... All the artists of the world are united ... all illusory frontiers created by men break down" (Mondragón 1969). Finally, in Mehrotra's declaration to Jussawalla, he expresses – apparently not for the first time – a sense of affiliation beyond literal geography, a "heart's theory" about the "emotional" intimacies of continents. His "bulimic" approach to Latin American literature and his efforts to be read in the same form of delirious consumption express a desire for reciprocity. In addition to this vision of looking-glass solidarity in the present, Mehrotra, like Kapur, posits Latin America as a rearview mirror "from which we ought to learn."

If this "heart's theory" explains *why* Paz appears on Mehrotra's countershelf, there is still a sociological question of *how* the Latin American special issue of *Mundus Artium* came together in the first place. How did these poets end up in the hands of an Indian author? It is well known that the general translation and promotion of Latin American literature in the United States in this period was tied to soft diplomacy in the Cold War (Cohn 2012; Iber 2015). Deborah Cohn shows that many of the specific translations Mehrotra references – indeed, both Lysander Kemp's translation of *Sunstone* and Spanish-language translations appearing in *Mundus Artium* in this period, even the very idea of publishing a "Latin American poetry number" – were supported by money from the Rockefeller Foundation with an explicit geopolitical purpose (Cohn 2006). The delirious fantasy, a "heart's theory" of identification thus becomes available to Mehrotra through the frank realism of Cold War politics, for which the concept of world literature in *Mundus Artium* was a convenient tool. These are the grounds of literary solidarity between these two areas. The "real" never invalidates the imaginary. They sit together awkwardly, even here, in the most underground of venues.

The Mexico City Sutras: tornado *and Baroque Citation*

Frank realism also intervened to frame Octavio Paz's circulation from India at the end of 1968. A page from the 1969 issue of the little magazine *tornado* offers a strange commentary on that moment, though in an oblique, fantastic mode. When Nerlekar gives a sense of the total little magazine scene of the 1960s and 1970s, the magazine *tornado* marks out one extreme. It has, she writes, "the deliberate appearance of the hastily handmade, complete with hand-drawn images along with the poems" (Nerlekar 2016, 193). In fact, it's hard to overstate how strange *tornado* looks – how strange it is. Time-consuming design choices include stamping the word "HAPPINESS!" in purple ink over a red paste-in triangle pointing to the title of a Seamus Heaney poem called "Fuck America." These labor-intensive production choices are part and parcel of the anti-commercial, limited-circulation values of so many of the little magazines. They have to do, too, with the use of foul language and other intentionally provocative gestures, like a full-page amateur portrait of Hitler, that occasionally descend into what we call, in more modern parlance, edgelording. It's not surprising that such a crowd would have been attracted to the very insidery forms, both cryptic and ludic, that characterized Paz's Indian writing.

Among these and other gestures, the 1969 issue, *tornado 5: tariq-e hind*, also contains what it calls "a page from: Mexico City Sutras by david-dougald" (dougald 1969a). These words are printed inside an empty square on the page's upper left corner. They are mirrored on the far right by a second square containing the poem's dedication "for julio reyes martinez" (dougald 1969a). This is followed by an equivalent amount of blank space (nearly a quarter-page) and about ten lines of text from the opening of the poem, partially obscured by an overprinting of the magazine's frenetic logo. The following words are underlined: "it never occurs to me that each time i come back i spend most of the day getting drunk" (dougald 1969a, emphasis original). And here, beneath a series of asterisks, the excerpt ends. Despite the promise to reproduce a full page of the poem, the last third is devoted to other writers.

What does this mean? Why is it here? Perhaps these are the wrong kind of questions to ask of such an intentionally disorienting venture. Still, *tornado*'s citation of the poem does offer something more than what appears on the surface, something recoverable, or perhaps decodable, with Paz as the key. *Tornado*'s particular reproduction of "Mexico City Sutras" makes it seem like a poem about a Canadian hippie on vacation coming to the gradual realization that he is, in fact, an alcoholic. The only thing that seems to connect such a poem to India is the generic definition of this writing as a "sutra," a common-enough, empty-enough gesture among white North American writers. But a fuller version of the poem was published almost simultaneously in the Berkeley-based *Aldebaran Review*, and it gives a startlingly different impression of its significance.[18] Far from the navel-gazing reflections of a new-age dirtbag that it becomes in *tornado*, the *Aldebaran Review* version of "Mexico City Sutras" is an explicitly political eyewitness account of the Tlatelolco massacre of 1968 (dougald 1969b).

Indian readers – or, at least, the circle of little magazine readers addressed by *tornado* – would have recognized the Tlatelolco massacre as the occasion for Octavio Paz's departure from India. Immediately after the massacre, Paz wrote a letter of protest to the Olympic Committee in Mexico City. Subsequently translated and published in *El corno emplumado*, the letter marked the beginning of the end for that little magazine. Responding from Delhi to an earlier invitation to write a poem on the occasion of the Olympics, an invitation Paz declined, he writes, "The recent turn of events has made me change my mind" (Paz 1969). He follows this with a bitingly ironic, furious poem, "México: Olimpiada de 1968" ("Mexico: The XIX Olympiad"):

> Clarity
> (maybe it's worth
> writing it down on this clear
> white paper)
> Is not clear
> [...]
> (City employees wash away blood
> In the Plaza de los Sacrificios.)
> Look at this,
> Stained
> Before having said anything
> Worthwhile,
> Clarity. (Paz 1969)[19]

The idea of "clarity" ("limpidez") as a blank and then stained page reflects the obsession with the void, the surface in potentia that shape his Indian project in *Blanco*, *Topoemas*, and "*Al pintor Swaminathan*." But while the politics of those pieces are sublimated in baroque play, these are explicit. The game has changed.

If Paz is the circumstance through which "Mexico City Sutras" becomes appealing to the editors at *tornado*, his is also arguably the aesthetic through which they choose to reproduce it. In this view, the reprint of "Mexico City Sutras" is a baroque citation. In this reading, the two squares might represent the photographs of gathering protesters and dead bodies that accompanied the original poem, lending it documentary power. Indeed, the line of asterisks marks out precisely the space where the first of these explicitly political photographs would have been.

Like Paz's invocation of Góngora, or Mehrotra or Nandy's invocation of Paz, these citations do contain a politics, but only for the player, the initiate. One cannot tell this is a political poem unless one has independent access to the whole thing.

"Innocence": The Cost of Literary Sainthood

For Anglophone poets of the 1960s and 1970s, a certain Paz-inspired obscurity was a core value: a value of circulation (only among friends) and a value of citation (only comprehensible to insiders). Obscurity is also their fate. In one sense, their story is the story of almost all Indian Anglophone writing before 1981: a minor aspect of the total Indian literary scene and an equally minor aspect of the English literary field. As recounted in the Introduction, the rise of Rushdie signaled a sea change in Anglophone South Asian writing. That discontinuity remains, even when we bring back in an account of the 1960s and 1970s. Latin America played a significant role in both literary moments but in different ways: not just the difference between poetry and novels but the difference in the manner and scale of circulation. In other words, what the *sathottari*s did inchoately, Rushdie does iconically.

When we do turn back to them, though, the *sathottari* authors are incredibly appealing to a critical apparatus for the way they seem to actively reject the kind of market circulations that later South Asian Anglophone writers embrace. Thayil, for example, contrasts his own recovery project in *The Book of Chocolate Saints*, and the aesthetic project of the *sathottari*s themselves, to a sensationalist roman á clef about the group that is "available in the bestseller section of an airport bookstore" (Thayil 2017, 94). Here he raises the common bugbear of South Asian fiction as both commercial and globally circulating.

The little magazines insist otherwise. As Bulson writes, "no matter how high the circulation, little magazines were never part of a totalizing world system" (Bulson 2016, 7). Produced by many of the most important Anglophone authors of the era, these were the locations where the terms of their linguistic affiliation, their worldliness, were established. They are objects intentionally set against a wide circulation. They eschew sales and advertisements in favor of individually mediated exchanges with other little magazines around the world. They actively reject the possibility of being sold and thus "sold out." Their collusive aesthetics "write out" a large portion of their potential audience in English. Even their form is anti-reproductive, all artisanal slowness and system-gumming friction.

Perhaps this is the answer to the question posed by Thayil in the opening to this chapter: "why has no one written about the Bombay poets of the 1970s?" Of course, as we have seen, this is true not literally but only proportionally to the rest of the field. The reason seems to be reflected in the unfolding of Thayil's novel. Like Bolaño's exploration of the fate of the recalcitrant infrarealist ("infra realista") poets of the 1970s in Mexico in *The Savage Detectives*, *The Book of Chocolate Saints* follows a disjointed series of interviews, recollections, and purportedly "discovered" unpublished poems – a structuring that reflects the original circulation and haphazard archivization of the little magazines and independent imprints in which both groups of poets primarily circulated.

No artefact better exemplifies this than *tornado*, each individual copy of which is distinct, collaged, hand-printed, flawed in slightly different ways. The single issue archived in the British Library has a little white feather pasted into the margin over the word "innocence." You can stroke it with your finger. Soft and yet the opposite of smooth, as we imagine the flows of capital to be smooth. Perhaps this is what we scholars want: the absolute innocence of a literature that refuses to circulate, that cannot circulate, except through bonds of friendship (Fisk 2018) – the intentional roughness of a form with no exchange value whatsoever.

Yet these are also pieces you can only access at the British Library or somewhere similarly locked away. As Nerlekar writes, "Mehrotra and Jussawalla, between them, hold the archives of the little magazines . . . . Mehrotra rightly notes that the work of canonization and archivization has fallen onto the shoulders of the poets themselves" (Nerlekar 2016). They all but disappear from the historiography, while the arc of Anglophone literature veers off in another direction. The major writers of this era, what we would otherwise call canonical Anglophone writers of the period, have not really been canonized.

Or if they have been, it is in the sense that Thayil invokes in the title of his novel: they have been turned into saints. Miriam Ticktin argues that contemporary political thought is "embroiled in a search for a space of purity, a space outside corruption and contamination, a space emptied of the power that can ground both tolerance and action; innocence provides us with such a conceptual space" (Ticktin 2017, 578). The problem with innocence, however, is that it operates at the expense of agency. Hence the animating concept of Thayil's novel: that he and his fictional protagonist take on the "encryption" work of memorializing and repopularizing a group of writers who were not able to make their own mark. In order for the *sathottari* poets to maintain their saintly innocence from the dirtying, commercial side of worldliness, they must perforce remain forgotten to the canon.

Consider, too, Chaudhuri's assessment of Kolatkar at the beginning of the chapter. Part of Kolatkar's authenticity, for Chaudhuri, emerges in his apparent reluctance to be published. When Chaudhuri first met Kolatkar,

Jejuri "was not only not published internationally, but it was only available ... in limited print runs at a couple of bookshops .... *Jejuri*'s author was, by all accounts, content, even determined, that this was how things should continue to be" (Chaudhuri 2005, vii–viii). Chaudhuri portrays their negotiations to bring out an English reprint of *Jejuri* almost as a drama of seduction – with Kolatkar the coy, blushing virgin. Jussawalla responds to another critic perpetuating the same "rumor" that Kolatkar "wrote poems to share with friends not publish, implying that, had it not been for his friends, *Sarpa Satra* and *Kala Ghoda* Poems might have remained unpublished" (Jussawalla 2004). Contrary to the elevation of "friendship" over public renown, he asserts, "Arun always planned to bring out books of his work ... He needed no friends to persuade him" (Jussawalla 2004).

The values of the *sathottari* literature fulfill everything we dream world literature might be. They are multilingual, both within and outside of India. They circulate through intimate, egalitarian friendships instead of commerce. Most of all, they are utterly, astonishingly unexpected. But that other value, the monetary one, they cannot claim it. Instead they bear the cost – the cost of being forgotten, unread, uncirculated. And there is a cost, too, to the pervasive scholarly imaginary that world literature must always, only appear in this guise, that one can only have moral or monetary value but never both.

But the *sathottari*s have not been forgotten by everyone. They pop up in some of the most canonical places – including the writing of their purported nemesis, Rushdie. In 1995, the same *Vrishchik* crew that turned Paz from a stranger into a friend made a similar gesture of affiliation to the younger novelist. The multilayered meaning of that interaction is the subject of Chapter 3.

CHAPTER 3

Displacee
The Andalusian Allegory and Dreams of a Shared Past

> Many of the painters who came to sit at great Aurora's feet earned their livings in other professions and were known within our walls as – to name only a few – the Doctor, the Lady Doctor, the Radiologist, the Journalist, the Professor, the Sarangi Player, the Playwright, the Printer, the Curator, the Jazz Singer, the Lawyer, and the Accountant.
>
> (Rushdie 1995, 202)

This scene appears in the middle of Salman Rushdie's fifth major novel, *The Moor's Last Sigh* (1995), which comments on the fragile cosmopolitan politics of mid-century Bombay by refracting them through medieval Spain. Art historian Sonal Khullar suggests that we can decode the acolytes of the fictional painter Aurora as specific Indian artists working from the 1960s to the 1990s: the Professor is Gulammohammed Sheikh; the Curator, Geeta Kapur; the Accountant, Bhupen Khakhar (Khullar 2015, 171). In other words, this passage pays homage to the artists-cum-editors-cum-writers of Chapter 2 through whom Latin America joined the conceptual map for Indian cultural life. This is the community whose aesthetic affiliations prefigure Rushdie's, while also being effectively incinerated in his explosive rise. The temporal move forward – and the decisive shift toward the Anglophone novel – necessitates a turn to Rushdie. This chapter and the two that follow each address one of his books. Here the aperture changes, so that Rushdie hovers mostly in the background. The focus remains on other authors, demonstrating that his pet themes and styles follow tides that rise and fall far beyond him.

In this case, *The Moor's Last Sigh* participates in a much longer South Asian tradition – indeed a global tradition – of displacing local political conflicts onto the medieval "moorish" kingdom of al-Andalus in Spain. This chapter explores several other contemporary displacements toward al-Andalus, arguing that they constitute an earlier type of countershelf in

Displacee: The Andalusian Allegory

South Asian letters. Like later gestures toward Latin America, the references to Spain emerged as an explicitly "contrary" move, responding first against colonial-era Islamophobia and later to moments of Hindu-majoritarian fervor in South Asia. And, indeed, these two countershelves ultimately became fused, as writers of the 1990s reflected on the 500-year anniversary of two related global traumas: the expulsion of Muslims from Europe and the incursion of European Christians into the Americas.[1]

Among the artists mentioned at the start of this chapter, Rushdie's gesture was read in their own idiom, as a collusive, baroque joke. The *sathottari* poet Adil Jussawalla wrote to Rushdie about his own veiled role in the novel, noting that "everyone who has read the book is trying to guess who's who" (Jussawalla 1995).[2] Yet, Rushdie's version is not nearly so demanding, so exclusive. Instead of a dense amalgam of citations, each requiring its own laborious interpretive gesture, the whole text acts as a diaphanous overlay that parts at the lightest touch, open to recognition. It operates in relation to a single key, one massive displacement. Not a baroque language game, but a simple allegory.

In response to Rushdie's invocation, Bhupen Khakhar, "the Accountant," painted an allegory of his own. He recast Rushdie as "The Moor," a sharp-nosed, heavily balding, but ultimately charming version of the author. In this way, he seems to enact the same kind of transmedial friendship suggested in Chapter 2 by Octavio Paz's poem "Al pintor Swaminathan," laying a coauthorial claim to the novel as if it were always already baroque ekphrasis.

The background of Khakhar's painting invokes the basic plot of *The Moor's Last Sigh*, which follows the fate of a family of Catholic and Jewish traders in Kerala and Bombay who can trace their antecedents to the final ruling family of medieval Spain. It is divided between modern Mumbai on the left and a coastline with palms – date palms, perhaps? – on the right. It might be Kerala or might be Spain. The figure wears a shirt rendered transparent by an unseen light, revealing flesh so deeply divided between pale peach and dark umber that it suggests the "by now familiar Rushdien celebration of bastardy, mongrelhood and hybridity" animating the novel's core plot (Coetzee quoted in Didur 2004, 554). In the bottom right corner is a figure of the painter Aurora, working on her own version of Rushdie's portrait. Her presence suggests the self-referential reflective perspective common to baroque painting, in which the audience finds itself in the place of the painting's subject, as if before a mirror. The shapes of the painting – its vertical symmetry, its vividly rendered central figure, its playful perspective both mirrored and, characteristic of Khakhar, radically frontal and flat – all suggest a formal engagement with the genre of allegory as a game of hiding and revealing, of displacement and affiliation sitting side by side.[3]

In an Anglophone context, especially a British one, Khakhar's recapitulation of Rushdie's title invites a reading of the painting through Shakespeare – not Caliban this time, but another character of ambivalent colonial belonging, Othello (Loomba 1998; Morey 2007). It thus resonates with a typical postcolonial reading of Rushdie as a figure "writing back" to Empire. This reading is underscored by the fact that Khakhar's painting now represents Rushdie in the British National Portrait Gallery, where the painter's unambiguous Indianness perhaps shores up Rushdie's own more ambivalent – must we say "hybrid"? – affiliations.

But the resonances of both the title and its allegorical displacement echo elsewhere, too. Rushdie's surname, often invoked as a stand-in for Indian literature as such or even Anglophone literature as such, is itself neither Indian nor English. It is a derivation of Ibn Rushd, the medieval philosopher of Muslim Spain (Rushdie 2012). Rushdie would later write that he "bore the name [Rushdie] for two decades before [I] understood that [my] father ... had chosen it because he respected Ibn Rushd for being at the forefront of the rationalist argument against Islamic literalism in his time" (Rushdie 2012, 23). He returned to Ibn Rushd and the origins of secularism in *Two Years, Eight Months, and Twenty-Eight Nights* (2015). Set in 1195, the reader comes upon Rushdie's Rushd living in exile from the center of Muslim life in Córdoba, having become outspoken in his defense of secular rationality – a clear overlay of Rushdie's own experience in the wake of the 1989 fatwa and consequent exile from India. Thereby reauthorizing his father's identification with the surname, Rushdie embraces a tradition that spans at least a century of South Asian cultural production: the Andalusian allegory.

Al-Andalus is the name given to the parts of the Iberian Peninsula held under Muslim rule from the early 700s until the conclusion of the Catholic *Reconquista* in 1492. In contrast to the mass expulsion of religious others and the infamously repressive Inquisition that followed, al-Andalus has acquired a reputation as an uncommon medieval site of religious tolerance and cultural harmony (*convivencia*) that, in turn, supported one of the most advanced societies of its time.[4] This popular understanding probably overstates the historical record. Yet the idea of a just, cosmopolitan Islamic empire contrasted against a brutal, intolerant Christian one has remained a common thread in the retelling of al-Andalus all over the world. In this regard, al-Andalus is not merely an historical empire. It has become, for generations of authors and in many different regions, an ideal allegory – an extended narrative in which a hidden, "true" meaning resides below another surface – onto which to displace any number of political desires.

Rushdie represents the Andalusian allegory synechdotally in *The Moor's Last Sigh* through the work of the protagonist's mother, the painter Aurora, in whose salons Khakhar, Sheikh, and Kapur briefly appear. Indeed, Khakhar's painting underscores Rushdie's own habitual use of painting as a concept metaphor in *The Moor's Last Sigh*. Painting both articulates the novel's central theme and comments on its layered construction – image on image, present on past. "[Aurora] was using Arab Spain to reimagine India, . . . her metaphor – idealised? sentimental? probably – of the present, and the future that she hoped would evolve" (Rushdie 1995, 227). Aurora here enacts the kind of rear-view mirroring, retrospection as futurity, that also often inheres in South Asian descriptions of Latin America.

But there is a dramatic irony to Aurora's use of the allegory. We know, and Rushdie knows, that this cosmopolitan dream will fail, rather spectacularly, in the 1992–3 Bombay riots – incited by the brick-by-brick destruction of the Babri Masjid in Ayodhya – at the novel's end. We know, too, that the tolerant, idealized Muslim empire in Andalusia also ends, abruptly, emptied out into the fanatical religious intolerance of the Spanish Catholic *Reconquista* and the Inquisition. As much as the Andalusian allegory suggests utopian hope and willed affiliation, it also always encodes its own end: a tragic but inevitable fall. In this sense, Rushdie performs what Natasha Eaton calls "proleptic nostalgia," in which authors invite their readers to see through a current wholeness into a future ruin-scape (Eaton 2013, 129).

Aamir Mufti references *The Moor's Last Sigh* to write briefly but suggestively about "the famous, and for non-Muslim Indian nationalists, often perplexing, attachment of Indian Muslims to Arab Spain" (Mufti 2007, 44).[5] For Mufti, the Andalusian allegory offers a location to work through successive waves of Muslim trauma in the subcontinent. He argues that British imperial discourses framed South Asian Muslims as a "minority" population, one with no claim to native belonging in India. This cast Muslims as "mobile" and set up the preconditions for their forced migration during Partition (Mufti 2007). The expulsion of Muslims from Spain after the *Reconquista* is a ready-to-hand allegory for this experience.

At the same time, as many other scholars have noted, literary references to a golden age of Muslim sovereignty in Spain offered a potent counter-narrative to British accusations of Muslim despotism and decadence – the claims through which British imperial rule was so often justified in India

(Russell 1992, 132; Pritchett 1994; Noorani 1999; Shamsie 2016; Yaqin 2016). Mufti's emphasis on forced mobility risks occluding the affective investment in the earlier history of voluntary Muslim migration, a consistent pride in the ability to root where planted. This theme is often cued, as in Khakhar's painting, through the metaphor of trees, especially date palms. Indeed, as much as it encodes the violence of abstraction and decontextualization, the displacement inherent in allegory itself is also a gesture of chosen affiliation, the recognition of sameness beneath outward difference (Teskey 1996).

This makes the authors who reference al-Andalus "displacees." Yet this is not necessarily connected to authors' position in exile or the diaspora, figures who have become nigh-synonymous with South Asian postcolonial writing since the 1980s (Said 2000). Rather, such a label identifies these authors' investment in the harmony between physical and formal displacement and the insight this comparative move enables. It also gestures toward the recurrent concept metaphors through which such insights are articulated: dreams, veils, footprints, tree roots – even the linguistic layering implied by puns.

Scholarly engagements with *The Moor's Last Sigh* have emphasized Rushdie's obvious investment in layered painting as a form of palimpsest. This line of inquiry suggests that Rushdie somehow innovated the "postcolonial" use of the Andalusian allegory and its key gestures, primarily in conversation with the renovation of allegory and the palimpsest as concepts in critical theory of the same period.[6] Instead, both the fact of reference to al-Andalus as an allegory for South Asian political violence and the concept metaphors through which that displacement was expressed had already been in common use for at least a century. They appear in Urdu writing including Hali's *Musaddas* (*The Ebb and Flow of Islam*) (1879), Abdul l'Halim Sharar's *Flora Florinda* (1899), and especially Mohammad Iqbal's poetry from Spain (1935). These affiliative projects were then creatively recapitulated in the late twentieth century, not only by Rushdie but in the writing of Intizar Husain, Tariq Ali, and Zulfikar Ghose.

Like Havana in the Introduction or Machu Picchu and Valparaíso in Chapter 1, Córdoba and Granada here operate as a location for literary affiliation. As a countershelf gesture, the Andalusian allegory offered a stage from which to speak back to dominant British colonial discourses of the nineteenth century. When the problematization of Muslim belonging in South Asia foreclosed the return to "native" literature, writers reached for this "third space" – not between colonizer and colonized, *pace* Bhabha, but *beyond* them. To a lesser extent, the Andalusian allegory relies on references to particular authors – Rushdie's fantasized identification with Ibn Rushd is exemplary. Finally, as with any countershelf gesture, books themselves play an outsized symbolic role – hence the way these authors condense the brutality and cultural erasure of the *Reconquista* through the burning of books at the fall of Granada in 1492.

But, of course, 1492 does more than mark the end of Muslim sovereignty in Europe. It is also the date in which "Columbus sailed the ocean blue." It thus simultaneously invokes the violent discovery of the "New World" and the creation of a maritime planet (explored by Paz in Chapter 2) as much as it does the violent closure of the "old" one. In associating these events in the present, South Asian authors recognize how such projects were ideologically fused for the conquistadors themselves. As Alan Mikhail writes, Columbus was first "a common soldier in Isabrella and Ferdinand's conquest of Granada," and – more than scientific curiosity or even simple avarice – his journey West was motivated by the desire to displace that religious aggression onto "a new front in Spain's war against Islam" (Mikhail 2020, 2). It does not escape the notice of South Asian Muslim authors that the intended target of his aggression was "the Indies."

The chapter ahead first establishes the connection between physical displacement in the wake of (re)conquest, the narrative turn to allegory, and the particular metafictional symbols through which various authors comment on their relationship. It then identifies some key tropes about the Andalusian allegory as they consolidated in Mohammad Iqbal's famous 1935 poems about Spain, "Hispania," "Abdul Rehman ...," and especially "Masjid-e Qurtubah." These tropes are refreshed in Intizar Husain's 1995 novel *Āge samundar hai* (The Sea Lies Ahead) and Tariq Ali's *Shadows of the Pomegranate Tree* (1992). In roughly the same moment, writers from the Americas, Octavio Paz and V. S. Naipaul, were using the same types of tropes to make an inverted argument about the relationship of the conquest of Tenochtitlan and the history of Islamic rule in al-Andalus.

When authors of this period merged these two countershelves, they gestured toward a historiographic argument about colonization, the onset of modernity, and the relationship between South Asia and Latin America in the deep past. This was the same moment when such relationships were first articulated, and later rejected, as a way of organizing the boundaries of the "postcolonial world." The progressive exclusion of Latin America and its literature from that category can be largely traced back to this disagreement about history. Whereas the Introduction used the countershelf to drive a wedge between world literature and world history, the layered historical fictions of this chapter suggest a need to reevaluate postcolonial historiography on its own grounds.

"An Irksome Layer": Ruins, Memory, and the Aesthetics of Displacement

Although Muslim Spain had long been a site of fascination and interest, the modern use of the Andalusian allegory emerged during the nineteenth century when European colonization of Muslim territories was at its height (Yaqin 2016). For Europe, the Andalusian allegory has been a story about the foreign, exotic element within the self (Fuchs 2011). For Spain in particular, it has often been a story about its glorious and powerful past precisely at the moment when actual political power has waned. So common was this trope that it was given its own name: "Andalucismo" (Hirschkind 2016, 209–232). For the Arab world, the Andalusian allegory has been a site to work out various ethnic identities and nationalist projects (Granara 2005; Laouyonne 2007).

South Asian Muslims can claim a more specific link with the history of Islamic Spain, since the Muslim conquests of Sindh (now in southeast Pakistan) and Andalusia occurred at almost exactly the same moment – 712 and 711, respectively (Naipaul 1981; Hashmi 2016). For many authors, this suggested a kind of "psychic connection" between Spain and India. It is the same type of connection produced between India and the Caribbean by Columbus' original misrecognition.

Yet the conquest of Sindh has also been used as an ideological weapon against South Asian Muslims. Studying the afterlives of a thirteenth-century account of that conquest, the *Chachnama* (*Story of the Chach*), Manan Ahmed Asif shows how the British transformed this history into a paradigmatic example of Muslim "despotism" in order to justify their own takeover of Sindh in 1843 (Asif 2016). These uses of the text played a key part in furthering two narratives essential to British colonization: first, that Muslims had come to the Indian subcontinent as brutal conquerors and remained as selfishly tyrannical rulers, unworthy in the face of superior British governance; second, that, despite the long duration of their residence in Indian territory, Muslims remained essentially alien in both cultural and ethnic terms. Mufti and Gaurav Desai demonstrate how critiques of colonial rule in South Asia often picked up on these discourses about Muslim foreignness as they mobilized around concepts of indigeneity as the primary justification for independent sovereignty (Mufti 2007; Desai 2011). Desai argues that logics of indigeneity, otherwise so important within anti-colonial rhetoric, were in this case used to justify violent and exclusionary policies toward minority populations deemed "foreign" – South Asian Muslims (Desai 2011). South Asian authors have turned repeatedly to the Andalusian allegory to work through and combat both colonial and postcolonial accusations of this type.

Arguments about sovereignty and belonging tend to emerge most forcefully around the Indian Uprising of 1857, which began among a contingent of Indian soldiers in the British Army and grew to engulf whole swaths of North India with the aim of overthrowing the power of the British East India Company in the region. The ultimate defeat of that effort had just the opposite effect, prompting Britain to formalize its colonization of the subcontinent and declare India part of the British Empire. Just as 1492 acts a synecdoche for the fall of Granada and, with it, the empire of al-Andalus, 1857 stands in for the formal end of Mughal power in India and the massive displacement of Muslim populations in Delhi and Lucknow.

British retribution for the 1857 rebellion fell heavily on the centers of Muslim life in South Asia (Russell 1992; Pritchett 1994; Taneja 2018). In addition to direct violence against the citizens of these cities, the British also exacted symbolic revenge on the cityscape itself, razing entire neighborhoods, expelling nearly all Muslim residents, and either destroying or desecrating Mughal landmarks (Russell 1992; Pritchett 1994; Taneja 2018). In a sense, then, the physical geography of Delhi and Lucknow was so deeply altered that it was as if the cities themselves had been "displaced." Longtime residents found themselves suddenly moving through alien territory. As the Urdu poet Mir wrote of Delhi, "I could not recognize the houses and lost my bearings. Of the former inhabitants there was no trace ... the houses were in ruins .... Everywhere there was a terrible emptiness" (Mir quoted in Eaton 2013, 130).

For many on the subcontinent, but especially Muslim residents of Delhi and Lucknow, communal violence and forced migration during the 1947 Partition were experienced as an echo of the devastation after the 1857 uprising. As mobs targeted entire neighborhoods with violence, once-salient topographies were emptied of their former inhabitants and were overwritten by the influx of migrants from the other side of the newly created border. Space was once again reordered, and for those who remained or returned, the cities became uncanny.

In the 1990s, South Asian Muslim authors joined the two crises of 1857 and 1947 with two more: 1991 – the American invasion of Iraq, which presaged a renewal of Christian–Muslim confrontation on the world stage; and 1992 – the destruction of the Babri Masjid and resulting pogroms, which ushered in a new era of communal politics and uncertainty among Muslims in India. It seems probable that the turn to allegory – specifically, the displacement of stories of anti-Muslim violence onto a new territory – arose as an aestheticized response to this experience of topography.

After each wave of violence, formerly lively spaces for Muslim socialization and worship were emptied out and reclassified as historical "monuments" – literally termed "dead" by both colonial and postcolonial versions of the Archaeological Survey of India (Taneja 2018, 11–13). The effect of this change, writes Taymiya Zaman, means that the viewer is primed to see "monuments built by the Mughals as remnants of an earlier time that no longer exists," in which their contemporary inhabitation "present[s] as an irksome layer" (Zaman 2018, 699). Notice Zaman's language, in which history is physically distilled into a "remnant," a ruin, access to which requires a palimpsestic procedure of peeling back the "irksome layer" of the present. This is precisely the physical process through which the Andalusian allegory is imagined to function in the writing of South Asian authors.

Such ruination was a key rhetoric of British colonial power. By vitiating these spaces and freezing them in time, the British were able to celebrate the power of the previous empire while also posing themselves as its natural inheritor (Eaton 2013). According to Benjamin, ruination is also key to the operation of allegory. "In the ruin, history has physically merged into the setting. . . . Allegories are in the realm of thoughts what ruins are in the realm of things" (Benjamin 2009, 178). Idelber Avelar extends Benjamin by suggesting a connection between mourning and the process of "encryption" by which allegory becomes comprehensible as a mode of substitution. Following Abraham and Torok, Avelar explains that when the work of mourning cannot be completed, or when it is actively refused in melancholia, the psyche creates a "crypt" in which to protect the mourned object (Avelar 1999, 8). Encryption and decryption, then, are not merely etymologically linked to burial and mourning. Instead the encoding and transit of allegory in these texts freezes and empties out the original meaning of al-Andalus in its own time in order to make of it a refuge for South Asian Muslim lifeworlds.

"The Dream of Another Time": Motifs of Association from Iqbal to Ali

"The Trustee of Muslim Blood": Iqbal's Layered Landscape

No author and text is more closely associated with the Andalusian allegory in South Asia than Iqbal's "Masjid-e Qurtubah" ("The Mosque of Córdoba")

(1935). Iqbal visited Spain in 1933 on his way home from a conference in London, his mind still abuzz from discussions about the political future of colonial India. Over the course of several poems, he reflects on traces of Muslim life in Spain, its possible relationship to the subcontinent, and a history that could decenter the colonial European model of progress (Noorani 1999). "Masjid-e Qurtubah" gains power not only from its own internal symbolism but from the symbolic value of its origin story. Like the Mughal monuments in India, the Mesquita had been desacralized and "deadened" as part of the symbolic project of the *Reconquista*. Iqbal was famously the first Muslim given permission to pray there since (Yaqin 2016). In this way, he temporarily rescues the mosque from ruination, revivifies it.

The primary purpose of Iqbal's Andalusian displacement is to use allegory as a tool of political imagining. Thus, "Masjid-e Qurtubah" is most often read as creating new pan-Islamic historiography as a basis for political action in the subcontinent (Noorani 1999; Yaqin 2016). Iqbal calls up the now-familiar tropes of the righteous Islamic ruler, the Arab rider, whose image recalls the superior military prowess and noble mien of medieval Arab conquerors (Iqbal 1935b).[7] It is the same image that Rushdie invokes ironically in the titular "Moor" of his 1995 novel. Iqbal claims that this figure and the empire he created should be judged by his style of "governance" and its superiority to the medieval "darkness of Europe" (Iqbal 1935b).[8] Perhaps the most common strain of the Andalusian allegory uses this image of a superior Muslim ruler to combat enduring British narratives about despotic or decadent Muslim power (Iqbal 1935b).

"Masjid-e Qurtubah" offers a motif for how to read the landscape allegorically when Iqbal's speaker describes the layering of al-Andalus as a vision for the Muslim world – "the dream of another time" – over his view of the Guadalquivir river that runs alongside the Mesquita (Iqbal 1935b).[9] This gesture reminds the reader that the poem as a whole enacts a layering of past over present and distant over proximate, a folding of space and time specific to allegorical displacement. A second branch of the Andalusian allegory radiates out from this idea of layered dreaming, seeking out the living traces through which dreams can be transmitted generation to generation.

For Iqbal, the bold Muslim rulers of al-Andalus have left their mark in modern-day Spain as a genetic legacy:

> By dint of whose blood Andalusians are, even today
> happy-hearted and warmly friendly, simple and bright-faced
> Even today in that land, gazelle eyes are common
> and the arrows of glances, even today, pierce hearts (Iqbal 1935b)[10]

The same kind of argument reappears in "Hispania" ("Spain") (1935), in which Iqbal praises the peninsula as the "trustee of Muslim blood" (Iqbal 1935a).[11] Even the earth and the wind hide traces of the Muslim past to be recovered through the sensitivities of the poet. This is an invitation to read the Spanish landscape itself as allegory: an outward symbol that hides a deeper truth. In these gestures, Iqbal outlines what will become, for postcolonial writers, the major utility of the Andalusian allegory: the testing ground for a type of cultural and genetic rootedness to which Muslims might lay claim that does not rely on indigeneity. At a deeper level, these allegories seem to contrast Muslim forms of cosmopolitan rootedness in the subcontinent against the exclusionary and even expulsionary logics of the European conquest that followed in the *Reconquista* and the British Empire, respectively. These are also compared, in the most recent cases, to various exclusionary forms of space-claiming in the postcolonial present.

We might call these cultural characteristics and physical traces "Islamicate," in that they reflect the "social and cultural complex historically associated with Islam and the Muslims" without being directly related to Islam as a religion (Hodgson 1977, 59). Indeed, the longer the Andalusian allegory operates in South Asian writing, the less these features are associated with any concept of Muslim identity at all, until it comes to be associated, instead, with a connection to Latin America.

If blood is one living trace that connects Spain to South Asia, a second poem from Iqbal's Spanish journey offers another powerful image: the date palm. "Abdur Rehman Awwal Ka Boya Huwa Khajoor Ka Pehla Darakht" ("The First Date Tree Seeded by Abdul Rahman the First") is "a free translation" of an Arabic verse penned by the founder of Muslim Córdoba, Abdul Rahman I.[12] Here Iqbal makes his own countershelf reference to the actual literature of al-Andalus, as opposed to merely its history and physical landscape. The poem begins with the reflection that both the Syrian conqueror and his tree "feel homesick in exile."[13] But upon seeing how the tree finds roots and flourishes, the speaker reflects: "There are no frontiers for the man of faith / He is at home everywhere."[14]

"Every Date Tree Was a Tunnel": Husain's Rooted Consciousness

The same reference– the same Andalusian Arabic text and its counterpart in the landscape – offers the key metaphor animating Husain's 1995 novel

Āge samundar hai (*The Sea Lies Ahead*). Husain had long been known as one of Urdu's preeminent chroniclers of the physical and cultural displacements of Partition. *Āge samundar hai* explores these themes among a community of Muhajirs, Muslim immigrants to Pakistan from India after Partition, in Karachi in the 1970s. Through Iqbalian motifs of date palms and shared dreams, Husain makes an argument about the relationship between that place and time and successive waves of exile in Andalusia.

The whole novel is written as a reflective, deathbed dream of its protagonist, Jawad, and it moves back and forth in time through associative logic of layered memory whose primary operation is the root system of trees. For Husain, the date palm has two opposing characteristics whose unexpected harmony is at the heart of Muslim mobility. On the one hand, the rootedness of the date palms, their ability to draw sustenance from a specific place and endure there, performs the work of claiming belonging based on nativity as distinct from indigeneity. Citing Rahman I through the Urdu of Iqbal, Husain's narrator reflects that the trees "were not exiles in Andalusia. There, they had struck roots and flourished and could be seen all over the countryside" (Husain 2015).

At the same time, the palms also represent connection to a separate, non-Iberian past. Husain imagines them as a sort of portal between Arabic and Iberian peninsulas, one that continues to operate after the ships with which the first Arab conquerors might return home are burned at Gibraltar. "Every date tree was a tunnel; you could enter one and go back to your desert" (Husain 2015). In the same way, Husain's protagonist soon wanders into "an entire jungle [of his] imagination," using the idea of trees to transport him from the shores of Karachi back to the lush landscape of his childhood in North India (Husain 2015). Indeed, the whole narrative flows through these allusive underground channels, moving suddenly from the novel's present into the Indian past and the annals of Andalusian history. Through these same roots, Jawad's story becomes entangled with an ancestor or psychic companion, Sheik Abdul Hajjaj, an exile whose family and associates, like the Muhajirs, have experienced successive waves of displacement between 1235 and 1492 – Córdoba to Sevilla and Málaga – finally taking refuge in Granada in the face of the oncoming *Reconquista*. In this way, he literally enacts Iqbal's "dream of another time."

Like Iqbal's poetry, Husain's novel is bound up with the tension between hopeful metaphors of landscape as a living trace – trees in family courtyards and fields, nourished by the umbilical cords of generations of Muslim inhabitants – and despondent metaphors of landscape as a deadened ruin. One of the protagonist's friends recalls his father reciting Hali's *Musaddas*. Writing in the wake of the devastation of 1857, Hali exhorts his reader to "Go and see the ruins of Cordoba" (Hali quoted in Husain 2015). The narrator's friend recalls his father replying: "And what about our own ruins. The echoing Jama Masjid and its deserted stairs ... for 12 *kos* all around not a human being nor the flicker of a lamp. The lampless city of Shahjahanabad" (Husain 2015). For the father, the Andalusian allegory calls up the expulsion and destruction of the nineteenth century, mourning what would become "Old Delhi" when the British built their "new" capital in 1911. But in the mouth of his son in Karachi, these lines echo in the devastations of Partition. In this sense, Husain's novel posits Muslim survival as a mise-en-abyme: sinking down through layer after layer of crisis until they bottom out in Spain.

Husain's novel thus holds within it a countershelf of literary reference toward Spain. The futurity implied by these earlier Andalusian allegories had been, at least in part, a hopeful one: for Iqbal, al-Andalus could act like a rearview mirror that presages a glorious era of cosmopolitan Muslim sovereignty; for Hali, it could act as a looking glass through which South Asian Muslims could gain new perspective on their own predicament. Like Rushdie's Andalusian novels, however, Husain's novel ultimately relies on proleptic nostalgia for that kingdom's end. Husain's title, *Āge samundar hai*, projects that anxiety forward to Pakistan through an apocryphal saying attributed to General Ayub Khan. When asked about the options for Pakistan's political future, he used the titular phrase to suggest that it was "my way or the highway" (Jalil 2016). Connecting this to the burning of boats at Gibraltar, Husain's characters warn, "That time is long gone when our forefathers got off at the shore, turned their backs to the sea and burnt all their boats. Now the angry sea is not behind us but ahead of us, and we have made no boats" (Husain 2015).

By focusing on characters in both time periods who must leave newly conquered cities and cross newly created borders to find refuge in a strange land, Husain creates a clear parallel to Partition. But the dramatic irony of the Andalusian allegory suggests that an even larger crisis in Pakistan looms on the horizon. A dying Jawad exits his own body and steps out into what was formerly Karachi, here displaced to reveal Granada underneath. The final lines present a literal countershelf gesture as the ultimate scene of Muslim devastation, one that infamously marks the final transfer of power from Muslim to Christian rule: "A half-burnt page of some poetry collection, a book, the manuscript of a philosopher, a malfuzat of a sufi fluttered occasionally. The rest was all stillness" (Husain 2015).

"Culture on Fire": Tariq Ali's Encrypted Crisis

Tariq Ali's novel, *Shadows of the Pomegranate Tree* (1992), begins with the event on which Husain's closed: the infamous book burning in Granada, an act of symbolic violence that encapsulates the anti-intellectual fanaticism of the *Reconquista*. The patriarch of Ali's novel, Umar, recalls how the Christian Spaniards "emptied all our libraries and ... set our culture on fire" (Ali 1992, 21). He concludes ominously that "the fire which burnt our books will one day destroy everything we have created in al-Andalus" (Ali 1992, 21).

Naming a shelf or library is, naturally, the most concrete instantiation of a countershelf affiliation, and thus the book burning has become one of the most common metaphors through which authors render their connection to al-Andalus. Trees are unquestionably alive. Buildings, emptied out as ruins, can be unequivocally rendered dead. Books exist somewhere in between. As in Agha Shahid Ali's poem "The Previous Occupant" in Chapter 1, Tariq Ali suggests that texts retain their associative power even when they, like human victims of political violence, are missing and can no longer be accessed directly. Like Agha Shahid Ali's speaker, Umar introjects the loss of both texts and people by connecting them to poetry learned by heart. He recalls the lines of the Andalusian Arabic poet Ibn Hazm, a rationalist who, like Ibn Rushd, was exiled amid the increasing fanaticism of an earlier moment of the Andalusian empire.

> *The paper ye may burn,*
> *But what the paper holds ye cannot burn;*
> *'tis safe within my breast.*
> *Where I remove, it goes with me;*
> *Alights where I alight,*
> *and in my tomb will lie.* (Ali 1992, 24, emphasis in original)

In the final line, the symbolic operation of melancholia as "encryption" is transported literally to the crypt.

Set in 1500, just after the completion of the physical *Reconquista*, Ali's novel focuses on a noble Muslim family and their home outside of Granada in the remote village of al-Hudayl, still relatively untouched by the violent regime change that has just occurred in the metropole. The Hudayal clan lives in harmony with Jewish and Christian villagers, as well as more distant Christian secular and religious authorities – suggesting the kind of idealized cosmopolitanism that often characterizes prelapsarian stories of al-Andalus. Over the course of the novel, however, the concerns of the wider world find their way into the cocoon of al-Hudayl, culminating in a catastrophic final confrontation between the village and a demonic, red-haired Catholic mercenary that results in the family's annihilation.

Shadows of the Pomegranate Tree is the first novel of Ali's *The Islam Quintet*, each installment of which recalls a different moment of Muslim–Christian confrontation through which contemporary conflicts might be allegorically refracted. In this way, Ali participates in a long historiographic tradition in South Asian letters. One of the most common responses to the claims about Muslim rulers' degenerate culture after 1857 was the attempt to recover images like Iqbal's "Arab Rider" that embodied just and prosperous Muslim sovereignty from the deep past. For this reason, it is common to find the Andalusian allegory within larger projects of Islamic historiography. Along with Hali's *Musaddas*, referenced previously, the most famous nineteenth-century Urdu writing of this type was Sharar's series of historical novels. Among them, *Flora Florinda*, about the fate of an ethnically and religiously mixed woman in al-Andalus, was by far the most successful and popular (Russell 1992; Mukherjee 2002).[15] Half a century later, popular Pakistani historical fiction writer Naseem Hijazi recapitulated this allegory in a four-book series titled *The Fall of Muslim Spain*. The historical novel *Shaheen* (*The Eagle*) (1987) about the fall of Granada was also produced as a television serial in Pakistan.

Yet unlike the other authors in this chapter, Ali never directly ties his story of Andalusia to South Asia or any one moment of displacement for South Asian Muslims. He offers no particular mechanism – like Rushdie's painting, Husain's roots, or Iqbal's dream – to thematize such a reading. Instead, Ali suggests an allegorical dimension through his preference for questions, conversations, and motifs that speak equally to 1492, 1857, 1947, and, post hoc, 1992.

This reading emerges in part from the inverted "shots" with which Ali opens and closes the novel: a chess set, specially carved for the youngest Hudayal, Yazid, by the village's Jewish carpenter. At the opening of the novel, it stands at the center of life in al-Hudayl, a symbol for the family's innocence and playfulness, embodied by the young Yazid. At the end, it is a metaphor for the town's destruction, the bloodied black queen dropping from Yazid's hand as he falls, murdered by the red-headed captain. Readers familiar with South Asian literature may recognize these two scenes as a reference to the Hindi writer Premchand's short story "The Chess Players," published in Hindi as "Shatranj ki khiladi" and in Urdu as "Shatranj ki bāzi" (1924) (Premchand 2007). Even more particularly, the scene references the innovations to that story made by Satyajit Ray's filmic adaptation, *Shatranj ki khiladi* (*The Chess Players*) (1977).

"Shatranj ki khiladi" tells the story of two Muslim noblemen who become so obsessed with the game of chess that they ignore the annexation of Awadh by the British in 1856. Chess here carries a dual symbolic cargo: it is both a synecdoche for all of the other forms of Lucknowi decadence and an allegory, a visual miniaturization of the territorial conquest happening in the real world at the same time. It is not merely that Ali uses chess in the same way as a leitmotif in his novel; he actually makes a very explicit citation of Ray's film by zooming in on the chess set itself. More precisely, still, Ali borrows Ray's innovation on Premchand's original story with regard to the metaphor of the chess queen, known through the male term *vazir* (advisor) in Indian chess. In the final scene of the film, one of the titular players holds the white queen aloft and declares, "Get out of the way, Vazir. Queen Victoria has arrived" (Ray 1977).[16] This aspect of the chess metaphor coheres with, but is absent from, Premchand's original story. Ali seems to reference the chess queen innovation directly when he makes Yazid's black queen into a horrifying miniature Queen Isabella. "The black Queen's eyes shone with evil, in brutal contrast with the miniature madonna hanging around her neck. Her lips were painted the colour of blood. A ring on her finger displayed a painted skull" (Ali 1992, 2).

Between the brackets of the chess scenes, the rest of the novel has little to do with bloody direct confrontations between Christians and Muslims. Instead, Ali gives precedence to anguished debates among the inhabitants of al-Hudayl and Granada about the ability to continue in their religious and cultural traditions in a suddenly hostile territory. Ali positions his narrative in that fragile and ultimately fleeting historical moment in which the territorial *Reconquista* had been completed but forced conversions and the Inquisition had not yet begun. Ali reminds us that the original conditions of the surrender of Granada promised to uphold religious tolerance under Catholic rule, a promise to which many of the characters cling even as it is gradually eroded over years of religiously motivated violence. This is, of course, the same promise given to Muslims who decided to remain in India, one betrayed first by the exceptional violence of Partition and again by intermittent brutalities in the decades that followed.

The prominence of arguments about whether Muslim characters will remain in Spain – and very likely convert to Catholicism – or emigrate to another Muslim territory clearly echo debates among Muslims living in India about how to respond to Partition. Ali connects the plight of Muslims in 1500 and in 1947 by emphasizing the paradox of their relation to place. That is, like Husain's characters, the Hudayl clan are explicitly non-indigenous, recalling with pride the ancestor who brought their family into Spain through the earlier, Islamic conquest. At the same time, the family has been living on the same piece of land for the 500 years since, in a village that bears their name. They struggle to envision a possible future in Egypt or the Maghreb.

Ali seems at pains to emphasize the connection of al-Hudayl to specific forms of emplacement that signify a Hispanic rootedness against a more general Muslim identity: food, literature, and geography. This is most notable in the titular pomegranate grove, where many key actions of the novel take place and where various characters reflect on their attachment to Andalusian soil. In this sense, the pomegranate may be read just like the date palm in Husain's novel. But it also carries a second metaphor for the displacement and layering of allegory: not roots, in this case, but puns.

Many readers will know that the Spanish word for pomegranate, *granada*, is a false cognate with the Arabic name for the city of Granada, Gharnāṭah, which Ali uses habitually in the text. Although the association is a well-known mistake, a failure of translation, the pomegranate has nonetheless become emblematic of Granada. Rushdie's *The Moor's Last Sigh* plays up a similar punny misunderstanding inherent in the name Bombay, a city that, like Granada, had developed an overly rosy reputation for cosmopolitan tolerance. Formerly a bastardization of the Portuguese *bom bahia* (good bay), the 1992–3 riots presaged a rightward shift that resulted in the renaming of the city Mumbai after the patron-goddess Mumbai-devi. Rushdie aligns this renaming with the operation of allegory, in that both suggest the revelation of the true meaning – a Hindu-exclusive urban space – beneath the outward appearance of cosmopolitan tolerance (Thiara 2007). Ali similarly uses the space of his novel to ask whether the kind of misunderstanding in a false cognate can be culturally productive – whether one can build a stable society on the recognition of outward resemblances over inherent distinctions, the harmonies between names, and the gradual syncretization of habits and meaning.

If these questions animate the novel, then the end provides a resoundingly pessimistic answer. A "red-headed beardless captain ... stout and short ... not more than sixteen years of age" lays waste to the village and everyone in it (Ali 1992, 225). In the final lines, the only survivor of this massacre resolves to abandon the Peninsula for the Maghreb. The novel proper ends here, with the fate of the Hudayl clan uncertain in exile. We might imagine an epilogue that follows him south, perhaps suggesting a parallel to the fate of Muhajirs in Pakistan.

But the epilogue we get instead traces the fate of the red-headed captain who destroyed al-Hudayl and, through him, suggests a very different kind of allegorical connection to South Asia – one based not on Partition but on European colonization.

> Twenty years later, the victor of al-Hudayl, now at the height of his powers and universally regarded as one of the most experienced military leaders of the Catholic kingdom of Spain, disembarked from his battleship on a shore thousands of miles away from his native land.
> ...
> "Do you know what they call this remarkable place?" he asked, to test his aide, as the boat carrying them docked at the palace.
> "Tenochtitlan is the name of the city and Moctezuma is the king."
> "Much wealth went into its construction," said the captain.
> "They are a very rich nation, Captain Cortes," came the reply.
> The captain smiled. (Ali 1992, 273)

"With the Same Zeal as Cortés": Theories of Conquest across Three Continents

Cortés' unexpected appearance at the end of Ali's novel suggests that the roots of colonial oppression in Latin America are already immanent in the completion of the Spanish *Reconquista*. The reader who was particularly sensitive to history might even recall that the conquest of Mexico included many equally infamous bonfires of indigenous codices, seemingly modeled on the conflagration in Granada (Mignolo 1994). If we take the body of *Shadows of the Pomegranate Tree* as an allegory for South Asian Muslim displacement, then the turn to Mexico at the novel's end invites a link between two regions based on their shared experience of European colonization. As with Paz's recapitulation of Góngoran style to mediate between Mexico and India in Chapter 2, Spain is merely a convenient middle term.

Nor is Ali alone in associating the conquest of Tenochtitlan with Spain and India. Indeed, for a while, imaginaries of the fall of Tenochtitlan functioned as a sort of inverse Andalusian allegory. In place of an infinitely iterable model of cosmopolitan tolerance, the invasion of Mexico became the exemplary allegory of brutal conquest. Ali thus rehashes a common historiography in which Isabella's armies applied the ruthless tactics they learned in the *Reconquista* in the new context of the Americas. This occurs, most infamously, in historical descriptions of the conquest of Tenochtitlan, whose houses of worship are misrecognized as "mosques"

(Cortés 2012, 95).[17] The imaginary of the conqueror, as much as that of the conquered people, works through allegorical displacement.[18]

More than a decade after his sojourn in India, Paz raised Tenochtitlan in order to reflect on the harmonies of various global forms of conquest in *Sor Juana Ines de la Cruz: o, las trampas de la fé* (*Sor Juana, or, The Traps of Faith*) (1982). Paz conceived of this text during his time in India, and that origin leaves strange traces in his writing.[19] In a tiny digression in a book otherwise dedicated to the life and times of the Mexican baroque poet and philosopher, Paz claims that "it is not an exaggeration to see in the conquest and the evangelization of America a process in which the Muslim precedent was no less a determining factor than the Catholic faith" (Paz 1990, 28). The evidence for this claim, he suggests, emerges in the Indian landscape, the same way for Iqbal it emerged in the dust of Spain. "Anyone who [has lived] in India can see," he argues, the traces of a history in which "Muslims . . . destroyed Hindu temples with the same zeal that Cortés devoted to tearing down the idols of the great pyramid of Cholula; upon those ruins, sometimes with the very stones, they erected superb mosques" (Paz 1990, 28).[20]

Paz thus undertakes a three-way displacement where Spain acts as a middle term between central Mexico and North India. He claims that "anyone who [has lived] in India can see" that the geographies of India and Mexico have been equally shaped by the displacing power, the practice of razing and layering, that he argues is characteristic of Islam.[21] What's more, Paz repeats a trope about the reconstitution of mosques on the grounds of temples that contributed to anti-Muslim violence in the subcontinent. It was the accusation that it was erected on a Hindu temple marking the birthplace of Rama that prompted the destruction of the Babri Masjid. Strangely enough, this, too, is an Andalusian allegory that proposes a portable experience of Islamicate *hispanidad*. But rather than seeking to recover a glorious history of Islam, it Paz's association serves to denigrate it.

The Indo-Caribbean writer V. S. Naipaul makes this three-way comparison even more explicit in *Among the Believers* (1981). Naipaul begins with the psychic connection between Spain and Sindh:

> In the imagination, the Arabs of the seventh century, inflamed by the message of the Prophet, pour out of Arabia and spread east and west. In the west, they invade Visigothic Spain in 710; in the east, in the same year, they move beyond Persia to invade the great Hindu-Buddhist kingdom of Sind. The symmetry of the expansion reinforces the idea of elemental energy, a lava flow of the faith. (Naipaul 1981, 131)

Like Paz, Naipaul goes on to suggest a genealogical tie between the Muslim–Christian confrontation in Spain and the conquest style of Cortés, calling them "not accidental" (Naipaul 1981, 132). He writes: "The Spanish conquistadores were like Arabs in their faith, fanaticism, toughness, poverty and greed," as if Catholicism were itself an allegorical screen, peeled back to reveal Islam underneath (Naipaul 1981, 132). Naipaul explores these resonances in a comparative reading of narration of the conquest of Sindh in the *Chachnama* and the narration of the conquest of Tenochtitlan in Bernal Díaz's sixteenth-century *Historia verdadera de la conquista de Nueva España* (*The True History of the Conquest of New Spain*).

Naipaul's reading is, in a strange, unappealing way, a postcolonial one, in that it returns to accounts of conquest in order to offer a theory of the logic of colonization. This ambivalence is perhaps appropriate for Naipaul himself, a figure who is at once foundational for postcolonial criticism – his novel *The Mimic Men* (1967) provides the namesake for Bhabha's most frequently cited essay and is one of the primary vehicles for the discussion of the Macaulay Minute – and the object of a thoroughly reciprocated disavowal. In *Among the Believers*, Naipaul presents Islamic and Christian armies as united, the aggressive conquering forces so that Hindu India and indigenous Mexico – and, by extension, the rest of Latin America and the Caribbean – can be united together as the colonized victim with whom the postcolonial author and his audience are meant to identify. Yet Naipaul, like Paz, uses this structurally postcolonial analytic to reinvigorate colonial-era tropes about Muslim despotism and violence.

Naipaul's comparison extends beyond the violence itself into other reprehensible tropes about Muslim fanaticism. "There is a difference between *The Conquest of New Spain* and the *Chachnama*," he admits (Naipaul 1981, 133). "[The latter has] no extra moral or historical sense ... no new *wonder* or compassion, no idea of what is cruel and what is not cruel, such as even Bernal Díaz, the Spanish soldier, possesses" (Naipaul 1981, 133, emphasis added). In this reading, Islamic conquest is uniquely brutal, not just due to its immediate violence but because of the total absence of wondering as a faculty of independent thought.

This is what makes Ali's renarration of conquest so striking. By implicating the very same person, Cortés, in the conquest of al-Hudayl and Tenochtitlan, he creates a genealogy of conquest that unites the two regions in such a way that Muslims are victims of colonial violence, rather than perpetrators. Given the overarching parallels with South Asian history in the rest of the novel, Ali seems to suggest colonial Latin America, in addition to Andalusia, as allegories for European, rather than Muslim, conquest in South Asia. He deftly responds to the core of Paz and Naipaul's premises – that world history contains a tripartite connection between Latin America, Spain, and South Asia – while cleverly inverting the usual rhetorics that such a connection implies.

The "Western Route": Divergent Pathways for Literary and Scholarly History

In the midst of all the Andalusian allegories coming out in the early 1990s, the Anglophone South Asian author Ahmed Ali reissued his foundational novel *Twilight in Delhi* (1941) with a new introduction. The introduction was written in the temporal halo of the quincentenary of the "discovery" of the Americas – also, of course, the anniversary of the fall of Muslim Spain. In the lead-up to and immediate aftermath of this event, it does not surprise that both moments might become notionally fused. At the same time, and likely for equally nonincidental reasons, there was a relatively brief moment in the 1990s in which the historiography of postcolonial studies attempted to account for Latin America. The final work of the chapter is to explore how that fragile moment of unity came to an end.

Like the other texts in this chapter, Ali claimed that the "racial memory" of the Muslim people is encoded in particular locations, even when all that remains of them is a ruin (Ali 1994, xi).[22] As with them, he tells the story of the decline of Muslim life in the subcontinent between the end of Mughal sovereignty in 1857 and the division of the postcolonial state in 1947. He even provides a concept metaphor for these displacements through the image of a family courtyard dominated by a tree that has been nourished by generations of umbilical cords. But unlike the others, Ali makes no mention of the ancient Islamicate past in Spain anywhere within his text itself.

Why, then, does the second sentence of the new introduction route west, take us immediately to "Mexico and Peru," where "the Spaniards conquered vast Aztec and Inca empires in the early part of the sixteenth century" (Ali 1994, xi)? Ali then reminds us that European invaders of India "had been awed by Islam since the conquest of Spain" (Ali 1994, xi). Later in the introduction, he describes the Tories supporting the East India Company as "hungry for souls, like the Spaniards" (Ali 1994, xiii). And in redescribing the horror of 1857, Ali reaches for the anachronistic term "conquistadores" to name the British, casting their Muslim victims "as paupers and a vanquished people, like the Aztecs and Incas of Mexico and

Peru three hundred years before them" (Ali 1994, xv). These comparisons to Latin America and Spain were not natural to the novel's critique of colonial rule when it was initially published in 1941. But through a stroke of incredibly bad luck, the majority of the first imprint of *Twilight in Delhi* was bombed out of existence during World War II (Ali 1994). The novel was only narrated into the Indian Anglophone canon after its recovery much later in the twentieth century. This makes all the more striking Ali's framing in the new introduction, which poses Latin America as a necessary inclusion, not merely as part of a vast postcolonial world but as the historical origin point and direct predecessor for that story in the early 1990s.

The necessity of this connection was equally felt among postcolonial scholars of the same period. So, for example, Mary Louise Pratt's *Imperial Eyes*, published in 1992 itself, remains foundational for postcolonial studies even though most of the book's archive focuses on Latin America, including its opening meditation on the sixteenth-century Inca intellectual Guaman Poma de Alaya (Pratt 1992). Stephen Greenblatt's *Marvelous Possessions* (1991), which takes as its point of departure and central example the aesthetics of Columbus' writing about the Spanish conquest of the Caribbean, was published almost exactly 500 years after of Columbus' first landing (Greenblatt 1991). Similarly, Robert Young's review of the field, *Postcolonialism: An Historical Introduction* (2001), begins in Hispañola in 1542 with Bartolomé de las Casas' *Brevísima relación de la destrucción de las Indias* (*A Short Account of the Destruction of the Indies*) and marks the Cuban revolution in 1959 and the Tricontinental Conference in 1966 as major events for modern postcolonial thought (Young 2016). Bill Ashcroft, Garet Griffiths, and Helen Tiffin, in *The Empire Writes Back* (1989), also insist that postcolonial literature include Latin American literature by virtue of including "all the culture affected by the imperial process from the moment of colonization to the present day" (Ashcroft, Griffiths, and Tiffin 2002, 2). Yet by the end of the 1990s, this historiography of the field had all but disappeared, and with it the possibility of a shared literary world.

Instead, major fault lines had developed between postcolonial studies and the then-nascent "decolonial turn" (Grosfoguel 2011; Maldonato-Torres 2011) around the location from which colonization and its aftermath should be theorized. Although the theoretical heart of those debates cue location as epistemology – whose modes of knowing sustain the field – its more practical arguments center on location as a question of historiography.[23]

In essence, both fields strove to align the timeline of European colonization with the development and theorization of modernity. Yet choosing a temporal starting point for modernity also implied a geographic preference. Stuart Hall famously summarized these conflicts over the temporal-spatial implications of the term in his 1996 essay "When Was the Postcolonial?" "Is Latin America postcolonial, even though its independence struggles were fought ... long before the recent stage of 'decolonization' to which the term more evidently refers, and were led by the descendants of Spanish settlers who had colonized their own 'native peoples'" (Hall 1996, 245)? Hall intends the interrogative tone of his title and this series of queries as a genuine conceptual opening in the field. But they have more frequently been read as "a polemical closure" (Hall 1996, 245).

Thus, in her popular field-survey *Colonialism/Postcolonialism* (1998), Ania Loomba represents the more common postcolonial position that Latin America must be excluded from the timeline of colonialism proper, since "modern colonialism" is distinguished by its imbrication with modern, industrial capitalism in France and Britain (Loomba 1998, 9). Decolonial scholars like Walter Mignolo, meanwhile, argue that the definitions of modernity and modern capitalism must be pushed back to account for the central role that the "discovery" and subsequent exploitation of the Americas played in the global economy (Grosfoguel 2011; Mignolo 2011). At the same time, Aníbel Quijano and Enrique Dussel use the ambivalent decolonization of Latin America – an early formal freedom from Spain in the nineteenth century paired with colonial social structures that endure into the present – to emphasize the duration of coloniality and the unfinished "transmodernist" project of decolonization (Dussel 1992; Quijano 2000). Both of these moves push back against the implied temporal "post-ness" of postcolonial.

While these tensions erupted in many parts of the theoretical landscape, they were perhaps nowhere more prominent than in the breakup of subaltern studies in the late 1990s. The movement ultimately fractured in no small part due to the perceived theoretical intransigence of the dominant South Asianist wing of the collective against innovations proposed by their counterparts focused on Latin America (Grosfoguel 2011). Postcolonial scholars in the present do not seem to register the level of anger that still exists about these events among those who theorize the experience of Latin American colonization, nor how sharply pointed it can be. In assessing the breakup of the movement, Gustavo Verdisio surveyed former participants in the Latin American Subalternist group in 2005. A full third of his questions deal explicitly with the perceived rivalry with South Asian studies, including the tellingly phrased "Why do South Asian subalternists ... *olympically* ignore the work of their Latin American peers?" (Verdesio 2005, 7, emphasis added).[24] In these discussions, South Asia is not merely one part of the postcolonial world from which the Latin American historical experience has been excluded. South Asian writers are, quite specifically, the antagonists in the drama of that exclusion.

Where does this leave an analysis of South Asian authors' obsessive return to medieval Spain and colonial Latin America – or any of the numerous "perplexing attachments" explored in the rest of this book? In part, they once again underscore the argument in the Introduction that global history and literary history are not one and the same. Yet, in the way that these fictions make explicit claims over the narration of history itself, they also do something more. They suggest the need for a more flexible form of field-making that includes authors as subjects and not just objects of theory. In part, they seem to harken back to the desire Hall expressed for postcolonial studies: "to identify what are *new* relations and dispositions of power which are emerging in the [post-independence or post-decolonization moment]" (Hall 1996, 246, emphasis original). As postcolonial studies has ossified, the term Global South, with its emphasis on willed affiliation, seems to leap into the breach.

In this light, perhaps the power of these stories lies precisely in their ability to leave behind the "realist" epistemologies of theory on which both decolonial and postcolonial historiographies are based. As we have seen, the central project of the Andalusian allegory – locating a safe haven for cultural survival through a connection to other places and times – has little to do with discovering what "really happened" back then. It reveals instead a fantasy about the present and the will to create or justify new relationships now.

This will is perhaps clearest in a brief, belated addition to the Andalusian craze of the 1990s, Ghose's short story "Arrival in India," published in *Veronica and the Góngora Passion* in 1998. "Arrival in India" tells the story of a resident of Granada named José Abbado Megid who becomes obsessed with India after reading travel accounts in Arabic with his mentor, the fictional character Ibn al-Rashid – perhaps an anachronistic countershelf gesture to the same twelfth-century philosopher who fascinates Rushdie. Like Ali's novel, the short story opens on the book burning in Granada, where Ibn al-Rashid's accounts of India are burned along with millions of other volumes. Like Ali's Umar, Ghose's José deals with this loss through a safeguarding act of encryption. He sets out to recover Ibn al-Rashid's texts by experiencing India itself, stowing away on a ship that will bring him to the subcontinent through an as-yet-untested western route. The reader immediately realizes what Megid fails to grasp even as he jumps ashore with arms outstretched at the story's end and declares himself in "Hindustan": that he has inadvertently and quite unconsciously "discovered" the Caribbean (Ghose 1998).

For most of the story, the book burning is the only relevant connection to the *Reconquista* and the idea of Muslim endurance. Only in the last pages do we learn that José Abbado Megid is the Hispanicization of Yusuf Abdul Majeed, marking Megid as a "Morisco," a false Catholic convert whose individual flight to "India" presages the wholesale expulsion of Muslims from Iberia. His identity, an allegorical Catholic layer that encrypts and protects the Muslim self, is a microcosm of the layering that misrecognizes the Caribbean as the Indies.

It is possible, too, that this revelation refers back allegorically to Ghose's own name. Like Rushdie's father, Ghose's father also adopted a different surname for his family than the one he was born with. But rather than reclaiming a connection to the deep Muslim past, in the wake of Partition the name "Ghose" was meant to shield the author's Muslim identity beneath a Hindu veneer. This experience of hiding, rather than open identification, is what pulls him toward Spain, and through Spain to Latin America. Chapter 4 follows up on Ghose's explorations of Latin American magical realism and the connection to the Americas he and other South Asian authors left hiding in plain sight.

CHAPTER 4

Pilgrim
Journeys to the Roots of Magical Realism

> If we were to forget about "Commonwealth Literature," we might see that there is a kind of commonality about much literature, in many languages, emerging from those parts of the world which one could loosely term the less powerful, or the powerless. *The magical realism of the Latin Americans influences Indian-language writers today.* . . . Much of what is new in world literature comes from this group.
> (Rushdie 1992, 68–69, emphasis added)

In his 1983 essay "Commonwealth Literature Does Not Exist," Salman Rushdie offers one of the clearest articulations of the countershelf as an instrument through which an Anglophone author can cast off the Anglophone tradition in favor of an imagined sphere of world literature "in many languages." Long before Amitav Ghosh would reject the Commonwealth Prize for literature on similar grounds, sounding the death knell for that term, Rushdie's essay pushes back against an academic comparative framework through which his own novels were being read and promoted at the time (Sadana 2012, 169–171). Nor is it by accident that the polemic between the multilingual world and the Anglophone globe should find its testing ground in the circulation of "the magical realism of the Latin Americans." By the middle of the 1980s, such an argument would have felt more or less self-evident, validated jointly by Gabriel García Márquez's 1982 Nobel Prize and Rushdie's own ascent.

Moreover, the globalization of magical realism in the early 1980s coincides with the moment in which the term "postcolonial" overtook "the commonwealth" as the world imaginary for texts like Rushdie's in the US academy. Ato Quayson offers 1983 as the latter's "totemic date" (Quayson 2012, 342). While postcolonial literary scholarship has also traditionally focused on the rereading of colonial-era British literature and the recovery of earlier twentieth-century writers in the colonies, the flood of post-Rushdie magical realism in English appears in just the right time – and language – to become iconic of the postcolonial contemporary. As Chris Warnes reminds us, these two categories are often perceived to be constitutively related, even one and the same. In the most positive sense, as Homi Bhabha writes, "'Magical realism,' after the Latin American Boom, becomes the literary language of the emergent postcolonial world" (Bhabha quoted in Warnes 2005, 6). In a more negative vein, Francis Barker, Peter Hulme, and Margaret Iversen state, "The most dangerous and shallow use of the term 'postcolonial' [is] as roughly equivalent to 'magical realist'" (Barker, Hulme, and Iversen quoted in Warnes 2005, 4).

Ironically, Rushdie's own writing would be used to validate a critical turn by which the possessive preposition linking "magical realism" and "Latin America" would be actively severed in postcolonial studies. As Wendy Faris wrote in 1995, "Rushdie's *Midnight's Children* ... exemplifies the mode of magical realism best for my purposes here – among other reasons because it is quite real, quite magical, *and not from Latin America, where the genre is usually imagined to reside*" (Faris 1995, 164, emphasis added). Ursula Kluwick is more pointed still, using Rushdie's status as "one of the most important representatives of magical realism *outside Latin America*" to stage an explicit polemic against tying postcolonial magical realism to a genealogy from that region (Kluwick 2011, 1, emphasis added). While Faris, Warnes, and others are more measured in their approach, the impact of this turn in the field has been to radically deemphasize Latin America as an intertextual contributor in any sense. And while there is, to be sure, much value to tracing the disparate sources of literary magic in various world areas and languages, the cumulative effect of these projects has been to sharpen the "local" and "abroad" dyad in postcolonial studies, while quietly editing out any inconvenient contributors from the rest of the literary world. Even the name of Faris' 1995 essay, "Scheherazade's Children," roots Rushdie's creative endeavor in a supposedly more "authentic" source for a South Asian Muslim author – *The Thousand and One Nights*.

Rushdie himself warns against this tendency as "the bogy of Authenticity," which "demands that sources, forms, style, language and symbol all derive from a supposedly homogeneous and unbroken tradition. Or else" (Rushdie 1992, 67). Undergirding his analysis, Rushdie says, is the writing of "the Indian art critic Geeta Kapur" (Rushdie 1992, 67). He is referring to Kapur's "In Quest of Identity" (1973) (discussed in Chapter 2), where she develops her idea of a genuinely indigenous art practice for India from the font of Latin American literature.

In the same way, Rushdie is among many South Asian magical realists who act as "pilgrims," staging textual journeys to Latin America as a way of highlighting their consciousness of the long tradition of magical realist writing outside South Asia. In direct contrast to scholars like Kluwick, who see in this association only a lurking accusation about "slavish imitation" of models from abroad, South Asian authors mark their own participation in that narrative mode as a deliberate act of South–South affiliation (Kluwick 2011, 1).

Within the larger debates about magical realism's origins and itineraries is an argument about its politics. In his affiliation with a possible world literature from "those parts of the world which one could loosely term the less powerful, or the powerless," Rushdie seems to uphold a common line of criticism in which magical realism offers a premier location of aesthetic resistance to cultural dominance of the Global North (Rushdie 1992). Kumkum Sangari sums up this strain in her pathbreaking comparative study of Rushdie and García Márquez, framing magical realism as "a transformative mode that has the capacity to both register and to engage critically with the present and to generate new ways of seeing" (Sangari 1987, 162). And yet, over time, that faith was vitiated by the very material success of magical realism and what Timothy Brennan calls "the saleable 'Third-Worldism' it represents" (Brennan 1989, 65). This has led to what Jerónimo Arellano terms its "theoretical malaise" in the present (Arellano 2010, 96).

But this is not solely Rushdie's story. Here, as elsewhere in this book, he provides an entrée into a greater problem in South Asian letters. At the same moment in 1984 that Rushdie was using "the magical realism of the Latin Americans" to take a stand against the Commonwealth, another South Asian magical realist, Zulfikar Ghose, lamented to his friend, Thomas Berger: "By setting so many of my books in South America, I have accidentally made myself meaningless to the Commonwealth" (Ghose 1984). These inverse statements – made by two authors in very different positions in an Anglophone literary market – nevertheless take on the same critical category through the same gesture of affiliation to a literary elsewhere.

Among the *sathottari* Indian writers discussed in Chapter 2, Ghose had already developed a reputation as one of the most important Pakistani Anglophone poets. He was regarded as by far the most accomplished contributor to the Oxford University Press compilation called *First Voices: Six Poets from Pakistan* (1965). Transnational readers also received with pleasure his South Asia–themed memoirs, *Confessions of a Native*

Alien, published the same year. Ghose capped off the 1960s with two successful realist novels about Pakistan, *The Contradictions* (1966) and *The Murder of Aziz Khan* (1967), the latter of which remains his most celebrated text (Mukherjee 1966).

In essence, Ghose was already a canonical figure when he moved from London to Austin, Texas, for a professorship in 1969. The move coincided with a dramatic shift in his writing. Turning even more conclusively toward prose, Ghose turned away from realism and toward magical realism. Quite unexpectedly, the geographic ambit of his novels shifted too: from South Asia to Latin America. He followed *The Incredible Brazilian* trilogy (1972, 1975, 1978) with a string of other more-and-less magical realist novels set in Hispanophone Latin America: *A New History of Torments* (1982), *Don Bueno* (1983), and *Figures of Enchantment* (1986), leading finally to *The Triple Mirror of the Self* (1992). In effect, his entire fiction-writing imagination seems captivated by Latin America, especially García Márquez, whom he called "the true and only begetter of literary magic" (Ghose 1998, 258).

In this context, Ghose's lack of material success – his "meaninglessness" to the institutions of canonization – offers a counterweight to the argument that magical realism will always act as an eminently mobile market good. Sara Brouillette has, indeed, made such an argument about the market dynamics of postcolonial fiction, using Ghose as her reluctant hero. For Brouillette, it is quite significant that his 1972 turn to Latin America seems to coincide with a drop-off in critical attention to Ghose's oeuvre. This choice signals a type of "writing back" to the Anglophone market, which, for her, requires "the situating of postcolonial authors and their works within clearly differentiated political locales" associated with their origins (Brouillette 2007, 145). This makes Ghose, ironically, one of the only canonical Anglophone Pakistani writers of his era while also "effectively invisible" to the categories through which such literature achieved canonicity in the West (Brouillette 2007, 145).

As Amit Chaudhuri did with the *sathottari* poets (discussed in Chapter 2), Brouillette explicitly contrasts Ghose's middling reception with the outstanding success of Rushdie. Both arguments rely on commercial failure and aesthetic recalcitrance as the guarantors of political innocence and what Gloria Fisk calls world-literary "goodness" (Fisk 2018). Within this market critique, Brouillette offers an argument about Ghose's ambivalent place in the ascent of postcolonial studies as an academic "institution" – one that made space for both South Asian literature and its authors in the classroom. But, as we will see, Ghose was not alone in refracting his concern about such institutionalization and what it means for identity through a turn to the south. This chapter both draws on and ultimately diverges from Brouillette by looking instead at what Rushdie and Ghose have in common in their stated investment in Latin American magical realism. They share that investment with other South Asian writers Anita Desai and Sunny Singh, who experimented in that form.

To look at the variety of these engagements is to see, as Mariano Siskind argues, how Latin American magical realism offered authors in South Asia "a *mirror* that reflected what they perceived as their own postcolonial reality" (Siskind 2012, 860, emphasis added). The following sections trace South Asian authors' journeys back "through the looking glass" to Latin America. An opening section examines conflicts within the study of magical realism. It highlights how South Asian gestures of pilgrimage locate politics within the narrative mode. The following sections examine the commonality between Rushdie and Ghose's commitments to the "realism" in magical realism, highlighting their attachment to truth rather than the fantasy generally thought to be transacted in the form. This proposes Latin America as a funhouse mirror that reflects back a hyperbolically distorted but ultimately referential image of postcolonial political life. We then turn to the way that both Ghose and Anita Desai approach Latin America as a concave mirror, one that allows them to invert the implied political meaning of institutional affiliation in "America" by redirecting their attachment to the continent southward. Finally, Sunny Singh provides the grounds on which to interrogate the postcolonial critical desire for magical realism to act as a transparent window onto traditions of home, negotiating instead the terms of likeness and difference in Latin American and South Asia as "looking glass twins: in many ways opposite and yet apparently identical" (Singh 2001, 53). These authors, moreover, sit at very different places in the matrices of commercial success and literary prestige. A final section uses this variegated group to reapproach the critical problem of magical realism's marketability, arguing for neither an ideal politics of resistance, nor an evacuation of politics into commercialism, but a "politics of the possible" for globally circulating texts written in English.

"At Every Step One Finds Such Wonders": The Possible Politics of Literary Magic

Studies of magical realism, like studies of world literature, often get bogged down in taxonomy. Without going the Potter Stewart route of "I know it when I see it," the description of magical realism here is brief. Other scholars have elaborated a definition of magical realism in order to trace it as an omnipresent representational mode with different points of emergence all over the world. This approach is intentionally different.

As the anxious repetition of "not Latin America" in these kinds of studies suggests, the critical turn to taxonomy in the study of magical realism is quite openly a move of historical and geographic abstraction. It replaces a necessarily untidy world-literary history with a set of ostensibly neutral – and certainly ahistorical – classificatory tools. As it became common in the study of magical realism in the 1980s and 1990s, this critical gesture reinforced the "bogy of Authenticity" in which postcolonial authors certify their political resistance by recovering the cosmogonies and narrative traditions of their "own" geographic, ethnic, or religious backgrounds. Taxonomy also has the impact, if not the intent, of deemphasizing or even outright excluding Latin America from any necessary geography of literary style, once again tidying up the link between literary and political history for postcolonial studies. Ironically, the turn to taxonomy uses one of the most obvious and pervasive gestures of world-literary affiliation to reinstate precisely the kind of tired "local/abroad" bind that authors turn to the countershelf to cut through.

But nor is this chapter overly concerned with the kinds of detailed historiographies of the term offered by William Spindler, Faris, and others. Instead, it takes as its point of departure Siskind's insistence that magical realism cannot be coherently studied when uncoupled from its early development in Latin America. While the term originates in Franz Roh's early-twentieth-century German milieu, Siskind recounts, it gains its recognized form and internal coherence – not least its identification as a literary mode – through the subsequent decades of Latin American innovation (Siskind 2012; Siskind 2014). Following this overarching assertion, Siskind is quite pointed about the Anglophone "globalization" of the mode. How can one argue for theories of independent emergence, he asks, when the efflorescence of Anglophone magical realism coincides so tidily with García Márquez's 1982 award of the Nobel Prize (Siskind 2014, 91)?

What is really at issue here is the way a specific set of South Asian authors site magical realism within particular Latin American landscapes, which they then further associate with specific Latin American authors. In doing so, they make one of the most recognizable "contrary" moves in South Asian Anglophone fiction, recirculating a popular aesthetic mode that, as both Franco Moretti and Pascale Casanova argue, shifted the world-literary "center of gravity" to the Global South for the first time in modern history (Moretti quoted in Kristal 2002, 69; Casanova 2004). They likewise evince a shared commitment to political claims made on behalf of magical realism by its most famous theorist, the Cuban novelist Alejo Carpentier: first, that magical realism is an ideal mode for registering the epistemological clash of colonialism; second, that it harbors a cryptorealist truth about the hyperbolic experiences of the Global South. In this way, the authors all become embroiled in the controversial association of these politics with a heightened emotional experience of fantasy and wonderment.

For our purposes, the definition of magical realism begins from Faris' first two assertions in "Scheherazade's Children": that magical realism is primarily defined as a text that "contains an irreducible element of magic," in which, nevertheless, "realistic descriptions create a fictional world that resembles the one we live in" (Faris 1995, 167, 169). Put another way, Warnes argues that "the key defining quality of magical realism is that it represents both fantastic and real without allowing either greater claim to truth" (Warnes 2005, 3).

That's it. Other literary elements that Faris includes – like metafictionality and verbal play – are not inherently related to magical realism. Rather, there is great conceptual utility in bracketing these other elements apart and tracing them, instead, through transnational circuits of modernist writing – the subject of Chapter 5. These characteristics draw just as much from Latin American literature but depend on other, non-magical-realist novels and persist in texts without magical realist content. By the same turn, both before and after the temporal high point of magical realism that Faris describes, that mode appears in relatively linear narratives that eschew modernist experimentation.

Perhaps it is too simple to say that magical realism is merely the balanced representation of both magical and real. Instead, it is the alchemical reaction between these ontologies, the affective charge produced when two worlds – or, at least, two worldviews – come crashing together, that sets apart magical realism and lends it narrative power. The form engages, as Arellano puts it, "two distinct wavelengths of *emotional intensity* (one directed toward vehement or intense emotions, the other toward forms of affect that are unremarkable and inconspicuous)" through which its primary charge is one of "*affective dissonance*" (Arellano 2010, 97, emphasis original)

Arellano emphasizes how Carpentier locates magical realism's affect in the "unexpected," "unusual," and "unforeseen" elements of magic in the ordinary, whose product is wonder (Carpentier cited in Arellano 2010,

96).[1] Wonder, then, requires the suddenness of surprise, the quick shift from low to high emotional intensity that occurs when things do not go as predicted. Its epistemology is an "ongoing, fragile project of making sense" that stands in contrast to the more static, preexisting "knowing" proper to theory (Fisher 1998, 8).

That startling jolt of wonder emerges out of a particular and somewhat essentialist understanding – sometimes called "anthropological magical realism" – of the dissonant orders of knowledge and cosmological systems belonging to various inhabitants of the colonized Americas (Spindler 1993, 80). The very force of these dissonances make magical realism particularly apt for describing the "epistemic violence" of colonial and neo-imperial projects (Spivak 1988; Warnes 2005; Siskind 2012). Ironically, though Carpentier ties them to specific realities in Latin America, the idea of magical realism as a mode of registering culturally situated, non-elite perspectives has become one of its most portable features.

But what kind of a thing is wonder, anyway? How does it operate? As a noun, it suggests an exoticizing, essentializing optic, a commodity to be transacted from South to North (Greenblatt 1991; Beverley 2008). As a verb, it refers to the capacity of openness to new experiences and new interpretations at the heart of cognition itself (Fisher 1998; Rubenstein 2008). The way various actors answer that question determines, to a large degree, how they approach the political cargo of magical realism as a narrative form.

For Sangari, as we have seen, wonder is a powerful tool for articulating difference. It "answers an emergent society's need for renewed self-description and radical assessment, ... questions the Western capitalist myth of modernization and progress, and asserts without nostalgia an indigenous preindustrial realm of possibility" (Sangari 1987, 162). For her, wonder's surprise forces us to "question" oppressive perspectives on the Global South, engaging alternative traditions without the affective baggage of the known, "nostalgia." If literariness appears at all, it is in the negative, an opposition of rational forms of "assessment" and "description" to "Western myth." This is markedly opposed to a second strain of criticism, represented by Franco Moretti, for whom the same affective engagement "is to be found in 'a complicity between magic and empire.' *One Hundred Years of Solitude* absolves the West of the guilt of colonial violence by recounting 'those hundred years of history as an adventure filled with *wonder*'" (Moretti quoted in Kristal 2002, 23, emphasis added). Notice again the way that affect emerges as a primary site of contest through servile and "complicit" appeals to sensibility, the substitution of a negative affect, "guilt," with the positive "wonder." All of this is transacted through the ambivalent narrative mode of "history," here less in the modern, factual sense but rather drawing on its etymological roots as "historia" – an account.

Moretti's use of "history" is a marked choice. One cannot help but imagine that he was here thinking of accounts of conquest, especially Bernal Díaz del Castillos' *Historia verdadera de la conquista de Nueva España* (*The True History of the Conquest of New Spain*) (1632), that describe their often hyperbolic or outright fantasized accounts in such "realist" (*verdadera*) terms. Moretti echoes critiques made by Stephen Greenblatt of the "rhetoric of the marvelous" that root wonderment in the Americas to Columbus' *Indian Diary* and other "historias" of the conquest (Greenblatt 1991). As we saw in Chapter 2, the Spanish baroque value of "asombro" – surprise or startled wonderment – translates the territorial act of discovery into a "discursive" one (Johnson 2010, 174).

Carpentier openly avows this association. In the original version of the essay in 1949, "*De lo real maravilloso americano*" ("On The Marvelous Real in America"), he writes that Díaz's account is "the only honest-to-goodness book of chivalry that has ever been written" and concludes that the fantastically real experience of indigenous Mexico revealed to Díaz the way that "events tend to develop their own style" (Carpentier 1995b, 83). He continues, "We must recognize that *our style* is reaffirmed throughout *our history*, even though at times this style can beget veritable monsters" (Carpentier 1995b, 83, emphasis original). Here, again, literary style is imagined to emerge organically out of a singularly Latin American reality.

In the updated version of this essay in 1975, "Lo barroco y lo real maravilloso" ("The Baroque and the Marvelous Real"), Carpentier both deepens and clarifies his reference to Díaz: "When Bernal Díaz del Castillo laid eyes for the first time on the panorama of the city of Tenochtitlán, the capital of Mexico, the empire of Montezuma [sic], it had an urban area of one hundred square kilometers – at a time when Paris had only thirteen" (Carpentier 1995b, 104). The misrecognition of this landscape as fantastic, he argues, derives from "a dilemma that we, the writers of America, would confront centuries later: the search for the vocabulary we need in order to translate it all" (Carpentier 1995b, 104). This is the second element that magical realists from around the world carry forward out of Carpentier – the idea that seemingly fantastic or hyperbolic descriptions are actually cryptically real. Their apparent excesses emerge as a flaw of "translation": the insufficiency of Eurocentric vocabularies to describe the world outside Europe. As Rushdie recounted:

> People would say about Gabriel García Márquez, if you know the history of South America, all kinds of things in *One Hundred Years of Solitude* become

plain which otherwise seem like fairy tales; *they actually describe real events* . . . . I guess that's what I think about my stuff, really. It's true that if people know about India, there are certain nuances that they will hear. (Viswanathan 2008, 29, emphasis added).

The ambivalence of "history" is also at the root of specific South Asian anxieties about magical realism and other forms of fantasy. They return us, once again, to the Macaulay Minute and the debates that brought English literature to the center of colonial education in India. Among other things, that education was meant to ameliorate the faulty epistemologies of other language traditions and their inappropriate attachment to fantasy: "history abounding with kings thirty feet high and reigns thirty thousand years long, and geography made of seas of treacle and seas of butter" (Macaulay 1835). This rhetoric furthers the long-standing idea that earlier Indian ways of knowing and representing were pathologically decadent and politically inert – the very accusation Muslim writers of the previous chapter displaced and then worked through in al-Andalus.

These anxieties continued to haunt South Asian writers even a hundred years later. As the Hindi novelist Premchand wrote in his inaugural address to the All-India Progressive Writers Association: "In earlier times we might have been impressed by fairy tales, ghost stories and accounts of star-crossed lovers, but those have little interest to us anymore" (Premchand quoted in Anjaria 2012, 1). These "earlier times" span everything from millennia-old Sanskrit religious epics like the Mahabharata and their almost innumerable vernacular retellings; to compilations based on oral storytelling traditions like the *Dastān-e Amir Hamza* (*The Adventures of Amir Hamza*); to literature of the previous century – both narrative and poetic – that favored the hermetic gardens of the *ghazal* or the imaginative escapes of romantic love.

It is true, as Ulka Anjaria argues, that Premchand's address does not unquestioningly reproduce British colonial accusations of Indian aesthetic immaturity, nor does it endorse the will to knowledge–power ostensibly encoded in European realist forms (Anjaria 2012, 7). Instead, in its own moment, the address valorized realism as a tool with which to reveal the cruelty of British imperialism in its own idiom. And yet, when Anjaria polemicizes against the elevation of magical realism and other kinds of nonrealist aesthetics at the expense of realism in postcolonial criticism from the 1980s onward, she glosses over the fact that excitement about Rushdie and others was, in fact, a response to the political privileging of novelistic realism immediately prior. Indeed, she gestures at this when she acknowledges that part of that scholarly backlash has to do with realism's close "association with ... Indian nationalism" that would have underscored its ostensible political transparency in the immediate wake of independence (Anjaria 2012, 7). The year 1981 rang out as a banner one in part because there had long been a sense that no positive politics could emerge from an engagement with India's diverse imaginative traditions (Pritchett 1994; Coppola 2018).[2]

Likewise, Indian nonrealist fiction from the early twentieth century – to say nothing of numerous European fictions about India – was often shaped by a desire to see India as a stereotyped location of Eastern magic. These desires informed the copious use of magic in texts like Sarath Kumar Ghosh's *1001 Indian Nights: The Trials of Narayan Lal* (1902) and many European representations of the subcontinent (Bhagat-Kennedy n.d.). Awareness of these stereotyped expectations almost certainly continues to inform the way South Asian authors write globally circulating narratives even today (Nambisan and Nambisan 2005; Chakravorty 2014).[3]

Concern about this kind of stereotyping became particularly acute in reference to the popularity of magical realism. When Brennan sweeps aside Rushdie's affiliation to Latin American literature in *The Jaguar Smile* (1987) as a saleable gimmick, he pooh-poohs the transnational transaction of a style that "required the adoption of a specific attitude toward the colonial legacy. Part of that attitude had to do with the invocation of 'fantasy'" (Brennan 1989, 65). There is little sense of how, following Octavio Paz, realism and fantasy might act as allies.

Brennan's language suggests how the progressive politics of magical realism became a victim of the mode's popularity. Since the late 1990s, the obvious (and continuing) market success of magical realism seems to have vitiated its political viability among scholars and literary critics. In fact, by the time the South Asian "boom" was truly underway in the mid-1990s, literary critics had begun to view the styles and themes associated with magical realism as "out of fashion," "derivative," and full of "gimmicks" (Nambisan and Nambisan 2005; Squires 2007). Siskind similarly argues that the globalization of the genre has allowed its former political specificity to descend into kitsch (Siskind 2014). The very expectedness of the form in postcolonial writing emptied out the power of its notionally unexpected juxtapositions.

Yet, on closer examination, this disillusionment seems less about the exhaustion of a particular style than a cynicism among postcolonialist critics about the progressive potential of aesthetics as such (Bahri 2003;

Sorensen 2010; Aubry 2018). After the 1973 Chilean coup, Arellano suggests, Latin American authors quickly lost faith in vehement passions like wonder to act as political vehicles, turning to realist "minor affects" instead (Arellano 2010). As Debjani Ganguly argues, something similar characterizes postcolonial scholarship in the same era, which entailed "a position of radical anti-aestheticism that denounced any intellectual gesture that hinted at literary and cultural autonomy from the realm of imperial interest" (Ganguly 2016, 20).

Despite these often legitimate suspicions, it is striking that the variously situated authors in this book continually drew on culturally and historically specific forms of wonder to make sense of the movement between their realms. Recall from the Introduction how the poet Faiz described his unexpected experience of Cuba as a series of "a'jūbe" – oddities or wonders. "Ajīb" also marks something worthy of narration, as encoded in the idea of "ajīb-o-gharīb" ("strange and wondrous"), a common phrase for introducing the subject of a story in South Asian narrative traditions. In Chapter 2, Paz used the terms "extrañeza" and "enigma" to describe his time in India, negotiating difference not by domesticating it but by exploiting its disorienting power. And in Chapter 3, V. S. Naipaul excoriated the writer of the *Chachnama* for his failure to "wonder," cueing the sometimes exoticizing trope instead as a critical faculty, a type of openness to possibility akin to thinking itself. In the same way, Ghose and the other writers in this chapter draw on the wonders of Latin American magical realism as a category of practice to reopen conceptual spaces that have been covered over by a common sense of how the world works. They estrange their audiences from a preexisting understanding of its place in the world, while offering a set of conceptual tools to negotiate that estrangement.

"Plenty of Fantasy": Rushdie's Anti-Realist Investment

In Rushdie's *The Jaguar Smile*, a travelogue about the aftermath of a socialist revolution in Nicaragua, the author's first impression of Latin America comes from a blurb on a tourist map in the Havana airport. In place of the sights Columbus expected to find in "the lands of the Great Khan," it explains, "another, also rich, beautiful, and plenty of fantasy, was discovered: America" (Rushdie 2008, 6). In this moment, Rushdie deploys the familiar trope of psychic connection (discussed in Chapters 2 and 3), where Columbus' mistake sets the groundwork for a fantasized link between the Latin American landscape and its newly arrived "el escritor hindú" ["the Indian writer"] (Rushdie 2008, 14). The word "fantasy" operates alongside "beautiful" and "rich" as an exoticizing gesture in which Latin America embraces a self-definition as wondrous – here explicitly Columbus' "rhetoric of wonder." It also marks out the grounds of Rushdie's primary investment in his Latin American journey: not so much the socialist governance it purports to trace, as questions about the circulation and meaning of literary style.

Brennan uses "invocation of 'fantasy'" and a few other brief references in *The Jaguar Smile* to cast aspersions on Rushdie's affiliative gesture toward Latin American magical realism (Brennan 1989, 65). He lays emphasis on the colonial baggage of Rushdie's "rhetoric of wonder" and reduces its politics into sales figures. In one sense, this analysis is correct. Rushdie's invocation of Latin American literature depends not only on his own access to it in English translation but also on the fact that such literature is popular and well circulated enough to be equally familiar to his audience. Whereas the *sathottari* poets made baroque, intentionally obscurantist gestures to a corpus of Latin American literature most Indian readers would not know, South Asian magical realists seem to work from the assumption that one's likely readership instantly recognizes these iconic names and locations. Indeed, by the mid-1980s, those figures would precede any firsthand knowledge a South Asian reader might carry with them: "When I started reading Latin American literature, for example, works by Borges and [García] Márquez," Rushdie recounts, "I had never been to Latin America at that point" (Rushdie quoted in Viswanathan 2008, 29). In contrast to Brennan, however, the fuller exploration of South Asian "pilgrims" suggests that it is not "fantasy" that is at stake in their writing. It is instead, following Carpentier, a commitment to the cryptorealism of literary portrayals of the region.

Nicaragua requires many such citations to become comprehensible to its South Asian visitor and his Anglophone readership. While Brennan focuses only on the references to García Márquez, which suggest that "in Matagalpa, Macondo did not seem so very far away," Rushdie is equally interested in Latin American experimental fiction (Rushdie 2008, 75). A walk through the covered markets of Managua prompts Rushdie to recall "the Argentinian writer Julio Cortázar ... the author of the fiendishly esoteric and complicated Rayuela ('Hopscotch')," who had "been on first-name terms with many market traders" (Rushdie 2008, 103). Cortázar is not, interestingly enough, an author like Gabo or Neruda whose name stands iconically for a whole tradition. Nor is he glossed as the inspiration for Michelangelo Antonioni's 1966 film *Blow Up* or a writer in the long Argentinian tradition of uncanny short fiction (Kristal 2002). Instead,

Rushdie seems to gesture back toward the ludic insider style of the *sathottari*s when he names the Argentinian's ambitious 600-page "hypertext" novel in the original Spanish. These affiliations not only point toward magical realism but invoke modernist narrative time as it is discussed in Chapter 5.

Rushdie's hosts on his trip have their own ideas about the literary relationship between their two regions and what stylistic inheritances that relationship entails. Throughout his time in Nicaragua, Rushdie continually confronts the unexpected popularity of the Bengali poet and novelist Rabindranath Tagore. For many decades, Tagore was the only author writing in a non-European language to win the Nobel Prize in Literature (Lahiri 2020). As with Neruda's award (discussed in Chapter 1) and, indeed, the animating role of García Márquez's win on the subject of this chapter, the Nobel propelled Tagore into global fame and significantly changed the tenor of his reception. The award was also informed by Tagore's self-translation into English, a move that famously made him available for both praise and later censure by Yeats (as discussed in Chapter 2). More significantly, however, this turn to English allowed Tagore's poetry and persona to circulate in the wider world outside Europe, itineraries that make him, for Madhumita Lahiri, the pioneer of "Global Anglophone" writing that "utilize[s] English without perpetuating its guiding regimes" (Lahiri 2020, 60).

Yet this alone does not explain his degree of notoriety in Latin America. The passion for Tagore that Rushdie encountered emerged from the fact that he was championed by the Argentinian poet Victoria Ocampo and was ostensibly plagiarized by a young Neruda just before he departed for his sojourn in South Asia in the 1920s (Das 2001). And it was, in part, through these experiences that Tagore developed his own concept of world literature, *vishwa sahitya*, a term that is notably more cognate with the Spanish near-equivalent, *literatura universal* (Tiwari 2011; Chakravorty 2017).

"What was old Rabindranath doing here," Rushdie wonders, "with this accent on his final e" (Rushdie 2008, 55–56)? In his subsequent literary debates, Rushdie uses the accent to distinguish between the real, two-syllable "Tagore," whom Rushdie considers, at best, a distant and relatively irrelevant predecessor, and the Latin American three-syllable "Tagoré," whom his hosts deem the most important, if not the only, literary force to come out of India in the last century.

Rushdie uses Tagore/Tagoré as an opening to consider the contradictions of worldly consciousness and visions of realism among his hosts in

Nicaragua. "India, to most Nicaraguans, always accepting the followers of Rabindranath, seemed an exotic, camelious, elephantine place; they were amazed when I drew parallels between that fantasyland and their own country" (Rushdie 2008, 167). In contrast to Brennan's simplistic reading, in which it is Columbus' "plenty of fantasy" that connects "both Indies," Rushdie here expresses frustration with that very concept. Yet "the followers of Rabindranath," though they are better versed in Indian realities and their parallels to Latin America, are no better off in Rushdie's account, because their literary associations are all the wrong ones. His qualms have not to do with the "camelious" or "elephantine" but with the "realist."

"Many people think of Latin America as the home of anti-realism," Rushdie tells the poet who first introduces him to "Tagoré" (Rushdie 2008, 40). This, of course, is no mere observation but a declaration of Rushdie's own sense of affiliation to the Latin American literary genealogy of magical realism, part of what prompted his pilgrimage to Latin America. However, the Nicaraguan poet seeks to correct both Rushdie's pronunciation of the poet's name and his impression of Latin American literary values. "You must not write fantasy. It is the worst thing. Take a tip from your great Tagoré. Realism, realism, that is the only thing" (Rushdie 2008, 40–41).[4]

The relatively innocuous accent, for Rushdie, encapsulates a great misunderstanding between himself and the Nicaraguan poet. It misrecognizes Rushdie as part of an unbroken literary tradition that connects him to older generations of writers in South Asian vernaculars. Not only does "Tagoré" explicitly overdetermine the type of writing that can circulate between Latin America and South Asia in Rushdie's travelogue, but the idea of Tagoré also threatens to overtake Rushdie himself during his three-week visit, where he is introduced as "the *hindú* writer or even, quite often *poeta*" (Rushdie 2008, 14). Of course, while this description comfortably fits a writer like Tagore/Tagoré, Rushdie is at pains to emphasize that he is very much not a Hindu, nor is he, despite his penchant for wordplay, a poet. Indeed, much to Rushdie's chagrin, Nicaraguans of the 1980s still harken back to the *modernista* poet Ruben Darío and do not seem to have gotten the memo that novels, not poetry, are now the predominant "global" form.

The Nicaraguan reverence for Tagoré upholds realism as a politically potent representational style. From Rushdie's perspective, it thus recapitulates the great anxiety of the middle generations of South Asians writing in the twentieth century: that realism is the only literary mode whose politics are sufficient to the ongoing work of decolonization. When he rejects this legacy, emphasizing instead his right to inherit "anti-realism" from Latin

America, it is on the basis not only of his Western, liberal vision of writerly "freedom" but also of the more radical belief in the political potency of wonder.

"The Master of Latin American Realism": Ghose's Cryptorealist Hyperbole

Ghose performs a similar pilgrimage to Latin American sites of historical importance in order to stage a related debate between realisms in his novel *The Triple Mirror of the Self* (1992). Infamously, as Brouillette recounts, this was Ghose's last published novel (Brouillette 2007). It went through a torturous process of rejections, was a dismal commercial failure, and effectively seems to have derailed his career.[5] This was quite a dramatic turn of events for a writer who had been productive and reasonably successful since the 1960s. It is also not sufficiently explained by Ghose's failure, for nearly twenty years prior, to write about a literary location that made him, according to Brouillette, legible within a postcolonial critical apparatus. After all, Ghose was already quite established by the time he shifted focus. This line of criticism ignores, moreover, the warm reception for many other South Asian authors whose later novels focus on protagonists and locations outside of the subcontinent. This includes, for example, the later work of Vikram Seth in *An Equal Music* (2000) and the Indian-American author Jhumpa Lahiri, with *Unaccustomed Earth* (2009) and *In Other Words* (2015).

Latin American landscape does not appear in Ghose's text unrelated to literary style. As with *The Jaguar Smile*, Ghose's later oeuvre uses place as an opening onto a countershelf of literary relation. We can sense these debts right from the mirror-work figure of Ghose's title, *The Triple Mirror of the Self* – a version of the looking glass by which Latin America frequently becomes the location of unexpected self-recognition for South Asian authors.

The novel is divided into three equal parts, each of which tells a different moment in the life of what seems to be a single character, each moment delving further and further into the past. The first section, "The Burial of the Self," is set closest to the present at the end of the protagonist's life. It takes place in Suxavat, a mysterious Amazonian village on the border between Brazil and Peru. It reads like a diary of the day-to-day experiences of the protagonist – here known as Urim. These events include Urim's sexual frustrations with a much younger love interest, Horuxtla, as well as a more general record of the villagers' struggle to establish an egalitarian, secular, and hybrid society in the jungle. These reflections are interrupted by the sudden, catastrophic invasion of a mining company and the ensuing massacre of which the protagonist is apparently the sole survivor. The text ends with what may be the protagonist's dying vision, in which what formerly appeared to be the Amazon jungle is peeled away to reveal a mountain range he vaguely recognizes as the Hindu Kush.

The second section of Ghose's novel, "Voyager and Pilgrim," is told from the perspective of an American academic named Jonathan Pons – who may be another avatar of the protagonist. It implies that part or all of the Suxavat narrative from the first section may be a fabrication by the author, here referred to by a different name, Zinalco Shimomura, "Shimmers." Pons, in turn, uses a combination of archival research and imaginative recreation to fill in the previous decades of Shimmer's life. These narratives, which record Shimmers' work at an American university and the loss of his Peruvian wife and child to political violence in her home country, seem to explain why Ghose's protagonist would have found himself in the Amazon in the first place.

Finally, the third section, "Origins of the Self," is narrated in a third-person omniscient style and moves back to the protagonist's young life in Bombay as part of a pluralistic gang of friends at a Catholic private school. The ending tears the fabric of their formerly cosmopolitan lives. This section provides a level of detail and a more standard verisimilitude that marks it as the most "real" of the three sections. The novel closes with a vignette from the early life of the protagonist – here named Roshan – that circles back to the apparent vision of the Hindu Kush mountain range with which the first section concludes. In doing so, it seems to imply a strong allegorical connection between the plots of these two sections, both of which, like the novels discussed in Chapter 3, revolve around the tenuous formation and ultimate disintegration of cosmopolitan communities on opposite sides of the world.

Suxavat is the only location described in this chapter that is not tied to a specific, real-world analogue. Even so, there are at least two locations of literary significance for which Suxavat may act as a site of pilgrimage. They are related to two writers brought to prominence in the Anglophone world by the Latin American "boom": Carpentier, the foundational theorist of Latin American magical realism, and "boom"-superstar Mario Vargas Llosa.

In the contemporary Anglophone world, Carpentier is almost exclusively read as the theorist of magical realism. But in his own place and time he was much more famous for the novel *Los pasos perdidos* (*The Lost Steps*)

(1953). Both texts draw on Carpentier's interest in anthropology, reflecting his belief that a specifically American artistic style arises naturally out of Latin American cultures and territory. *Los pasos perdidos* focuses on a nameless protagonist, whose time in the United States has alienated him from his rather ambiguous origins in the Global South and whose creative faculty is renovated by a journey to the Amazonian interior. This is an identity position very like the one Carpentier inhabited himself. It is also very obviously resonant with Ghose's experience as an American professor and fairly easy to locate in the shapeshifting "self," Urim/Shimmers/Roshan, whose trajectories more or less match their author's.

Moreover, based on its location in the jungle and the inner conflicts of the protagonist who makes his way there, Ghose seemed to closely model Suxavat on Santa Mónica de los Venados, the Amazonian village at the heart of *Los Pasos Perdidos*. Like Suxavat, Santa Mónica de los Venados is a remote jungle village organized by a group of people from ethnically and socially diverse backgrounds who share a utopian dream of retreating from contemporary society. Both locations are also exceptionally remote, and the precise means of arriving there vague; thus, once the protagonists leave, it is never possible for them to return.

Similar, too, is the role of Urim's love interest, the seductive teenaged Horuxtla, to Carpentier's Rosario. Both embody the same qualities – remote but welcoming, unselfconsciously natural, even primitive – that each narrator seeks in the village itself. Finally, Ghose's first-person narrator shares with Carpentier's narrator a desire to keep a written record of his experiences and insights. For Carpentier's protagonist, this takes the form of a symphony. For Ghose's, it is the diary entries that become the first part of the novel. These scriptural tendencies are fundamentally at odds with the intentional primitivism of the rest of the community and serve in part to drive each protagonist away.

But a second, equally important textual predecessor for Suxavat seems to be the nineteenth-century separatist community in Canudos, Brazil. Although the community and its ultimate destruction by the Brazilian government are both matters of historical record, their memory was returned to the global popular imagination in Vargas Llosa's novel *La guerra del fin del mundo* (*The War at the End of the World*) (1981). Canudos is located in the northern desert rather than the Amazonian jungle, but, like Suxavat, it was founded by a group eager to break away from contemporary society, intentional in their primitivism. And like the residents of Suxavat, the citizens of Canudos were ultimately massacred with the blessing of the Brazilian government.

We know from Ghose's correspondence with Berger that he was an avid reader of Vargas Llosa, "having read almost all of his work" (Ghose 1990a). In 1982, he wrote:

> I'd heard of Vargas Llosa for years as one of the novelists of the South American boom, and had read a much admired novel of his called THE GREEN HOUSE which, though I thought it the work of a serious and intelligent mind, I had not liked ... the man who struck me as an operator furthering his career with an eye on the Nobel Prize (all the major Latin American writers are obsessed with the Nobel, by the way, from Borges to Paz to [García] Márquez). (Ghose 1982a)[6]

In this passage, Ghose demonstrates a canny awareness of the way the Nobel operates as a major answer to the literary-sociological question of "how" Latin American literature ends up on the South Asian countershelf. García Márquez would win later that very year; Siskind credits that event with inaugurating magical realism as a global phenomenon (Siskind 2014). As the story of Neruda's reception showed in Chapter 1, his own Nobel win likewise significantly expanded his global reception while changing its political tenor. Of the four authors Ghose discusses, only Borges would be snubbed in Stockholm. Even as Ghose expressed suspicion of Vargas Llosa's relationship to the market and lamented the decline of his new work around the time Ghose wrote *The Triple Mirror of the Self*, it's clear that he still respected earlier writing like *La guerra del fin del mundo* (Ghose 1990a).

Whether or not there is an association between Suxavat and Canudos, it is likely that the Peruvian Vargas Llosa informs "the renowned master of Latin American realism, Valentin Sadaba," a Peruvian novelist who becomes an essential character in the second section of Ghose's text (Ghose 1992, 101). It is Sabada who passes the Suxavat manuscript on to Pons, setting off the main action of "Voyager and Pilgrim." At the same time, Sabada's presence initiates, within the text, a central argument about the genre characteristics that Ghose inherits from Latin American writers and its relationship to the nature of the "real."

It may at first seem strange that, in a novel and a larger oeuvre that are both obviously influenced by magical realism, Ghose chooses to lionize a "realist" as the primary stand-in for his Latin American literary forebears. Yet, in the scenes leading up to the transfer of Urim's text, Sabada convinces Pons to follow him around Peru, first to the location of a secret, semi-mystical Incan rite and then to his home in the slums of the capital city. Pons expresses his incredulity: How, after the ravages of conquest, could there still be a genealogical link to the Incan throne? Why does one of the most famous authors in the world live in a Lima slum? Sabada replies:

> "I know of so many things, many of them unbelievable to anyone else!"
> "You are the great realist. The maestro of realism. The whole world knows that."
> "And that is precisely why I keep nine-tenths of my experience to myself."
> (Ghose 1992, 109–110)

In this exchange, Ghose rehearses the same argument offered by Carpentier and echoed by Rushdie – that Latin American reality is itself so implausible or extreme that it exceeds the traditional, Eurocentric definition of the real. Those other writers respond to this ontological difference by resorting to a semi-fantastic style of representation: magical realism. Sabada's more traditional realism employs the inverse strategy. It conceals "nine-tenths" of the real to fit expectations of verisimilitude. Still, the inference is the same: Latin American reality somehow overflows the category of the "real."

Ghose had rehearsed many of the beats of Sabada's story in an ode to García Márquez appearing in a special issue of the scholarly journal the *Latin American Literary Review*. Unlike other acts of literary pilgrimage, the explicit purpose of the resulting story, "Lila of the Butterflies and Her Chronicler" (1985), was to root magical realism in a Latin American landscape and associate it with its most famous practitioner. The titular "Lila" – whose unconscious, ageless body births a cloud of yellow butterflies every twenty-eight years – is a figure classically in keeping with Carpentier's competing cosmologies, having assumed her place "long before Pedro de Alvarado marched into the kingdom of Quito" (Ghose 1998, 239).

Again, the story's narrator is an unnamed Indian academic visiting South America from his post in a US university – this, too, a clear stand-in for Ghose himself. He originally comes to South America for a conference in Quito, chaired by Jorge Luis Borges (whom Ghose had met at the University of Texas three years earlier) and attended by "the great international democracy composed of the aristocrats of literature" (Ghose 1998, 240).

When García Márquez does not appear at the conference, the protagonist goes in search of him. He ultimately arrives at a large, remote gothic house reminiscent of the Buendía family compound from *Cien años de soledad* (*One Hundred Years of Solitude*) (1967). Inside, he encounters a series of fantastic tableaus that recall iconic moments from the novel: naked children with the tails of pigs, close relatives caught in endless incestuous couplings, and a trail of blood that travels in a path of its own volition. He even meets a grotesque version of himself, a bald scribbler who speaks in perfectly fluent Indian-accented English and quotes "Caliban's famous words" to his double, the story's one nod to more traditional postcolonial modes of writing back (Ghose 1998, 246).

Finally, the narrator comes across Lila's "chronicler," whose image he realizes he has seen before "on the back of the English translation of a book called *El otoño del patriarca*, published by Harper & Row in 1976" (Ghose 1998, 248–249). As with so many other South Asian authors, Ghose names his countershelf in the original Spanish, underscoring the contrarian desire to tie his Anglophone practice to non-Anglophone sources. The emphasis on translation and publication venue likewise underscores Ghose's canny awareness of the modes of circulation through which García Márquez became available to him as a model. But most strikingly, the presence of Lila's "chronicler" draws on what was, at that time, García Márquez's most recent, purportedly nonfiction book, *Crónica de una muerte anunciada* (*Chronicle of a Death Foretold*) (1981). His belated appearance and generic marker as a "chronicler," a mere recorder of fact, authorizes and makes sense of an apparently magical Latin American landscape as actually real.

"I Knew Nothing About It Except from Literary Sources": Desai's Journey South

Brouillette's analysis of *The Triple Mirror of the Self* focuses primarily on Ghose's semi-autobiographical reflections on an unsatisfactory life as an American professor, refracted through a journey to Latin America. For her, these passages offer a clear-eyed condemnation of the role that academia plays in creating conditions of acceptance within what Ghose calls "the great industry of Commonwealth Literature" (Ghose 1984). Kalyan Nadiminti furthers this critique by arguing that contemporary Anglophone fiction as a body is overdetermined by the enfolding of creative writing within American institutions of higher learning (Nadiminti 2018). In this context, Brouillette casts Ghose's Latin American pilgrimage as a uniquely resistant literary gesture.

But Ghose was hardly alone in refracting his ambivalence about his imbrication with US academia through a literary journey to the South. As we saw in Chapter 1, Agha Shahid Ali's "I See Chile in My Rearview Mirror" (1991) makes the same gesture at the same moment in the early 1990s, reflecting on his own position at the University of Arizona through the very same mirror-work figure. An equivalent gesture appears to an even greater extent in Anita Desai's novel *The Zigzag Way* (2004), which projects her experiences teaching creative writing at the Massachusetts Institute of Technology through an American academic's pilgrimage to a mining town in Mexico.

Desai appears briefly in Ghose's correspondence, in much the same arch tone in which he dismisses Latin American authors "obsessed with the Nobel" and more legible Commonwealth authors who are "immediately the subject of papers at conferences" (Ghose 1984). He wrote: "There's an Indian novelist named Anita Desai ... who has quite a reputation in this country and whose latest novel [*In Custody*] was a runner up for the Booker award in London last year.... It's a dull piece of work, quite worthless in fact" (Ghose 1985b).

Despite this dyspeptic comment, Ghose and Desai were rather alike. They were both part of that lost generation of Anglophone writers coming up in the 1960s and 1970s, the ones who felt adrift from South Asian traditions and cast their nets further afield. In fact, it is arguably Ghose's generational affiliation, rather than his geographic one, that limited his popularity vis-à-vis a much younger writer like Rushie. Both Desai and Ghose made their sojourns in US academia more or less permanent and then used visits to Latin America as a stage on which to reflect on the intimate compromises of life as professors. Both wrote about protagonists who feel out of place in the American academy, struggle to write, and are somehow renewed by a journey south. While neither author has any native claim on Latin America, both experienced visions of their roots there: Ghose's protagonist through a death-bed vision of the Hindu Kush, and Desai's through an unexpected discovery about his origins, one mediated by a ghost.

Yet, unlike other writers in this book, Desai was not attracted to Latin America because of a preexisting passion for Latin American literature. Where Rushdie and Ghose view their landscapes through the prism of the "boom," Desai's references consist of a much more expected gesture for an Anglophone author, British writing about Mexico. "I knew nothing about [Mexico] except from literary sources – D. H. Lawrence, Malcolm Lowry, etc." she recounted (Desai quoted in Izcue 2008, 83). As such, what she discovers is not a confirmation of these writers' insights but rather the opposite. "My experience bore no resemblance to theirs. Instead, the very minute I arrived there, stepping off the plane in Oaxaca, I felt as if I had come home and also, conflictingly, as if an entirely new world had opened before me" (Desai quoted in Izcue 2008, 83).

Desai describes arrival in Mexico as a conceptual opening onto wonder. She quite explicitly frames her experience as unexpected, in the sense that her Anglophone literary models leave her quite unprepared for what she actually finds in Mexico. The particular phrasing of a "new world" suggests that Desai's wonderment is tinged with colonial-era expectations about the novelty of the Americas. Nevertheless, Mexico also invites Desai "through the looking glass," in that she invokes the common trope of surprised self-recognition – the sense that she had "come home." The very frisson of the juxtaposition between the low-intensity homey sensibility and high-intensity otherworldliness evokes the emotional stakes of magical realism, if not its ontologies.

These are the energies which power *The Zigzag Way*. But like Ghose's preview of *The Triple Mirror of the Self* in "Lila of the Butterflies and Her Chronicler," Desai took a first crack at the same material half a decade earlier in a short story called "Tepotzlán Tomorrow" (2000). The story and the later novel share the central conceit of a protagonist trying to refresh his stagnating doctoral thesis through a journey to Mexico. But in the earlier story, that landscape is explicitly connected to Latin American literature through the figure of Paz, whom the protagonist, Luis, is studying in relation to "Hindoo philosophy" (Desai 2000, 143). Playfully inverting Paz's own use of baroque ekphrasis in India, Desai peppers her journey through Tepotzlán with unattributed citations of Paz's poetry. Upon seeing a hummingbird, for example, Luis recalls Paz's short poem "Exclamación" ("Exclamation"), composed in India:

> Stillness
>   not on the branch
>   in the air
>   Not in the air
>   in the moment
>   hummingbird   (Desai 2000, 148)[7]

Like the Indian poets of her generation, Desai offers these lines as an unattributed, collusive gesture. Only the relatively small Anglophone readership already familiar with Paz's writing would fully appreciate them or their relationship to his interest in "Hindoo philosophy."

The Zigzag Way changes the locus of its literary enchantments. Gone is the intertextual playfulness of Paz's citation. In its place is a serious consideration of the competing cosmologies thesis that authors all over the Global South adapted from Carpentier. The title derives from the path that indigenous laborers took to navigate the treacherous paths inside the now-abandoned mines. That indigenous knowledge is then reflected in the architecture of the book itself. In a structure very similar to *The Triple Mirror of the Self*, *The Zigzag Way* shifts abruptly between locations, times, and focal characters, moving progressively further into the past. But more self-consciously than Ghose, Desai uses the structuring of her book to both draw on and critique the culturalist form of magical realism that informs the unification of timelines at the novel's end.

The first section, "Eric Arrives," concerns the journey of the present-day protagonist – an academic from Boston – to an abandoned mining town in Mexico. At the novel's opening, Eric, like Luis, has just secured funding to expand his doctoral thesis and finds himself confronting a crippling writer's block. Seeking inspiration and an escape from the bleak Boston winter – exactly patterned on Desai's own experience as a professor at MIT – he follows his scientist partner, Em, to Mexico. Here Desai most clearly echoes the sentiment in Ghose's "Voyager and Pilgrim" and Ali's "I See Chile in My Rearview Mirror," that Latin America offers an ideal contrarian space in which to step back and reflect on one's imbrications with Anglophone institutional authority.

The second section, "Vera Stays," focuses on the mid-century transformation of another immigrant, the erstwhile Austrian cabaret performer who will become the ersatz anthropologist Eric has followed into the Sierras. The appearance of this faux social scientist unsettles any sense of easy affiliation in the text. Again, it is worth recalling that in *Los pasos perdidos*, Carpentier structured his protagonist's physical journey to the Latin American jungle as a journey to find the origins of music in the deep past. To his credit, Carpentier ultimately ironizes this gesture, and later Latin American writers like García Márquez are even more pointed in their embedded critiques of these sorts of developmentalist ideas (Arellano 2010). Still, Desai's plot, which moves from present to past as her protagonist journeys from metropolitan Boston to the remote Mexican interior, risks recapitulating this highly problematic "denial of coevalness" to Latin America. As she shifts focus to Vera's self-serving obsession with Huichol cultural traditions, Desai casts a suspicious eye on an overly romantic embrace of indigenous cosmology as a source of re-enchantment for readers in the Global North.

The third section, "Betty Departs," tells the story of a young Cornish woman at the turn of the century who finds herself inexplicably drawn to the harsh Mexican landscape where her husband has come to work as a miner, deciding to remain there when political upheaval drives the rest of the Cornish back home. She dies birthing Eric's father, and the brief final section "La Noche de los Muertos" ("The Night of the Dead") recounts Eric's attempts to find and honor her grave. As with Ghose's invocation of García Márquez's *El otoño del patriarca* (*The Autumn of the Patriarch*) (1975), the insertion of Spanish itself interrupts the smooth flow of the Anglophone prose and forcefully suggests a "contrary" affiliation. Through this zigzag movement, Desai's plot picks up on ideas worked out through the affiliative gesture of the countershelf: the sense of a psychic connection to a land not one's own, and the strangeness of being native but not indigenous.

While the majority of the book is written in a verisimilar style, it is explicitly structured as Eric's pilgrimage to find his roots. His journey coincides both with a peyote pilgrimage specific to the Huichol and the more general syncretic "pilgrimage" to the graveyard that characterizes the *Día de los Muertos* festival. It is here, in the cemetery, that Desai indulges in her one interlude of literary magic, allowing Eric a brief encounter with the ghost of his grandmother. This is a gesture that unifies past and present in an alternative, marvelous reality only possible through the particular cosmologies of Latin America.

"A Looking Glass Twin": Singh's Negotiation of Likeness in Literary Style

When he updated his articulation of "lo real maravilloso" in 1975, Carpentier theorized it as an aspect of the baroque, thereby radically expanding its geographical and temporal ambit. Validating the claim that "the baroque has flourished in all ages," Carpentier writes that "to cite clearly typical examples that everyone knows, I'll say the baroque – and this is obvious – flourishes in all aspects of Indian culture" (Carpentier 1995b, 94). This statement carries an echo – and not at all an incidental one – of the associations made by Paz (discussed in Chapter 2). Referring to similar features of Indian architecture in 1968, Paz had written to Tomás Segovia that the harmony between Indian and pre-Columbian art "is not a matter of influence or historical contacts, of course" (Paz 2008, 114). And yet, he goes on, they share "an aesthetic vision that is nourished from the same sources," concluding that India and Mexico are like "two photos of a pair of twins, each one in a different landscape, dressed differently" (Paz 2008, 114).[8]

In these reflections, both Latin American authors offer a discourse on the meaning of likeness, of aesthetic affinity, that does not emerge from a single genealogy and yet somehow is "nourished from the same source." Such statements resonate with Anita Desai's observation that traveling to Mexico for the first time felt like "coming home." A similar discourse emerges with regard to magical realism and the debates about how to narrate its emergence as a hallmark style in South Asian Anglophone fiction in the 1980s and 1990s.

As Ignacio Sánchez Prado argues, "critics in the English field ... generally sidestep the lineage running from Anglophone and Francophone postcolonial production to the Latin American Boom – even though they are interwoven" (Sánchez Prado 2018, 82). In the case of magical realism, Anglophone scholars have increasingly narrated the form as a "universal tendency" emerging simultaneously and independently all over the world (Menton quoted in Siskind 2012, 859). This allows Michael Bell, in his discussion of magical realism as a "world literary" mode, to state unequivocally that "there is no intrinsic connection of the genre per se with Latin America" (Bell 2010, 183). Because, again, there is such a widespread critical understanding that "postcolonial production" takes shape around magical realism, this elegant "sidestep" has the impact of editing out the untidiness of the Americas, safely delimiting the geography and, in effect, the language of postcolonial literature to the Anglophone and its purported "globe."

This larger critical context casts a different light on the tendency in South Asia–focused criticism to reroot magical realism in traditions of home, especially Hindu cosmology. Priya Joshi, for example, renarrates *Midnight's Children* as emerging from the *Mahabharata*, rather than Macondo (Joshi 2002). Others have identified earlier authors as magical realists *avant la lettre* or suggest that earlier, nonrealist narrative modes should be read as the true predecessors of South Asian magical realism (McLain 2001; Anjaria 2015; Khair and Doubinsky 2015). While this research is certainly valuable, the preponderance of scholarship in this line risks reinforcing the idea that South Asian magical realism may *only* emerge from these sources.

Sunny Singh's *Nani's Book of Suicides* (2000) would initially seem to fit into such a tradition that locates magical realism in existing "fantastic" narrative traditions of India. Singh's novel follows a globe-trotting young woman trying to outrun her fate as the latest in a matrilineal line of Indian sorceresses. The story of each chapter is modeled around a female "suicide" from Indian history or Hindu tradition: for example, Sita, heroine of the Ramayana, being swallowed by the earth, or the medieval devotional poet Meera Bai drinking poison (Singh 2000).

Yet the novel is also structured by the protagonist's flight from India, her ambivalence about conforming to the models of American higher education in Boston (where Singh attended college), and the ultimate resolution of these conflicting modes through the discovery of a complementary magic in Mexico. Singh reflects more explicitly on her experience in Mexico in a 2001 talk called "'Twin in the Mirror': India and Mexico" – an intentional echo of Paz's 1968 letter. Singh adds a layer of precision to Paz's remark by calling Mexico India's "looking-glass twin, in many ways opposite and yet apparently identical," adding another surface of self-reflection to Ghose's "triple mirror," Ali's "rearview mirror," and Hamid's "funhouse mirror" (Singh 2001, 53).

Like Desai, Singh complains that European and American sources did not prepare her for the unexpected sense of belonging she found in Mexico. She writes, "Mexico serves as the great escape for Europeans and North Americans.... It merely serves to remind an Indian of home" (Singh 2001, 52). Even though Singh's book is most explicitly about Hindu cosmology and traditions of "home," she – like Ghose, Rushdie, and, briefly, Desai – insists upon the centrality of Latin America to the development of magical realism as a global form. She rehearses the same idea articulated by the other authors in this chapter, that Latin American and South Asian realities are defined by their exuberant excess of "Eurocentric" realism – what she codes as "myth."

> If there is any element of Latin America that I have relied on in developing my storylines, and my craft, it is that of mythmaking. ... Myths can be based in history and tradition, but they need not have factual precision or even comply with the restrictive ideas of "truth." ... So while much of the Eurocentric world tries precisely to document and rationalise historical data, Mexico works by creating myths. (Singh 2001, 52)

But Singh's generation of magical realists was not just impacted by the ambiguous origins of its chosen narrative form. When she and Desai take up magical realism in the early 2000s, they participate in a more general shift from masculine to feminine, one that often seems – quite coincidentally, no doubt! – to attend lamentations about the decline and fall of the form.

This was the era of more popular magical realist fare like Chitra Banerjee Divakaruni's *Mistress of Spices* (1998). Both this novel and *Nani's Book of Suicides* revolve around intergenerational female conflict as a foil to male–female romance and sexuality. These books and others of their era have tended to be read as stylistically flattened and politically evacuated, signaling the risk that the formerly prestigious mode of magical realism will backslide toward the capital-"G" "Genre" of Fantasy.[9] The association of fantasy with wish fulfillment and a more hearty embrace of sexual pleasure also creates an uncomfortable proximity to the feminized, low-brow genre of Romance. In an era marked by a general critical suspicion about the form, magical realism by South Asian women was all the more likely to be portrayed as offering itself up willingly for transnational commodification.

"The Usual Penguins": Magical Realism and the Problem of "Mass Appeal"

One of Ghose's last short stories, "Errors and Afflictions" (1998), contains a brief scene in a bookshop in the Caracas airport that speaks to just such commodification. Ghose uses his protagonist as a mouthpiece to lament the usual offerings of this shop, "popular British and American writers who have done nothing but degrade the English language with their vile preoccupation with mass appeal" (Ghose 1998, 108). The airport bookshop and its Anglophone contents are, of course, a favorite concept metaphor for scholarly critiques of the homogenizing effect of "world literature" and "Global Anglophone" alike (Damrosch quoted in Watroba 2018, 54). But instead of the expected (Anglophone) dreck, the "usual Penguins by the Anglo-Americans," the narrator finds "nothing but English translations of works originally written in Spanish" (Ghose 1998, 108). Here, as with his invocation of "the English translation of a book called *El otoño del patriarca*, published by Harper & Row," Ghose articulates a contrarian attachment to literature in translation as a guard against the commercialism of Anglophone publishing companies.

In this incident, as in his letter about the "great industry of Commonwealth literature," Ghose expresses a strange mix of resentment and bravado that characterizes much of his approach to literary markets. Within the space of a paragraph, Ghose describes with admiration the style of new, popular novel by a recognized Commonwealth author (often Rushdie); denigrates the stylistic ambit of popular Commonwealth literature; celebrates his own insouciance from such market pressures; and bemoans his invisibility to a set of institutions which he has just refused to address (Ghose 1981). Echoing concerns that Desai registers through the character of Vera, he complains that popular Commonwealth writers give preference to subject matter at the expense of literary style. "[Commonwealth] writers are studied because they appear to be anthropologists and not because they pretend to be novelists" (Ghose 1981). Despite the denigration of "anthropological magical realism," in other quarters, for Ghose it is precisely the embrace of magical realism, as against more straightforward styles, that can rescue Anglophone postcolonial literature from its academic fate as mere social-scientific evidence.

For Brouillette, such a resistance is furthered by the affiliation to a literary location that does not "belong" to him as a Pakistani writer. She endorses his self-description here and elsewhere as a brave iconoclast willing to sacrifice institutional recognition and financial recompense to stay true to the dictates of his conscience and taste (Brouillette 2007). This characterization minimizes some of the other problematic aspects of his final novel's reception.

Writing to Berger in 1985, Ghose describes what will years later become the third section of *The Triple Mirror of the Self*. "A paragraph began itself the other day, touched off by a memory from the forties in Bombay and at the end of it I saw the potential for a whole book, but I stopped myself, unsure that I want to have anything to do with India" (Ghose 1985b). He declines to write it at that time in part because of the "glut of good work by Indian writers in England" and the sense "that people are beginning to get sick and tired of India" (Ghose 1985a). The first half of this statement is remarkably sensitive to the explosive potential of the South Asian "boom" nearly a decade before it takes its recognizable shape. But the second half is astonishingly wrong. Importantly for the present argument, Ghose – contra Brouillette – openly admits that he is interested in appealing to market pressures and flying "the 'banners' of geographical affiliation" if it will garner the correct type of attention (Brouillette 2007, 61).

In this section, Ghose abandons the magical realist mode and Latin America for the verisimilar Bombay of his childhood. It's marked that, in a full chapter dedicated to this novel, Brouillette makes barely any mention of the final, most politically legible section of *The Triple Mirror of the Self* referenced earlier. Indeed, it is strange to think that this final section of the novel would not have been legible to early-1990s postcolonial critics when it is so overtly invested in themes of cosmopolitanism and hybridity. Hybridity often manifests thematically through unexpected sexual couplings, a hallmark of Rushdie's most famous novels as well. But nowhere is this idea more literal than in *The Triple Mirror of the Self*, where the protagonist's motley interreligious crew solidify their bond of friendship by masturbating together into a shared vessel, not once but over and over again. There are other aspects of this section – especially a romantic dalliance with a high-school teacher – that, as with Horxtula in the first section, strike the reader as primarily serving the protagonist's sexual self-esteem. It is striking that such wish fulfillment on the part of a male author does not automatically draw Brouillette to comparisons with the commercialism of a Romance novel. Considering that the second and third sections are overtly autobiographical – mid-life as a professor in an American university with a South American wife; adolescence as a Muslim minority in Bombay – the whole book feels uncomfortably confessional and self-aggrandizing.

Brouillette, suspicious as she is of the category of "the literary" and attendant evaluations of quality, might not be particularly troubled by these features (Harlow et al. 2016). But *The Triple Mirror of the Self* received a slew of rejections from publishers. It caused Ghose's longtime agent to quit and, upon its release, was received with barely a whisper of praise. In effect, it destroyed his literary career. Brouillette's argument pitting Rushdie against Ghose hinges on the idea that the latter is radically innocent of machinations toward material success. A perusal of his correspondence troubles that claim. She also suggests that Ghose is "irrelevant" in postcolonial studies primarily because of the location of his plots in Latin America (Brouillette 2007). But Rushdie and Desai likewise wrote late-career books set there. Rather than rivals in the literary marketplace, it might be more revealing to read them as allies, mutually invested – though with varying degrees of success – in the contrarian energy of the countershelf.

One thing such an association reveals is the critical bind that these writers have faced through the mere fact of writing in English. The "vile preoccupation with mass appeal" seems less an authorial than a scholarly obsession. How else to explain the diametrically opposed conclusions of Brennan – for whom an affiliation to Latin American magic constitutes a cynical appeal to "saleable Third-Worldism" – and Brouillette – for whom it furthers a brave embrace of institutional "invisibility?" And yet, for both scholars, and many more besides, the affiliative gesture is really beside the point. The real issue is to find the expected conclusion, in which Rushdie's conspicuous success and the sudden "mass appeal" of South Asian Anglophone literature from the 1980s onward can be pinned to a singular authorly "preoccupation": the market. The whole scholarly discourse is shaped by the knowledge that novels written in these styles have done well with international audiences. This is flipped so that style is taken as prompting success in a relatively transparent way. As Karolina Watroba argues, such deterministic readings of aesthetics inevitably praise the same aspects of recalcitrant literature that they excoriate in their more commercially successful peers (Watroba 2018).

Especially when it comes to magical realism in English, the outcome of analysis seems predetermined by the all-powerful agency of global capital and the unresolvable Macauley-ish origins of English-speaking. As Fisk incisively puts it, this cynicism is enforced by representing any dissenting criticism "as a dupe of the administration and possibly also Citibank" (Fisk 2018, 184). This approach to the possibility of literary enchantment is an enormously conservative gesture, one that protects the scholar from the unpleasantness of what Eve Sedgwick calls, in her own proposal for reparative reading, "bad surprises" (Sedgwick 2003, 130). Wonder, on the other hand, the affect that holds together the various texts in this chapter, requires embracing surprise. It entails an embarrassing credulousness, a willingness to believe in, oh, all manner of things – socialist utopias, anti-genetic lineages, cross-racial solidarities, and the political power of narrative magic.

CHAPTER 5

Revenant
Dictator Fiction and Mobile Modernist Form

> Obaid's head has been buried in a slim book since takeoff. I glance at the cover – a bawdy illustration of a fat woman. Part of the title is covered by Obaid's hand. " ... of a Death Foretold" is all I can read.
>
>   . . .
>
> "Why keep reading it when you know already that the hero is going to die?"
>
> "To see how [...] ."
>
> (Hanif 2009, 279)

A few pages from the end of Mohammad Hanif's debut novel, *A Case of Exploding Mangoes* (2008), the protagonist Ali Shigri urges his friend Obaid to disembark with him from the plane that will carry General Mohammad Zia-al-Haq back to Pakistan's capital. Obaid refuses, preferring to remain absorbed in a book that he, like us, is pages away from finishing. Minutes later the ill-fated plane explodes – just as we were told it would at the beginning of Hanif's book. Among the charred remains left to Shigri are a few scraps of his friend's fatal novel, an English translation of Gabriel García Márquez's novella *Crónica de una muerte anunciada* (*Chronicle of a Death Foretold*) (1981).

In drawing on this particular plot structure, Hanif's book joins a bevy of South Asian novels to come out in the past three decades, novels which likewise flash us the fact of their disastrous endings right from the start and spend the rest of the story stringing us along "to see how." Salman Rushdie's *Midnight's Children* or Arundhati Roy's *The God of Small Things* come immediately to mind as novels that follow the same general line. Nor is Hanif alone in crediting Latin American "boom" authors for this and other narrative tricks, though few other South Asian novelists are as blessedly explicit about their intertextual debts. Following Gloria Fisk, we might call this plot structure "prolepsis," but it might be better to borrow from García Márquez's translator, Gregory Rabassa, and use the more informal term "foretelling" (Rabassa 2005; Fisk 2008).

Narrative tricks like foretelling – stylistic tics identifiable as "modernist" – often lie dormant for decades or disappear altogether from previous locations only to appear, unexpectedly, elsewhere as "revenants." That is, borrowing Andreas Huyssen's coinage, the aesthetic qualities of modernism and their underlying ideologies about the nature and purpose of art have not been left behind in the contemporary, ostensibly "postmodern" moment (Huyssen 1984). Instead, they seem to be reappearing – perhaps they never left. While scholars like Michael North posit the endurance of modernism's key themes and modes as more or less continuous, Huyssen poses it more as a "comeback" (Huyssen 1984; North 2019). Though they take very different stances on its nature and temporality, more recent scholars of modernism like Susan Friedman and Michaela Bronstein share with Huyssen a sense that elements of modernist form do not so much endure as reappear, especially in their travels through the Global South (Friedman 2015; Bronstein 2018). The question may then become, who or what has called them back? What elements of the here and now, what particular narrative problems, seem to require the reanimation of these forms – itself a kind of proleptic shuffling of present and past?

In general, the scholarly tendency to elevate magical realism as a premier postcolonial narrative mode has occluded the endurance of modernist structures altogether. Liam Connell puts it baldly when he says that Western authors "are allowed literary forms called Modernism, where their non-Western counterparts can only write Magic Realism" (Connell 1998, 95). In fact, he argues, "the formal characteristics of a literature described as Magic Realist are hard to distinguish from the formal characteristics of early-twentieth-century modernism" (Connell 1998, 95). The first part of this chapter explores how this formal mix-up might have occurred.

But when it did happen, the identification of South Asian Anglophone authors as "modernist" created another key mode around which postcolonial literature could hang together as a critical category (Anjaria 2012, 3). This gesture tended to impute to such "modernism" a set of radically opposed political leanings. On the one hand, they might be "fetish[ized] . . . as the equivalents to specific political values of postcolonial imperatives" (Sorensen quoted in Anjaria 2012, 3). On the other, they could be denigrated as displaying "the complexities and subtleties of all 'great art'" that certify writers in the Global South as "aesthetically 'like *us*'" – purportedly an unproblematized, singular Western readership (Brennan 1989, 37, emphasis added).

Whatever the politics attributed to this gesture, the texts invoked as "modernist" were almost invariably framed as Connell casts them above, as the inheritor of "early-twentieth-century modernism." Within the last decade, such lineages are suggested by, among others, Rebecca Walkowitz's exploration of Rushdie, Aarthi Vadde's writing about Michael Ondaatje as related to James Joyce, Susan Friedman's examination of Roy as an ally of E. M. Forster, Rajiv Patke's reading of Arun Kolatkar and other *sathottari* poets through T. S. Eliot, or Jahan Ramazani's affiliation of Agha Shahid Ali with William Butler Yeats (Walkowitz 2006; Ramazani 2009; Patke 2013; Friedman 2015; Vadde 2016). All of these scholars and many others trace "cosmopolitan" and "transnational" literary developments as if modernism simply lay dormant for the half-century in between an origin in Europe and the United States and an arrival in English-speaking South Asia.

This line of criticism leaves unaddressed the central countershelf question of circulation. That is, the mere availability of texts in a particular place and language is necessary but not sufficient to explain why later authors take them up and redeploy them as part of a new aesthetic program. The half- or even three-quarters-of-a-century gap that divides the supposed models from their inheritors should prompt us to ask *why*. Why would the authors in this chapter reach back so far into the past to tell a story about dictatorship in the 1980s? The answer is, they didn't. The case of Hanif reveals that techniques credited to Anglo-American modernists actually arrived in South Asia not through their automatic connection to a shared language, nor through the ironizing gesture of "writing back," but instead through an affiliative movement toward an unacknowledged middle generation in Latin America. These Latin American intertexts were generally written less than a quarter-century before their South Asian recapitulation – sometimes they are separated by only a handful of years, or even months.

And yet, the connection to Anglophone modernism is not totally incorrect. South Asian authors draw on some of the most recognizable traits that "boom" superstars like García Márquez and Mario Vargas Llosa developed out of their own revenant readings of the North American modernist William Faulkner. This is an intertextual relationship as well established (even clichéd) among Latin Americanist scholarship as it is apparently totally unknown in the English-language context. Gerald Martin, foundational scholar of the Latin American "boom," wrote in 1989 that "most important Latin American fiction between the 1940s and the 1960s is recognizably 'Joycean' or 'Faulknerian'" (Martin 1989, 296). He went on to conclude that "it is equally arguable that since the 1960s many of the most important writers – Italo Calvino, Milan Kundera, *Salman Rushdie*, Umberto Eco – have had to become 'Latin American' novelists" (Martin 1989, 296, emphasis added). This chapter will demonstrate – beyond Rushdie, and beyond magical realism – how right he was.

Establishing this genealogy, however, does not imply that all identifiably modernist textual gestures route through this particular path or even that all types of modernism originate in a single place and time. Instead, as with the discussion of magical realism in the previous chapter, it flows from the avowed countershelf of particular authors and prompts a consideration of why such clearly articulated intertextual relationships have been so infrequently included in the scholarly conversation.

Even so, the question of why modernist revenants reappear in South Asian writing is not fully answered only by a more proximate model or even by the general countershelf tendency to affiliate with Latin America. In this case, Hanif draws on revenant modernism from Latin America to address the particular narrative "problem" of General Zia and his fiery demise. This is, strikingly, the same "solution" hit upon by several other South Asian authors writing about Pakistani dictatorship, including Mohsin Hamid and, predictably, Rushdie. In this model, particular revenants like prolepsis become appealing because they are integral features of the "dictator novel" as it has been described in the Latin American case by Ángel Rama and in a comparative framework by Magalí Armillas-Tiseyra (Rama 1976; Armillas-Tiseyra 2019). This more specific, explicitly political framing helps narrow down from all of the various, self-contradictory gestures modernist style is taken to encompass and avoids the path of the swinging pendulum that alternately elevates and degrades the politics of modernist form (Friedman 2015, 19–21).

This chapter offers several reasons why revenants recirculate on the countershelf. First, it follows a common world-literary argument about affiliation and resonance between Faulkner and mid-century writers from the Global South. This is one made, in various ways, by scholars like Bronstein, Hosam Aboul-Ela, and Pascale Casanova and captured pithily in the title of an essay by Deborah Cohn: "He Was One of Us" (Cohn 1997; Casanova 2004; Bronstein 2018; Aboul-Ela 2020). All of these scholars have argued that Faulkner, as opposed to other Euro-American modernists, interwove his convoluted style with commentary on the spectres of "under" or "uneven" development, thereby modeling a world literature "from the South." When South Asian writers look to the Latin American literature avowedly inspired by Faulkner, they recapitulate a similar belief about that region's specific aptitude for representing dictatorship.

Second is the idea, suggested by Armillas-Tiseyra, that the revenant narrative structures discussed in this chapter offer a kind of epistemological counterweight to the dictatorial control of information. Based in part on its championing as a hallmark of mid-century literary "freedom" during the Cold War, modernist narrative complexity has often been cast as apolitical or even reactionary (Schwartz 1988; Larsen 2011; Iber 2015). In contrast, South Asian authors suggest that such styles undo the easy certainties the dictator offers and use language to challenge him on the grounds of the literal power to "dictate."

Third, this chapter addresses the apparent conundrum outlined by Aboul-Ela that "writers from the postcolony are interested in particularly that quality of the Faulkner text that makes it most *elusive* for many of his American readers" (Aboul-Ela 2020, 5, emphasis added). By the same turn, South Asian authors report using revenant styles to highlight the fictionality of their texts to quite literally elude their political adversaries. Rushdie called his Zia novel "a kind of modern fairytale," while Hanif reported emphasizing his novel's fictionality by filling it with "fantastical happenings" (Rushdie 1983, 68; Hanif 2019). These are the same Faulkner-inspired qualities that García Márquez would claim made his first dictator novel, *El otoño del patriarca* (*The Autumn of the Patriarch*) (1975), "deliberate hermetic, dense, [and] complex" (García Márquez quoted in Armillas-Tiseyra 2019, 90). As opposed to the pervasive critical assumption that authors from the Global South employ revenant modernist techniques in order to be legible in the Global North, García Márquez reports the opposite, tying these stylistic choices to the hope that "only those who have previously taken the work to learn literature will be able to stand it; that is to say: us, and a few friends" (García Márquez quoted in Armillas-Tiseyra 2019, 90). This recalls the form of literary collusion explored in Chapter 2 – writing for "a few friends." Similarly, in South Asian dictator fiction, certain revenant forms suggest a strategy to manage the "overheard" quality of writing in English – that is, as a way of addressing two totally distinct audience expectations at once.

"Many Years Later": Prolepsis as Prophecy from Faulkner to Hanif

In order to understand why revenant modernism reappears "many years later" in South Asian fiction, we must, like the novels themselves, make a detour back in time. If Huyssen and others argue that the revenant forms at the heart of this chapter underscore a continuity between modernism and postmodernism, Brian McHale argues the opposite. For McHale, literary forms of modernism and postmodernism can be definitively held apart based on their investment in questions of epistemology versus ontology, respectively (McHale 1987). Magical realism is therefore affiliated to postmodernism based on its claim to register competing ontologies, an argument pioneered by Alejo Carpentier's discourse on "lo real maravilloso" and, as we saw in Chapter 4, affirmed by many of his readers in South Asia (Carpentier 1995a; Carpentier 1995b).

Yet these claims about the clash between different worlds are exactly the opposite of what is at stake in, and what gets carried forward by, recurrent tropes like prolepsis. Instead, even in texts with a magical realist flair, epistemology is the central concern: what do we know about the life and death of a dictator, and how did we learn it? That is why the idea of an archive – the single fluttering page that survives the plane crash at the end of Hanif's novel – is another revenant element with an enduring legacy in Latin American fiction (González Echevarría 1990). Between them, these two revenants create a fundamental epistemological tension: prolepsis suggests the supernatural knowledge of prophecy, while the archive recalls the evidentiary standard of a juridical case.

McHale uses Faulkner's 1936 novel *Absalom, Absalom!* as an object lesson for his description of the relationship between modernist style and epistemology. This is a happy coincidence indeed, since *Absalom, Absalom!*, perhaps more than any other Faulkner novel, offers key elements that shape the dictator novel in the hands of García Márquez, Vargas Llosa, and ultimately Rushdie and Hanif. Faulkner's novel tells the story of the rise and fall of the house of Thomas Sutpen, a mysterious self-made man who pulls up and populates a plantation house in the middle of the Mississippi wilderness by sheer force of will. Despite his best-laid plans, Sutpen's design begins to crumble when his son Henry inexplicably murders Charles Bon, who was Henry's best friend and his sister's fiancé, at the gate to the family home. This is the central disaster that is proleptically revealed early in the novel. The "how" and "why" come out only much later: that the crime was necessary to prevent brother–sister incest, as Bon was Sutpen's son by his first wife, whom he set aside when he learned of her mixed-race heritage. McHale lists a number of structural and stylistic features that make *Absalom, Absalom!* representative of literary modernism, and it is worth quoting at length:

> Its logic is that of a detective story, the epistemological genre par excellence. Faulkner's protagonists, like characters in many classic modernist texts ... sift through the evidence of witnesses of different degrees of reliability in order to reconstruct and solve a "crime" .... *Absalom* foregrounds such epistemological themes ... through the use of characteristically modernist (epistemological) devices: the multiplication and juxtaposition of perspectives, the focalization of all the evidence through a single "center of consciousness" (the character Quentin) .... Finally, in a typically modernist move, *Absalom* transfers the epistemological difficulties of its characters to its readers; its strategies of "impeded form" (dislocated chronology ...) *simulate* for the reader the very same problems of accessibility, reliability, and limitation of knowledge that plague Quentin and Shreve. (McHale 1987, 9–10, emphasis original)

As we shall see, these very elements are the key revenants that characterize dictator fiction in both subsequent generations. First is the rudiments of foretelling – "dislocated chronology" in McHale's description, though its narrative purpose becomes much more central than merely one among many modes of "impeded form" in later generations. Second is the central role of an archive and its compiler through which "all evidence is focalized." This second element is sometimes related back to the "epistemological genre par excellence" of detective fiction. The influence of that genre is winkingly engaged by García Márquez's (usually unacknowledged) play on Agatha Christie's *A Murder Is Announced* (1950) in his *Crónica de una muerte anunciada*. It likewise appears in Hanif's intentionally punny "case" of pyrotechnic fruit. However, the archival witness is, for later generations of writers, only one of several gothic character and plot archetypes that can be traced through *Absalom, Absalom!* These include: incestuous siblings, doubles that appear both simultaneously (twins) or in subsequent generations (reincarnations), vindictive virgin aunts, labyrinthine mansions, and, most importantly, the patriarchal strongman figure, who becomes the caudillo or dictator in the Latin American generation.

It is, again, a commonplace in the scholarship on Latin American literature that these stylistic features played a primary role in shaping the "nueva novela latinoamericana" ("New Latin American Novel") of the 1960s "boom" (Martin 1989; Cohn 1997; Casanova 2004; Larsen 2011; Iber 2015). As such, García Márquez's 1967 breakout hit, *Cien años de soledad* (*One Hundred Years of Solitude*), adapts many of these elements into the story of a century in the life of the Buendía clan of Colombia. Their progenitors are José Arcadio and Ursula, distant cousins who defy their families to marry and establish a new community, Macondo, in the Colombian interior. The remote interior is historically similar to Faulkner's Mississippi, and, like Yoknapatawpha County, Macondo is a place to which García Márquez would imaginatively return throughout his career. In time, the nation, the town, their family, and the gothic house in which they live all develop. They do so not in a linear way but recursively, uncannily doubling and trebling Arcadios, Aurelianos, Ursulas, and Amarantas through couplings that draw ever nearer to that dreaded brother–sister incest – that act that is both threateningly generative and genetically doomed.

Both here and later in his career, García Márquez does not merely repeat but actively sharpens two essential revenant elements from Faulkner's oeuvre. The first of these is the intensification of the truth claims made by the archival sleuth. Roberto González Echevarría has famously argued that engagements with the authority of the colonial archive constitute a fundamental shared obsession among Latin American writers like García Márquez, Vargas Llosa, and Jorge Luis Borges, who, as we have seen, exert so much power over the South Asian imagination (González Echevarría 1990). He even identifies the earlier roots for these archival obsessions in Octavio Paz's *Piedra de sol* (*Sunstone*) (1957) and Pablo Neruda's *Canto general* (*General Song*) (1949), texts that, as discussed in Chapters 1 and 2, provided a blueprint for regional mythmaking for generations of Indian and Pakistani authors. González Echevarría identifies the manuscripts of the itinerant ghost Melquíades as the "archive" in *Cien años de soledad* and the doomed Aureliano Babilonia as their ultimate compiler/decoder. The completion of this project is what famously "simulate[s] for the reader" the spectacular textual revelation at the novel's end, suggesting that this canonical example of "ontological" magical realism can, instead, be read as a stage for modernist epistemology.

More significantly still, García Márquez develops a striking narrative habit, "foretelling," out of Faulkner's preference for prolepsis and recursive plot structures. Foretelling distinguishes itself by being both the temporal structure of the text and a hinge point of its action. That is, the clan, and the story, will meet their end when a Sanskrit text left to the first generation by Melquíades is finally decoded by the last. As we learn in the masterful final pages of the novel, that text and the one we hold in our hands are functionally identical – we step into the story at the very moment it self-destructs.

Traditional nineteenth-century realism depends on the establishment of laws, and the reader takes pleasure in the text to the extent its elements work consistently according to these laws. Personalities should be integrated and psychologically consistent, time should flow smoothly from beginning to end, and the mechanics of the narrative world should generally operate as they do in the world outside. As discussed in Chapter 4, magical realism is usually defined as the rupture of a subset of these laws to produce the fantastic, almost invariably those of physics and biology. As such, a scene from *Cien años de soledad* like Remedios the Beauty's bodily ascension to heaven along with the family sheets is identifiable as magical realism because it breaks with the laws of physics in a world where they are otherwise obeyed. What is notably similar about developments from modernism, and what contributes to the tangling of the two genealogies, is the fact that modernist narrative tendencies break the laws of time.

In *Absalom, Absalom!*, the radical absence of concrete knowledge about Sutpen and his progeny at the center of the novel produces a looping, hopping, folding kind of narrative time that ostentatiously interrupts reader expectations about chronology. Cohn emphasizes that "modernism's exploration of alternatives to linear time" appealed to mid-century Hispanophone writers because it reinforced their "efforts to express their preoccupation with troubled pasts that overshadow the present" (Cohn 1997, 159). Especially in the later two generations, narrative representations of time may produce a feeling of the fantastic. Various observers have, indeed, argued that representations of time reflect the ontological difference of magical realism. For some, temporal jumps indicate the complex and contested historiography of Latin America, and thus form part of the cryptorealism of magical realism (Cohn 1997; Kristal 2002). For others, they are a negotiation of the place of indigeneity and its cosmologies within a mestizo nation and thus the origin point of magic in colonialism's ontological clash (Sangari 1987). When Kumkum Sangari offers a very early comparison between García Márquez and Rushdie's magical realism, she emphasizes their shared obsession with narrative foretelling as "part of a complex notion of causality that takes into account both the perceived concurrence of mythic time with a cultural simultaneity and the felt experience of enclosure within a seemingly deterministic system" (Sangari 1987, 175).

Primarily, however, the feeling of magical time comes through in the habit of narrative foretelling evident in the much-discussed and oft-imitated first line of *Cien años de soledad*: "Many years later, as he faced the firing squad, Colonel Aureliano Buendía was to remember that distant afternoon when his father took him to discover ice" (García Márquez 2006, 1). This line is more iconic than any other in García Márquez's oeuvre, and yet its untimeliness arguably has nothing to do with the "magical realism" the author has come to represent. Revealing aspects of a character's future before the reader reaches that fate chronologically in the text is perhaps intended to feel like an element of the fantastic, a kind of prophecy. Aureliano, who is only a child in the "present" of the text, will die "many years later" before a firing squad – or so we are meant to think. And yet, structurally, narrative foretelling is not fantastic; it is merely disruptive. For any narrative in the past tense, the narrator must necessarily know the whole plot in advance, telling it, as he or she does, from a perspective at the story's end. It is merely a mimetic convention that prevents narrators in any realist fiction from revealing their knowledge ahead of time.

Similarly, dozens of scholars over the years have taken up Saleem Sinai's phrasing, "handcuffed to history," to describe how the postcolonial future in *Midnight's Children*, or, indeed, any of Rushdie's novels, cannot ever fully emerge from the past (Parameswaran 1983). This phrase encapsulates, for them, the ongoing relationship of thematic content to the style of its retelling. These narrative tendencies have come to be understood as hallmarks of Rushdian style, where Rushdie was, for decades, the hallmark postcolonial author. As such, explanations of Rushdie's "modernism" also trace a reference shelf that ties his digressive narrative style and thematic concerns back to borrowings from both sides of the authorized dyad: Indian sources like Bollywood and the Mahabharata, Islamicate sources like *One Thousand and One Nights*, Anglophone sources like Rudyard Kipling or Laurence Sterne (Batty 1985; Cronin 1987; Alter 1999; Joshi 2002; Morey 2007). Pranav Jani lists two entire pages of references that apparently shape Rushdie's reception "at the interstice where the postcolonial and the postmodern meet" (Jani 2010, 6–7). These include the inspirations for critical theory's "linguistic turn," the Frankfurt school, the Spivak–Said–Bhabha triad of postcolonial studies, W. B. Yeats, and, at a nod toward the official postcolonial canon, Chinua Achebe.

García Márquez and the broader category Latin American literature are nowhere to be found in these endless lists. Even Sangari's extended comparison between García Márquez and Rushdie only ever posits their writing as analogically related through a shared position in the Global South (Sangari 1987). It never asserts a genealogical link between them. Almost the only places in the astonishingly vast corpus of Rushdie scholarship where García Márquez appears are appended by some form of "not."

Thus, in a mid-1990s interview with Rushdie, Gauri Viswanathan states that "for a long time I've felt that to put you in a tradition aligning you with Gabriel García Márquez is not really doing justice to what I think is actually a far richer texture to your work – a texture which may have different genealogies" (Viswanathan 2008, 37). Like Connell, she is quite right to suggest that the focus on magical realism has occluded "different genealogies" in Rushdie's writing. Naming García Márquez as the figurehead of that tradition, however, actually furthers the very occlusion she decries. García Márquez belongs no more exclusively to magical realism than Rushdie does. These critical streams seem to miss how deeply and openly the habit of narrative foretelling, its relationship to historical consciousness, and the text's resulting untimeliness arise from a relationship to García Márquez.

This is not for lack of trying on Rushdie's part. As Mariano Siskind has noted, "The reader is presented with a meaningful rephrasing of the famous opening sentence of García Márquez's book" several times in *Midnight's Children* (Siskind 2012, 858). Rushdie writes of the novel's patriarch, Aadam Aziz, "Many years later, when the whole inside him had clogged up with hate, and he came to sacrifice himself at the shrine of the black stone god in the temple on the hill, he would try and recall his childhood springs in Paradise" (Rushdie 2006, 5). Halfway through the book, he repeats himself with Aadam's daughter, Mumtaz: "Many years later, at the time of her premature dotage, when all kinds of ghosts welled out of her past to dance before her eyes, my mother saw once again the peepshow man whom she saved by announcing my coming and who repaid her by leading her to too much prophecy" (Rushdie 2006, 97). In both cases, Rushdie suggests a necessary relationship between the magical realist content of the "foretold" plot points and the form of their (fore)telling: the hole in Adam's stomach echoing the hole in the throat of the ghostly Prudencia Aguilar in *Cien años de soledad*; the sieve of Mumtaz's mind, like that of García Márquez's prescient Melquíades, becoming a conduit for "too much prophecy." This unity of formal and thematic levels has led to readings that subordinate the epistemological claims of prophecy to its ontological status as a kind of literary magic.

Yet the association of magical realism with disrupted chronology and other features of modernist style is born of coincidence: they occur at the same time, and perhaps according to a similar law-breaking logic, but they are not, in fact, the same. This matters because narrative foretelling is one of the primary stylistic devices that both Rushdie and Hanif develop from their readings of García Márquez – and, in Hanif's case, from Vargas Llosa as well. In the case of dictator fiction, as Rama and Armillas-Tiseyra argue, the same narrative habit conveys a different mode of knowing and being: a certain cynicism about the notion of progress, particularly encoded in the inability to overcome anti-democratic politics. This is also what Sangari seems to reference through the "felt experience of enclosure within a seemingly deterministic system." As such, Hanif's later, non-magical realist innovation demonstrates how foretelling operates separately, representing a "different genealogy" out of Latin American fiction.

The passage of time matters, too, in terms of what counts, following Viswanathan, as the "tradition" of García Márquez. While García Márquez has a recognizable style – much more internally consistent than other "boom" writers like, say, Carlos Fuentes or Vargas Llosa – he also marked a major shift with the publication of *El otoño del patriarca* (*The Autumn of the Patriarch*) (1975), a lightly allegorized representation of Latin American dictatorship. Using the novel as an exemplar of dictator fiction, Ángel Rama writes that "the novel brings to its limit point the principle that was laid out in *Cien años de soledad* ... : that of a cyclical time that links its end with an earlier beginning" – prolepsis, in other words (Rama 1976, 54).[1] He goes on to validate this observation – one he claims is allied with the reincarnation-inspired "monotony" of Neruda's *Residencia I* (discussed in Chapter 1) – through a description of the novel's first chapter, which "departs from the death of the patriarch, half-eaten by cows and buzzards, his palace in ruins, in order to proceed to the reconstruction of an already-completed cycle of his existence" (Rama 1976, 54).[2] Here the connection between the corpse of the dictator and the ruins of his surroundings enact Eaton's concept of "proleptic nostalgia" (discussed in Chapter 3), another element Hanif echoes in his association of Zia with his exploded airplane. By "reanimating" the fallen dictator in the subsequent chapters – making him a quite literal "revenant" – García Márquez suggest the inescapable repetition of authoritarianism in the Caribbean (Rama 1976). These structures echo the death and ghostly reappearance of Sutpen and the original sins of the South that haunt the bitter, sterile survivors he leaves behind or propagate, mushroom-like, in the uncanny doubles of subsequent generations. If the centrality of this proleptic mode were not clearly enough a modernist trope, Rama is careful to make comparisons to Faulkner himself, noting that García Márquez "belongs to his school" (Rama 1976, 60).[3]

Crónica de una muerte anunciada, the subsequent 1981 novella that absorbs Hanif's fictional Pakistani cadet in 1988, was one of García Márquez's most famous and influential later works. Yet it is radically smaller than his most famous novels not only in length but in total ambition and temporal scale. Unlike the titular hundred years of his breakout hit, the main action of *Crónica de una muerte anunciada* takes less than twenty-four hours. And though it begins with a remarkably similar phrasing – "On the day they were going to kill him, Santiago Nasar got up at five-thirty in the morning to wait for the boat the bishop was coming on" – in this case García Márquez eschews the magical realism that such foretelling is supposed, necessarily, to entail, purporting instead to produce a work of journalism (García Márquez 2003, 1). Scholars like William Spindler who try to cram all of García Márquez's writing in the magical realist framework often run aground on *Crónica*, since it "do[es] not include supernatural or fantastic occurrences" (Spindler 1993, 79). Others, like Michael Bell, use García Márquez's later writings to argue that to pigeonhole him as a magical realist "is to occlude" some of the most significant and far-reaching of his contributions to world literature (Bell 2010, 183).

García Márquez closed out the 1980s with similarly nonmagical fare, returning to the theme of dictatorship, this time retaining the conceits of a much tighter timeline and a real historical archive from *Crónica de una muerte anunciada* and applying them to a novel about the grim final days of another military leader, Simon Bolívar, *El general en su laberinto* (*The General in His Labyrinth*) (1989).

The General in His Labyrinth: García Márquez and the Dictator Template

Hanif and Rushdie are joined by Hamid in attempting to neutralize the threat of General Zia by trapping him in stylistic labyrinths of their own making. Zia had gained power in a military coup unseating and ultimately executing the democratically elected socialist President Zulfikar Ali Bhutto in 1977. Zia held the position of president for the next decade under a program that combined aggressive Islamization and anti-Western sentiment with a cozy Cold War relationship to the United States. As Hanif's novel recounts, Zia's tenure ended in sudden and rather spectacular fashion in 1988 when the military plane carrying him and his entourage to Islamabad exploded – an apparent assassination. By making him the subject of their texts, and especially by focalizing part of the narrative through his perspective, all of the authors discussed in this section seem to draw on a tradition that, like magical realism, has deep roots in Latin America: dictator fiction. These are roots, moreover, of which they seem consciously aware – something that becomes especially clear when they redeploy García Márquez's catchy 1989 title as their own. They thus show an attraction to the revenant character of Faulkner's enigmatic strongman Thomas Sutpen as he sharpens into a dictator figure in the Latin American generation.

Still, the dictator novel of the Global South is not merely defined by the presence of a dictator at its thematic center (Armillas-Tiseyra 2019). Instead, dictator novels share an interest in narrative experimentation as a political act – one that disposes of the easy certainties and black-and-white thinking of authoritarianism. This is opposed to the anti-dictator "diatribe," as Rama had described them, since the latter, while politically righteous, do not formally interrupt the type of absolute truth claims that keep dictators in power (Rama 1976; Armillas-Tiseyra 2019). When Timothy Brennan briefly identifies Rushdie's anti-Zia novel *Shame* (1983) in a "tradition" with García Márquez and Vargas Llosa as writers who attack "current and identifiable political villains," in a "postmodern" form, he seems to inchoately address these same genre conventions (Brennan 1989, 141).

In engaging this argument, Rama, Armillas-Tiseyra, and Brennan participate in a larger debate about how to locate politics within modernist form in Latin American writing. Casanova, for example, argues that Faulknerian modernist innovations offered a path out of dominant strains of social realism in Latin American writing of the 1940s and 1950s, what she describes without irony as a "literary liberation" (Casanova 2004, 344). On the other hand, Neil Larsen draws on arguments by Lawrence Schwartz and Barbara Foley about the way Faulkner's canonization was instrumentalized as part of a Cold War efforts to delegitimize socially engaged literature in favor of apolitical modernist experimentation (Larsen 2011). Thus, for him, the "liberation" into revenant modernism defanged politically progressive "boom" authors at the same time that it helped them toe the line with the more conservative Euro-American readership. These debates carry forward into the perceptible politics of style in dictator fiction in South Asia.

A Garden of Forking Paths: Hamid's Dictator Hypertext

Recalling his youth during Zia's tenure, Hamid reflected, "The state asserted one notion of truth and one national narrative and rejected deviation. Writing ... in a novelistic form that broke things apart and reassembled them in new ways: it felt like precisely the kind of response I needed to the dogma I had grown up in" (Hamid 2017). As Armillas-Tiseyra notes, not all writing styles are equally capable of producing this epistemological resistance. It inheres, instead, in the specific act of "[breaking] things apart and reassembl[ing] them in new ways," the kind of "impeded form," especially "chronological interruptions," that characterize revenant modernisms.

Hamid made these links concrete in his own very brief foray into dictator fiction. His experimental short story, "The (Former) General in His Labyrinth" (2008), uses an overt reference to García Márquez's *El general en su laberinto* to offer his own oblique encounter with military dictatorship in Pakistan. Given its timing and precise title, the proximate inspiration for the (former) general is the more recent Pakistani dictator Pervez Musharraf, who took power in 1999 and was self-exiled around the time of the story's composition. But Zia seems to float in the background, too, and the intentional lack of locational and temporal specificity suggest an open relatability. In addition to the experimental form of the text, discussed later in the chapter, what qualifies Hamid's story as dictator fiction is its interest in the (former) general's subjectivity – as Rama says "not only what dictators did, but who they were and why" (Rama 1976, 10). Thus, rather than recount various atrocities at the dictator's hands, "The (Former) General in His Labyrinth," like its namesake, explores the psychology of a previously omnipotent ruler at the end of his power.

Framed by its title as an homage to García Márquez, the text and paratext nevertheless suggest several other, often more appropriate lineages for a Pakistani writer composing in English. Part of a digital storytelling project funded by Penguin and coproduced by the web designer Adrian Hon, "The (Former) General in His Labyrinth" operates as a choose-your-own-adventure story (see Figures 5.1 and 5.2). Readers are invited to click through various binary options to access different facets of the text. As they do so, the program maps their progress on a map in the lower right-hand corner, ultimately drawing a honeycombed pattern of rooms that form the general's "labyrinth." Snippets of text appear in a Mughal-inspired scalloped window overlaying a moon- and star-dappled sky – quite literally locating Hamid's often intentionally nonspecific and transnational writing in a "clearly differentiated political locale" (Brouillette 2007, 145; Hamid 2008). The website's paratext likewise claims the story descends – much as Rushdie's writing is purported to do – from the legitimate, Islamicate inspiration of *One Thousand and One Nights*.

But these structures also return pointedly to Latin American writing. They depend not so much on the García Márquezian title Hamid borrows but on an earlier intertext, Jorge Luis Borges' *Ficciones* (*Fictions*) (1944). In this sense, Hamid underscores a point made by Shital Pravinchandra that the short story creates its own vectors as a form of world literature – a trend

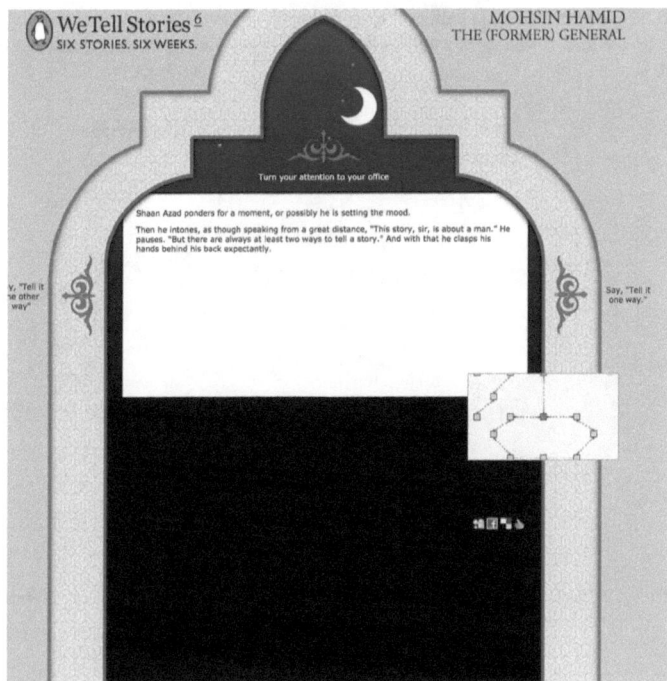

Figure 5.1 Cell 13 from Mohsin Hamid's "The (Former) General in His Labyrinth" (Hamid 2008).

for which she names Borges as exemplary (Pravinchandra 2018). Most obviously, Hamid's visual concept, in which a text also operates as a physical space, and where each page requires a choice between two branches, exactly recapitulates the short story "El jardín de senderos que se bifurcan" ("The Garden of Forking Paths"), published in 1941 and republished in *Ficciones*. Indeed, this story is often cited (sometimes alongside Cortázar's *Rayuela*, discussed in Chapter 4) as a conceptual origin point for hypertext literature (Wardrip-Fruin and Montford 2003).

Hamid adds to this the affective resonance of the story's framing conceit. Borges' protagonist Doctor Yu Tsun finds the key to his own ancestor's indecipherable texts in a foreign land, amazed "that a man of a distant empire had given them back to me" (Borges 1993, 76). In the same way, we might read the recapitulation of both Borges and García Márquez in "The (Former) General in His Labyrinth" as a meditation on the overriding mirrored theme of the countershelf: an unexpected encounter with the self in the tradition of another.

MAP OF STORY (Numbers [1] are cell text; arrows [->] are link direction; letters [AA] are link text; an asterisk [*] denotes a cell or link that changes during the story; and the ALICE reference is in Cell #5)

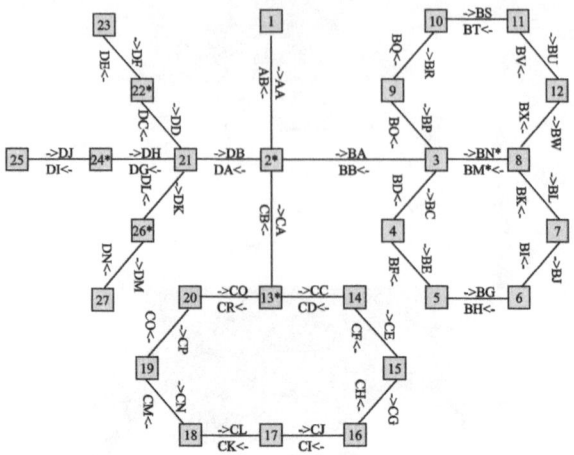

Figure 5.2 "Map of Story" from planning documents for "The (Former) General in His Labyrinth" (Hamid 2010, 321).

As the reader explores more and more of these possible paths, the hexagonal labyrinth that emerges recalls the honeycomb shape of Borges' short story "La biblioteca de Babel" ("The Library of Babel"), published in 1941 and republished in *Ficciones*. While the seemingly infinite, disconnected textual possibilities invite the reader into the position of the librarians who wander its endless halls, Hon recalls that Hamid insisted on producing a "conditional link," that appeared only after the reader had completed their first journey through the labyrinth, a new branch that allows the reader to "keep looping around forever" (Hon 2008).

Even the elements that seem, on first blush, to conform to the expectations of English-language readers about what kinds of intertexts "belong to" a Pakistani writer reveal themselves, on closer examination, to carry the mark of the Argentinian author. Rather than approach *One Thousand and One Nights* directly through his "own" Muslim heritage, Hamid's text seems to tease out its formal possibilities by means of Borges' famous infatuation with that text. This is especially true in the final story in *Ficciones*, "El Sur" ("The South"), first published in 1953 and appearing in the second edition of the collection, in which an impassioned reader of the text suffers a concussion and finds himself fatally drawn into the endless labyrinth of the Arabic tales.

But even more clearly, in "El jardín de senderos que se bifurcan," Doctor Tsun uses the *Thousand and One Nights* to form a preliminary theory of a hypertext, recalling "the night in the middle of The Thousand and One Nights when Queen Scheherezade, through a magical mistake on the part of her copyist, started to tell the story of The Thousand and One Nights, with the risk of again arriving at the night upon which she will relate it, and thus on to infinity" (Borges 1993, 74). Likewise, as Hon recalls about Hamid's story: "To the south is a narrative which can be read in forward or reverse; each direction gives the story a very different meaning" (Hon 2008). In both cases, the resulting "volume whose last page would be the same as the first" rediscovers, in this other source, the modernist prolepsis at the heart of so many dictator fictions (Borges 1993, 74).

Lessons of the Coup: Tariq Ali's Silenced Radio Play

Following a line of criticism suggested by Albert Braz, it's reasonable to assume that Hamid was at least glancingly aware of dictatorial parallels between Pakistan and Latin America when he set the climactic action of *The Reluctant Fundamentalist* (2006) in Chile. A mere half-decade before Zia's overthrow of Bhutto, Chile had experienced a remarkably similar turn of events, in which the right-wing, America-friendly military general Augusto Pinochet overthrew the democratically elected socialist government of Salvador Allende. The 1973 coup marked a radical loss of faith in Latin American cultural and political ascendency and is often credited as the final nail in the coffin of the "boom." Indeed, that event also presaged a wave of authoritarian power that overwhelmed most of South America in the decades that followed – the state of affairs upon which Agha Shahid Ali reflected in 1991 through the idiom of Neruda's *Canto general*. Unsurprisingly, the mid-1970s also saw the publication of three canonical Latin American fictions upon which the concept of the dictator novel is based: García Márquez's *El otoño del patriarca*, Alejo Carpentier's *El recurso del método* (*Reasons of State*) (1974), and Augusto Roa Bastos' *Yo, el supremo* (*I, the Supreme*) (1974).

Back in the 1970s, the coup caught the attention of Tariq Ali as a young Pakistani socialist living in London. In response, he wrote a 1974 pamphlet for the International Marxist Group titled *Chile: Lessons of the Coup, Which Way to Workers' Power?* In 1985, when his own home country had also fallen under dictatorship, Ali was invited by the BBC to compose a TV series about Zia's final confrontations with Bhutto before he ordered the latter's execution. The resulting work, *The Leopard and the Fox: A Pakistani Tragedy* (2006), does not demonstrate the same structural experimentation or intertextual debts as the others discussed in this chapter. Yet it does share with other dictator fictions the concern with Zia's psychological interiority that distinguishes it from a mere "diatribe." And it is hard to imagine that the political parallel of Chile was far from Ali's mind, just as the parallel of colonial Mexico subtly shaped his narrative of medieval Spain (discussed in Chapter 3).

Yet, on the eve of its production in 1985, the BBC scuttled *The Leopard and the Fox*. In the midst of the Russo-Afghan war, the British Foreign Office was reluctant to allow very public, very open criticism of an anti-Communist ally (Ali 2007, ix–xi). Ali was even threatened with a libel suit.

Other South Asian authors seem keenly aware of this "lesson of the coup." Unlike Hamid, they do not necessarily report a cheery faith in the epistemological challenge of revenant modernist tropes. Instead, they suggest that a certain kind of marked literary style helps their critiques hide in plain sight. This echoes the form of literary collusion employed by the poets in Chapter 2, the same insidery aesthetics that allow García Márquez to mark out the audience for *El otoño del patriarca* as "us, and a few friends." But unlike the clubby playfulness of their small-batch poetic expression in baroque poetry, collusive aesthetics have a much more serious duty in dictator fiction. They address the "eavesdropping" presence of unfriendly readerships with disproportionate political power (Elam 2020, 1).[4] In these contexts, Daniel Elam has identified "unintelligibility" and "opacity" as explicitly political aesthetics, ones that would allow revolutionary writing to circulate right under the nose of the oppressor (Elam 2020).

"A Sort of Modern Fairytale": Rushdie's Dictator Fantasia

By far the most well-known and important predecessor to Hanif's project in *A Case of Exploding Mangoes* is Rushdie's follow-up to *Midnight's Children*, *Shame*. Writing in an earlier moment, Rushdie shares with Ali a challenge that Hamid and Hanif did not directly face: how to write about an ongoing political crisis, one in which the opposing side has the advantage of censorship. For Rushdie, then, revenant modernist structures provide not so much intellectual humility about the limits of knowledge and narrative but something far simpler – camouflage.

As with *Midnight's Children*, *Shame* openly adapts the plot architecture of *Cién años de soledad*, in which a single, multigenerational family stands in as an allegory for the fate of the nation.[5] Yet aspects of this winking allegory seem much more specifically indebted to *El otoño del patriarca*, in which García Márquez offers himself plausible deniability by creating an allegorical composite of several real Latin American dictators: Rafael Leónidas Trujillo, who controlled the Dominican Republic from 1930 to 1961; Gustavo Rojas Pinilla, who was in charge of Columbia from 1953 to 1957; and Juan Vicente Gómez, who was in power in Venezuela from 1908 to 1935. In *Shame*, certain aspects of Pakistani history are displaced – Zia and Bhutto are dubbed with the historically loaded pseudonyms Raza Hyder and Iskander Harappa. Meanwhile, at other moments the pretense of a parallel world is abandoned altogether – Rushdie admits that the region of Q stands in for Quetta and doesn't even bother to rename Karachi.

Rushdie excuses his half-hearted allegory, even the idea of magical realism itself, as a form of protective disavowal in a potentially hostile political context. As Aamir Mufti argues, *Shame* is still "concerned with addressing actual audiences in South Asia with whom [Rushdie] might be able to declare a commonality of purpose and position" – a constituency he argues is underestimated in Western critiques of Rushdie's early work (Mufti 1991, 102). Trying to imagine how *Shame* will be received in Pakistan in the midst of Zia's dictatorship, Rushdie's narrator explains, "By now ... [a realist book about Pakistan] would have been banned, dumped in the rubbish bin, burned. All that effort for nothing! Realism can break a writer's heart. Fortunately, however, I am only telling a sort of modern fairytale, so that's all right" (Rushdie 1983, 68).

Brennan's book-length analysis of Rushdie's *oeuvre* seems to recognize this debt. He lists a dozen overlaps between the two novels, concluding with this same observation that Rushdie's recourse to "humorous fantasy" acts as a "stylistic veneer [for] matter-of-fact violence" (Brennan 1989, 66). And yet, as with Brennan's critique of Rushdie's *The Jaguar Smile* (1987), "fantasy" is all that is at stake in these various intertextual gestures. They only ever underscore a relationship to magical realism, though most of them have nothing to do with literary magic. That the same list begins, a page earlier, with "display a calculated and disorderly leaping into the future and past"– that is, narrative foretelling – seems merely incidental. Brennan misses the centrality of foretelling in the politics of Rushdie's dictator novel.

Excoriating the same proleptic narrative style that Brennan praises, Ajaiz Ahmad famously called the fatalistic approach to Zia's death, and Rushdie's investment in genetic doom more generally, "the aesthetics of despair" (Ahmad 1992, 155). Fisk writes similarly that the turn to narrative prolepsis has become a preferred narrative form for modern tragedy by creating a feeling of dread about the inevitability of disaster (Fisk 2008). Yet, in some of the most famous Latin American and South Asian cases, narrative foretelling operates, instead, as a kind of a structural joke. Because, of course, the disaster prolepsis portends in *Cien años de soledad* actually doesn't come to pass – Aureliano lives! In both *Shame* and *A Case of Exploding Mangoes*, prolepsis and tragedy part ways because the "disaster" both authors narrate is not actually sad – Zia dies! As Armillas-Tiseyra explains, the focus of the typical dictator novel rests on the impossibility of systemic change, for which the endurance of a dictator is a ready metaphor (Armillas-Tiseyra 2019). In contrast, in Rushdie and, later, Hanif's hands, at least part of the dread that we feel as audience comes not from the inevitability of the assassination but from the unexpected sense of suspense, a kind of pleasurable anxiety as the plot's recursive energy overrides our knowledge of the facts.

Rushdie's obsessive foretelling of the dictator's death reads not as fatalism but almost as wish fulfillment. Overloaded with metaphorical cargo, Zia is murdered by a series of revenant character tropes: incestuous triplets (doubles) by means of a haunted house (gothic mansions) on the nation's insurrectionist western edge (rural backwaters) while his daughter (a vengeful virgin) lays waste to the land below. Zia's death is hyperbolically overdetermined, as if Rushdie were expressing an anxiety that it could actually be accomplished at all. "How does a dictator fall?" he asks (Rushdie 1983, 277). It appears, at first, a rhetorical question. But it isn't, really. The narrator continues, "There is an old saw that states, with absurd optimism, that it is in the nature of tyrannies to end. One might as well say that it is also in their nature to begin, to continue, to dig themselves in and often to be preserved by greater powers than their own" (Rushdie 1983, 277). Then Rushdie suggests a necessary relationship between magical realism and other elements of his modernist, proleptic style. His narrator foretells that the "dictator will be toppled by goblinish, faery means. 'Makes it pretty easy for you,' is the obvious criticism; and I agree, I agree. But add, even if it does sound a little peevish, '*You* try and get rid of a dictator some time'" (Rushdie 1983, 277, emphasis original).

A Prophetic Moment: Hanif's First Draft

The publishers of *A Case of Exploding Mangoes* seem to be aware that readers might receive Hanif's novel in the lineage of *Shame*. A blurb on the cover likens it to "the magical realism of Salman Rushdie" – even though the novel itself has very little relationship to fantasy (Hanif 2009). Similar blurbs on the jacket and first pages likewise slot Hanif's novel into the increasingly expected shelf of English-language fiction "comp texts" and genealogies that are required to make a new, nonwhite voice salable in the Anglophone market (McGrath 2019).

The back of the book tells quite a different story. In a brief afterward, Hanif takes the somewhat unusual step of actually naming his influences, a real-life countershelf including, "*Fateh . . . The Bear Trap . . . Charlie Wilson's War. Ghost Wars . . . Aaj . . . The Feast of the Goat . . . Newsline . . . Chronicle of a Death Foretold*" (Hanif 2009). Vargas Llosa's *La fiesta del chivo* (*The Feast of the Goat*) (2000) and García Márquez's *Crónica de una muerte anunciada* are the only literary references that merit inclusion on this list. The three English-language monographs, while important to the book's content, are all nonfiction sources about General Zia and the Russo-Afghan war. *Fateh* (*Conquest*) (1990), an Urdu-language biography of Zia's second-in-command, General Akhtar Abdur Rehman, plays a similar role, though it is the only non-American historical source that Hanif credits directly. The other two publications he mentions are Pakistani periodicals. The first is the Urdu-medium literary journal *Aaj* (*Today*), whose 1991 special issue on García Márquez included a translation of *Crónica de una muerte anunciada* under the title *Ek pesh gufte maut ki rudād*. The second is the English-medium news weekly *Newsline*, where Hanif worked as a journalist for several years. In 1991 he published a review of *Fateh* under the title "The General in His Labyrinth" (Hanif 1991).

At the time, García Márquez's novel of the same name had been out a scant two years. Edith Grossman's English translation had appeared mere months prior. This suggests that Hanif's 1991 citation is the product of an intentional pursuit of García Márquez, rather than a casual encounter. Unlike Mohsin Hamid's later reference, which seems to play more on the "memeability" of the title than any serious engagement, Hanif's commitment to García Márquezian storytelling carries into the review itself.

> A few months before the C 130 crash that changed the course of history in Pakistan, General Akhtar Abdur Rehman stopped dead in his jogging tracks and told his son Ghazi Khan, "We have done what we had to, but they are not going to spare us now." (Hanif 1991, 140)

It is hardly necessary to underscore that this is precisely the same structure of narrative foretelling with which García Márquez opens *Cien años de soledad*, *El otoño del patriarca*, and *Crónica de una muerte anunciada* – the same proleptic introduction recapitulated by Rushdie and many others.

Hanif's opening is more than structurally similar. Like García Márquez, like Rushdie, he also suggests a necessary relationship between narrative foretelling and thematic prophecy, opening a world in which Akhtar's statement that "they are not going to spare us" has real predictive power, going so far in the following sentence as to call it a "*prophetic* moment" (Hanif 1991, 140, emphasis added). Already then, almost two decades before he will publish *A Case of Exploding Mangoes*, Hanif is framing the assassination of Zia and his associates in the structure of a García Márquezian epic.

The review also portends a future engagement with Vargas Llosa. Among the many incidents *Fateh* offers from the general's life, Hanif is particularly taken with a story in which General Akhtar abandoned a train full of partition refugees he was assigned to escort across the border, allowing them to be massacred by an angry mob. Hanif quotes Akhtar on the decision: "'We didn't stop the mob,' he told his regiment in 1987, 'because we didn't want to stop them'" (Hanif 1991, 141). Both the incident and the fact of its shameless retelling continued to resonate with Hanif. In *A Case of Exploding Mangoes*, he makes them the centerpiece of a chilling encounter between his protagonist, Shigri, and General Akhtar, one of the clearest statements in the novel about the intentional, rather than merely banal or even hapless, evil fostered by the dictatorship (Hanif 2009, 209–210). Yet in its later, extended treatment – the recapitulation of a well-known story about a civilian massacre at the border and the self-justifications of the general who enabled it – also very clearly seems to reference the scene in *La fiesta del chivo* where Trujillo rehashes for a group of cronies his masterminding of the massacre at the Haitian border in 1937 (Vargas Llosa 2001, 214–234). Indeed, the geographic echo of these two massacres, as well as their historical proximity a mere decade apart, must have been striking to Hanif when he read Vargas Llosa's novel.

"It Says So Right Here in the First Sentence": Witness and Truth in Proleptic Forms

"You might have seen me on TV after the crash," Hanif's protagonist, Ali Shigri, tells his audience in the first sentence of *A Case of Exploding Mangoes* (Hanif 2009, 3). Although it doesn't have the syntactical flair of some of the lines that inspired it, Ali's opening statement nevertheless announces the disaster to which the rest of the novel is merely the prelude. He thereby recreates that "cyclical time that links its end with an earlier beginning," which, for Rama, is the apotheosis of García Márquez's narrative contribution to dictator fiction. The rest of the novel alternates between Shigri and a group of unrelated plotters, each of whom is concocting a plan to assassinate General Zia, as well as tracking Zia himself in his final weeks as he grows increasingly paranoid about threats, real and imagined, to his already doomed existence.

Despite the biographical similarities between himself and Shigri – both were cadets in Pakistan's Air Force – Hanif is at pains to present his protagonist as something of a philistine. Shigri is an aspiring macho man, even a bit of a sadist with younger cadets, someone whose aesthetic tastes run toward *Top Gun* and *Playboy*.[6] Instead, it is his roommate and best friend Obaid who harbors a literary soul, the kind that inspires translations of Rilke into rhyming Urdu couplets. It is Obaid's capacity to be seduced by world literature that keeps him rooted to his seat reading García Márquez on Zia's doomed plane, and adds a surprising emotional heft to the otherwise foregone conclusion.

Why would you carry on with a book whose outcome you know "right here in the first sentence" Hanif's narrator wonders, a playful wink toward his own readers and the degree to which narrative foretelling has held their interest up till now (Hanif 2009, 279). While narrative foretelling is a shared feature for so much South Asian dictator fiction, the central role of García Márquez's novella suggests that Hanif's claims about epistemology, and thus the reason "why [we] keep reading," may emerge differently in this case. It seems to rely, as Debjani Ganguly argues, on the moral position of witnessing that has come to be central in contemporary novels (Ganguly 2016, 13). In other words, the ethical requirement "to see how" violence unfolded rather than merely "know already that" it has happened.

Crónica de una muerte anunciada was published in Spanish just before García Márquez won the Nobel Prize in 1982 and translated into English just afterward. The edition Obaid reads, with "the cover – a bawdy illustration of a fat woman," appears to be based on the 1983 debut of the English translation in *Vanity Fair*, accompanied with illustrations featuring the famously inflated figures of Fernando Botero. Its appearance in the novel thus suggests the sociological "how" of countershelf circulation, an object lesson in García Márquez's level of celebrity in the 1980s. And yet the novella is quite different from the epic texts on which García Márquez's fame had rested up to that time. It is structured like a piece of longform journalism, in which the narrator, Gabriel, returns to his provincial hometown in order to investigate a murder that happened many years before. In the process of the investigation, the narrator fulfills the revenant role of archival sleuth. He speaks with many witnesses to different pertinent events and even hunts down letters and other documentary evidence relevant to the case. Indeed, García Márquez claimed that the novella is based on research he undertook around a real event, and in calling it a *crónica*, a genre of narrative journalism in Latin America, he cues his readers to approach the text as nonfiction.

The concept of narrative "foretelling" as a distinct subset of prolepsis gets its name from Rabassa's now-iconic translation of the Spanish title of *Crónica de una muerte anunciada*. Yet, as Rabassa himself points out, the most faithful translation of the title is not "foretold," but merely "announced." That is, the intention to kill Santiago Nassar is literally announced over and over again by the two would-be murderers during the hours leading up to their crime. While the translation of "anunciada" as "foretold" is certainly poetic – and like so many García Márquez titles, almost infinitely memeable – it also suggests a major perspectival shift in how we receive the narrative. That is, "foretelling" suggests a location or mindset where prophecy has power – that is, a magical realist realm. Arguably the (mis)translated title is the most magical thing about the whole story.

Although this same narrative habit is used in *Cien años de soledad* and *Shame* to produce a feeling of uncanny foresight, it is less "magical" in the context of *Crónica de una muerte anunciada*. Instead, it recalls García Márquez's long years of work as a journalist. In the realm of crime, journalism also shares many of the same features of detective fiction or legal thrillers. The epistemological rules underpinning all of these genres have to do with an evidentiary standard required by law, whether upheld defensively by journalists trying to avoid a libel suit or in a prosecutorial sense by various arms of the justice system building a case. Ganguly argues that this form of "case" making, whose multiplicity of meanings Hanif cues in his novel's title, is "central to the act of novelistic witnessing in our violent times" (Ganguly 2016, 196). Raising these more traditional forms of fact within the modern novel, she argues, intervenes into "the history of what counts (and has counted) as fact in modernity" (Ganguly 2016, 194). Recalling Armillas-Tiseyra's argument mentioned previously, the "real" epistemology of case-making allows authors to recover the power to dictate truth in a context where the truth-telling function of both the media and the courts has been subverted by anti-democratic power.

When decoupled from thematic elements of prophecy, the same style of foretelling the most salient points of a story and then fleshing them out with interviews and archival evidence is the hallmark of the lede–body structure of a news story. It's not incidental that Hanif, who worked for many years as a reporter, picked up on this particular legacy in García Márquez's style. Like García Márquez, Hanif chooses to retell a story whose most important points – a dictator's death by plane crash – are "foretold" both by the existence of the real news event and by the structuring of the novel around its "lede."

Like a news story – and like those of the other writers before him – Hanif's novel is also organized around the revenant characteristic of archival sleuthing, shuttling between multiple source materials and personal perspectives on the same events. In this sense, he much more obviously takes up the mantle of archival authority that distinguishes Latin American mid-century writing and its relationship to history. At several moments, Hanif's narrator refers his readers to external materials that supposedly shore up the facticity of his version of events. These are accompanied by excerpts of the material itself – a Pakistani TV news recording, a CIA phone log – that suggest a different level of reality effect, even though said materials do not exist or could not have been accessed by the narrator/implied compiler of the text. At other times, Hanif takes care to point out how key pieces of information were left out of the official records – the moment a television crew stopped recording just before a critical confrontation, the fact that a guest of tremendous historical significance was slighted by the official photographer at a CIA party, or even the murder of a potential eyewitness. In later interviews, Hanif reported that some readers, especially in Pakistan, assumed based on these interludes that the novel had drawn on evidence not released to the public – that it was literally true (Hanif 2019).

These gestures seem to echo similar moments in *Crónica de una muerte anunciada* when the narrator mentions, for example, a tome-like court document about the central crime, several hundred pages of which were lost in a flood. And, indeed, both writers seem to engage the mode of mourning for lost texts, and their protective recuperation in memory, that characterize countershelf gestures peppered throughout this book.

At the same time that Hanif's account is meticulously correct, however, he also allows a baroque proliferation of plots against Zia, including the titular crate of exploding mangoes, two different kinds of poison, a collection of women's curses, and an extreme case of intestinal worms. Like *Shame's* fantastic final chapter, their accumulation evinces an anxiety about the impossibility of actually ending Zia's reign. He further organizes the text around a recurring motif from the story of Jonah, in which the Quranic whale is transformed into the ill-fated exploding plane, the dictator trapped in its bowels. In these episodes, Zia predicts his own death by randomly returning, over and over, to a single line in the Quran, a snippet of text that survives, miraculously unscathed, among the wreckage in which the novel ends. These and other "prophetic moments" suggest that a possible relationship to magical realism remains. It is a flirtation that ends without consummating embrace, an element that Hanif, again, adapts from *Crónica de una muerte anunciada*.

Both García Márquez's novella and Hanif's book evince an interest in the possibility of foretelling as a narrative element, the idea that signs about the disaster lurking in the future might be present in the retelling of the story and that they might be interpretable by certain figures within that story. Thus, for example, the mother of the victim in *Crónica de una muerte anunciada* recalls making a fatal mistake when she failed to identify an obvious omen about her son's death from a dream. Zia's death is likewise "announced" dramatically in his own obsessive readings of the Quran, in a declaration of his humiliated wife, who publicly shatters her bangles like a newly widowed woman, and by a rape victim he has sentenced to death, who damns him in the hearing of a curse-carrying crow.

Yet while all of these elements give the uncanny impression of predictive power, the actual deaths they portend come about through perfectly realist – if baroque – means. We are not in the realm of García Márquez's earlier novel, where Melquíades can write out the ultimate demise of a family line before it has happened, nor Hanif's later novel *Our Lady of Alice Bhatti* (2011), where Alice can look into a stranger's face and see the manner of their death. In neither case do the narrators clearly endorse foretelling as a true element of the world. Instead, like Rushdie's "faery means," Hanif recounts his style as a self-protective cover for suspicious Pakistani readers:

> I threw in a mango-eating crow and a poison-tipped sword for good measure. I had assumed that if you said on the cover that the book was a work of fiction, people would read it as a work of fiction .... It's almost frightening to think that people read a work of fiction full of fantastical happenings as a piece of history. (Hanif 2019)

There is, however, a significant difference between the narrative style of *Crónica de una muerte anunciada* and *A Case of Exploding Mangoes*. That is, whereas *Crónica de una muerte anunciada* is narrated exclusively by Gabriel, Hanif's novel is only partly focalized through Shigri narrating in first person. Alternating sections take up the third-person limited perspective of General Zia, General Akhtar, various CIA functionaries, and political prisoners, even occasionally hopping like a flea between major and minor characters who pass each other briefly in the same scene. These narrative choices point toward a second essential source of revenant Faulknerian style in Hanif's writing: *La fiesta del chivo*, a relatively late novel by the "boom" prodigy and recently minted Nobel Laureate, Vargas Llosa – the same Vargas Llosa, of course, whose writing acted as a site of pilgrimage for Zulfikar Ghose in Chapter 4.

La fiesta del chivo concerns the demise of Trujillo. Thematically, Vargas Llosa's Trujillo is an even closer model for the characterization of Zia than García Márquez's diminished version of Simon Bolívar in *El general en su laberinto*. While other explorations of Trujillo's dictatorship have presented him as a terrifyingly omnipotent villain – in *The Brief Wondrous Life of Oscar Wao* (2007), Junot Díaz likens him to the all-seeing Sauron from *The Lord of the Rings* – Vargas Llosa presents Trujillo as a threatening but ultimately pathetic, vain old man, impotent both literally and figuratively. Hanif recapitulates these characteristics in scenes that emphasize Zia's hypocritical lasciviousness, his childish paranoia, and his physical frailty. So devoted is he to undercutting the sense of Zia's power that Hanif ends up displacing some of the real villainy of the regime onto the much more menacing figure of General Akhtar.

While *Crónica de una muerte anunciada* offers a basic structure, *La fiesta del chivo* supplies the most direct model for the plot of Hanif's book – the assassination of a dictator in an impoverished country with deep but ambivalent ties to the United States. And while the multiple perspectives in *Crónica de una muerte anunciada* ultimately unify under the voice of the narrator/protagonist, the various chapters in *La fiesta del chivo* alternate between very different types of narration. Some focalize through a sympathetic protagonist, Urania Cabral, the privileged daughter of a prominent official in the dictator's government who is belatedly thrown into the role of archivist as she tries to piece together brutalities of that regime and her own level of both complicity and victimization within it. Other chapters are more loosely organized around the experiences of the would-be assassins and the dictator himself in the days leading up to his murder.

Hanif adapts this structure almost exactly. About half of the chapters are narrated from the present in first person by the protagonist, whose father, like Urania's, was a high-level government functionary, and who only belatedly confronts the evil of the regime that has kept them in comfort and privilege. The other chapters toggle between third-person narratives of many other characters, all of whom may or may not be implicated in the dictator's death. Hanif even recapitulates the titular images of a "fiesta" – suggesting both the standard translation, "party," and the etymological root "feast" through which Edith Grossman translates it – as an ironic metaphor for the assassination plot. The final section of his novel, concerning the immediate hours leading up to Zia's death, is titled "Mango Party."

"*You* Try and Get Rid of a Dictator Some Time!" Locating the Second Person in Global Anglophone Fiction

For both Rama and Armillas-Tiseyra, the relationship that informs a recourse to revenant modernism in dictator fiction is that between the author and his object. That is, writers and dictators are foils in terms of their approach to truth, certainty, and power (Armillas-Tiseyra 2019). Writers distinguish themselves from dictators through the epistemological openness of their style. The primary risk of writing dictator fiction, on the other hand, is the seduction of power and certainty – the author's potential identification with the dictator that Rama condenses into the slippage between "Yo" ("I") and (Él) ("He") in Bastos's *Yo, el supremo* (Rama 1976, 37).

But when Shigri addresses the reader as "you" in the opening sentences of *A Case of Exploding Mangoes*, he introduces a third person into the equation. Well, to be precise, more of a "second person": an audience. The same is true of the "you" who refers both to the (former) general, the subject of Hamid's story, and the reader/player who explores his labyrinth. Likewise, when Rushdie's narrator answers anticipated criticisms of *Shame* with the "peevish" lines "*You* try and get rid of a dictator some time!" he hails the imagined reader directly. An important question lingers in each of these gestures: where in the world is this readerly "you"?

The tricky thing about "you" is that, through a quirk of English grammar, it's always potentially plural (as it is in polite forms of Urdu, though not in Spanish). Thus, as with the recourse to baroque obscurity among the *sathottari* poets (discussed in Chapter 2), the choice to deploy revenant modernism can be read in relation to a bifurcation in the writer's anticipated audience. It has long been observed that South Asian Anglophone writing tends to offer gestures of orientation to an anticipated foreign audience in the guise of observations, even explanations, of things that would not rise to the notice of a reader in the subcontinent (Rockwell 2003). More pointedly, as long as South Asian authors have been writing in English, they have been haunted by the accusation that they produce exclusively for foreign, Western audiences wholly ignorant about Asia.

These critiques have merit, but they also ignore the way that Anglophone writing has enjoyed an increasingly robust readership among knowledgeable audiences "locally" in South Asia and among its diaspora. In the present, successful authors must find the virtue in narrative strategies that can, without favoring either, address both.

Beyond its relationship to the epistemological claims of dictator fiction, this is what the adaptation of narrative foretelling seems to offer for Hanif. That is, *A Case of Exploding Mangoes* is a work of historical fiction. In another context, an author might assume their audience possesses a baseline familiarity with the subject of their work. But in the case of recent Pakistani history written in English, Hanif, Rushdie, and Hamid are all wedged between one audience that knows their subject very well and another that might know nothing about it at all.

A Case of Exploding Mangoes uses foretelling to narrow the gap between its two audiences. By revealing the story's headline at the outset, Hanif brings his relatively ignorant audience up to speed. Several episodes in the novel revel in the irony of the earlier coziness between the United States and a Pakistani dictator committed to Islamization, as well as the Americans' positive glee about arming tribal leaders in Afghanistan. This tendency climaxes in the winking appearance of the future Taliban leader "OBL" at a CIA-sponsored party. Through the proleptic nostalgia of our current, post-9/11 age, these elements acquire a patina of dramatic irony and a sense that history is doomed to repeat itself. All these gestures seem primarily designed to force Western readers to confront the roots of their own geopolitical present in a historical incident they have been privileged to forget.

At the same time, the hyperbolic accumulation of apparently eyewitness and archival evidence in the novel conversely suggests to the familiar audience that they actually weren't as familiar with the story as they thought. When Hanif recounts that Pakistani audiences responded to the text as a potential source of new information about the assassination, they were, in a sense, following his lead. The revenant modernist focus on epistemology and the archive directed them there. Contra the assumption that novels about Pakistani dictatorship are aimed at creating "a certain frisson in the global reception" of stories about "jihadi Islam" (Mufti 2016, 174), the case of Hanif's novel shows that Anglophone texts are often written with the expectation that they are accessible in South Asia. They have a distinct political purpose among that audience, and they encounter distinct risks, in that they may be "overheard" by less friendly eavesdroppers (Warner 2002).

It was because of this risk – not of being ignored as irrelevant but of being taken too seriously – that Hanif's novel did not join the ranks of Walkowitz's "born translated" literature (Walkowitz 2015). Instead, Syed Kashif Raza's Urdu translation *Phatte āmōn ka kais*, produced in the early 2010s, was held back six years over concerns about its reception (Hadid 2020). And indeed, the newly released translation was almost immediately confiscated from bookshops, and the publisher sued for defamation (Hadid 2020). The book itself now joins the ranks of lost archives spectrally marshalled as evidence by lawyers and journalists. As Rushdie says, "Banned, dumped in the rubbish bin, burned . . . . Realism can break a writer's heart."

"One of Us": Intertextuality as Affiliation in the Global South

The key tropes of revenant modernism can make a literary narrative hard to follow. The paths these tropes have carved through literary time and space are equally winding. In response to such authorial acrobatics, editors and other professional mediators have created paratexts that help readers reorient. Most famous among these, perhaps, is the family tree Gregory Rabassa constructed for the English edition of *One Hundred Years of Solitude*. It's hard now to imagine getting through the novel without it. The work of this chapter, and of the book as a whole, is a little like Rabassa's: drawing out family resemblances that have, evidently, gotten lost in the critical shuffle.

Frederic Jameson once infamously reduced all "Third World literature" to a series of allegorical sagas about the family (Jameson 1986). In equal but opposite measure, most scholars of South Asian literature in its various global guises are markedly reluctant to call out family ties. To suggest that certain genres, narrative forms, or thematic foci have their origins elsewhere is to call forth that old spectre of "originality and secondariness" that has haunted South Asian Anglophone literature since its inception (Roy 1998, 72). Thus, otherwise pathbreaking comparative studies of literature in the Global South – like Sagari's early association of García Márquez and Rushdie – stop shy of making genealogical claims.

There is a reason for their reluctance. When the critical establishment has identified intertextual relationships like those presented by revenant modernism, it has usually understood them structurally as a satire, a travesty. According to this logic, a once-authentic style – considered authentic, of course, in its Northern, Western instantiation – is copied with its auratic center emptied out and nothing new put in its place. Like the anti-reproductive, threateningly incestuous couplings of so many of the novels in this chapter, indeed like the zombie-like "revenant" in its title, scholars see the recapitulation of style itself as an iterative rather than generative development (Jameson 1986; Brennan 1989). And as in those families, the results will become progressively deformed and ultimately sterile, until they arrive at the "dull new global novel" of the present (n+1 2013).

Hanif presents a useful "case" – though here a case of exploding *markets* – because his engagement with revenant modernisms and flirtation with magical realism trace two of the major stylistic contours through which South Asian authors succeeded on the global market. As this chapter and Chapter 4 have clarified, both are grooves initially carved by writers of the Latin American "boom." Moreover, the clear line between his novel's subject and post-9/11 geopolitics, not to mention Hanif's own itinerant movement through various publishing and scholarly institutions in Pakistan and abroad, likewise mirrors the various structures extrinsic to literary style through which global attention was directed to Latin American cultural production during the Cold War. These are not merely parallels – they actually suggest the endurance of many of the same structures between both "booms" (Kantor 2018).

Within this larger geopolitical and market reality, scholars tend to interpret South Asian authors' affiliative gestures with astounding cynicism. So when writers like Hanif and Rushdie turn to García Márquez, it is supposedly only as a model of globe-trotting, superstar authorship – the same model Larsen claims García Márquez derived, in turn, from Faulkner (Larsen 2011). And to be fair, García Márquez is a pretty good model for market success. But those who attribute these gestures to exclusively the market commit an act of interpretive violence.

In the first place, as Efrain Kristal argues, to see García Márquez's oeuvre as sycophantically oriented toward readers in Europe and the United States is to miss the way his narrative project emerged in conversation with long-standing traditions in Latin American letters (Kristal 2002). It is also to ignore, as Paulo Horta argues, the fact that supposed market masterminds García Márquez and, later, Roberto Bolaño actually ran long and tortured roads to their initial publication – and encountered even more resistance getting published in English translation (Horta 2019; Horta 2020). Perhaps more tellingly, these critiques cannot account for the far larger number of affiliative gestures toward Latin America whose primary purpose was to speak to "us, and a few friends," gestures which produced no special market success among South Asian authors.

Again, Brennan dismisses South Asia and Latin American writers together for appealing to "the market" by "producing writing that is aesthetically 'like *us*' – that displays the complexities and subtleties of all 'great art'" (Brennan 1989, 37, emphasis added). This recalls a question from the Introduction of this book: Who is "us"? Because, as we have seen in each chapter of this book, "us," "hum log," and "nosotros" are concepts that these authors are actively negotiating, new communities, new worlds they construct in the very act of writing. As Cohn's title puts it, "He Was One of Us." That is, she argues, earlier revenant modernisms in Latin America do not represent a desire to submit to the conditions of European taste but, on the contrary, a will to affiliate with the specific problems of peripherality, underdevelopment, and difficult histories that shape Faulkner's world as against other modernists (Cohn 1997). In the same way, by including those writers and styles on their countershelf, South Asian authors call up Latin American political history as a looking glass for their own experience. They seek out reciprocity, attracted even to exoticizing gestures among Latin American authors in South Asia, and read that way, in turn, as "another hand, unknown to you" that reaches out despite distances of time and space (Das 2001, 161).

As Anglophone South Asian texts experienced their own global "boom," the recognition they extend toward Latin American texts has slowly become mutual. Thus, Rushdie's engagement with Latin American dictator fiction in *Shame* went on to be a touchstone for Dominican American writer Díaz in his own foray into dictator fiction in *The Brief Wondrous Life of Oscar Wao*. As Armillas-Tiseyra illuminates, Díaz raises and debates Rushdie in much the same way Rushdie engages García Márquez, but even more explicitly: "Rushdie claims that tyrants and scribblers are natural antagonists, but I think that's too simple; it lets writers off pretty easy. Dictators, in my opinion, just know competition when they see it" (Díaz quoted in Armillas-Tiseyra 2019, 4–5). Coming in one of his characteristic postmodernist footnotes, the form of the observation underscores the theme of archival sleuthing and digressive, nonlinear, occasionally foretold storytelling that shapes *The Brief Wondrous Life of Oscar Wao*, just as it shapes the novels discussed in this chapter. Díaz's citation, moreover, is a gesture to his own countershelf. His naming of Rushdie seems to evince the same attraction that the *satthotari* poets felt for Paz: an appreciation not only for making available certain tools of the trade but for his investment in reciprocity, recognizing the other who has recognized something of value in your "own" tradition.

One way of narrating this citation – the cynical one – is as two authors who might, in other times, have written in two mutually unintelligible languages but who now both participate in the great cultural flattening of an Anglophone globe. But there is another way to see it: one that recognizes the endurance of worldly difference, its purposeful negotiation through stylistic affiliations that are not imposed but ethically chosen, and that produce their own tradition, within and yet "contrary" to Global English.

Epilogue

> I like the idea of an American reader coming upon [my novel] almost as a work in translation. Part of the appeal of such books (such as [Roberto] Bolaño's novels) is that they seem addressed to another audience.
>
> (Mahajan quoted in Majumdar 2016)

As much as earlier poets like Pablo Neruda and Octavio Paz and mid-century novelists like Mario Vargas Llosa and Gabriel García Márquez remain models for South Asian authors, their place on the countershelf has recently been eclipsed by Roberto Bolaño. Bolaño, of course, stands so centrally for the reception of Latin American fiction in a "post-boom" world that his name acts as an icon for globalization in the same way García Márquez once stood for magical realism (Kristal 2002; Hoyos 2015, ix). This informs the critical ambivalence that attends Bolaño's tokenized inclusion as the single Latin American author among various theorizations of "the Global" (Deb 2015; Kirsch 2017). And yet, it would be a profound failure to treat the excited reception of Bolaño and other world-striding Latin American authors only as some kind of false consciousness among South Asian authors. The notion of authenticity, of South–South solidarity, that their names and works invoke has real power, even now, in the realm of Anglophone letters.

When the Anglophone Indian novelist Karan Mahajan commented that he finds in Bolaño the warrant to write "almost as a work in translation," he challenges many of the unthought assumptions that surround "Global Anglophone" writing in its apparent opposition to multilingual world literature. Faiza Khan sums up this polemic when she aligns Latin American authors with those who write in other South Asian languages, who "engage with their local traditions; their writing, even when read in translation, is infused with the local idiom, it has its own distinct flavour" (Khan 2010). By contrast, she writes, "it must surely be excruciatingly difficult" for South Asian Anglophone authors "to write anything with real conviction when half of your efforts go into providing explications for a foreign readership" (Khan 2010).

This, Mahajan told me, is what he looks to the model of Bolaño's translation to avoid. In his imaginary, English and vernacular writers need not be rivals for global attention. Instead, he returns to an idea that South Asian Anglophone authors have long held: that Latin American literature might be the model for the popular reception of any tradition that wishes to address a global audience on its own terms (Karan Mahajan, personal communication, November 1, 2019). This is somewhat different from Rebecca Walkowitz's model, in which books written in English highlight the language's foreignness, its operation as a self-referential, even self-ironizing screen for some authentic vernacular version of self underneath (Walkowitz 2015). Instead, Mahajan suggests, English itself can be foreign, multiple, and culturally authentic (Majumdar 2016). Ironically, Mahajan's quote about Bolaño has been almost immediately rearticulated as a cynical market manipulation (Nadiminti 2018). In this reading, literally any representational strategy (e.g., realism, modernism) and any authorial position (including the expressed desire to become less transparent to audiences in the Global North) is only ever evidence of being a sellout.

Instead, Mahajan's contrarian statement forces the English-only establishment to acknowledge what happens beyond its boundaries. Although they favor different eras and styles, both Mahajan's realism and the revenant modernism of Chapter 5 are equally worldly, because both orient toward Latin American models. In the light of these reciprocal gestures, we must be wary of all that follows from Khan's assumption that "engag[ing] with ... local traditions" is the only way to be politically potent, as well as the accusation, echoed in Nadiminti, that addressing "a foreign readership" is anathema to writing "with real conviction."

Like Zulfikar Ghose in the 1960s, Mahajan found a significant source of support at the University of Texas at Austin, first as a student and later as a professor of creative writing. Through his Texas affiliation he came to know the Mexican journalist and fiction writer Antonio Ruíz Camacho, who followed the same trajectory. It is not just that Mahajan and Ruíz Camacho are fellow travelers in an academic network. It is that this network, like the others – fantasized and real – described in this book, allowed them to see something about themselves and their writing that otherwise might remain forever latent. This is the topic of their discussion in a 2015 interview conducted by Mahajan for *The Rumpus*. As Ruíz Camacho explains to

Mahajan: "I feel I have more to do with Latin American writers who live abroad than with other Mexican writers in Mexico or an American writer in America. I myself have more in common with you, though you write about India" (Ruíz Camacho quoted in Mahajan 2015).

Certain Latin American authors of Ruíz Camacho's generation possess one more important point of commonality with writers like Mahajan than they would have had in generations prior: they, too, write in English. In the interview, Ruíz Camacho reports that a literary agent who visited one of his creative writing classes told him in no uncertain terms that he would not find publishers writing in Spanish; his only choice was to switch languages (Mahajan 2015). And it has certainly been the case that his writing reaches a wider audience in English – including an Indian audience. Indeed, Ruíz Camacho is one of a small but growing contingent of Latin American authors to have participated in the Jaipur Literature Festival. With offshoots in London, Boulder, and New York, the Festival is now one of India's most visible engagements on the "global" literary stage – the self-proclaimed "greatest literary show on Earth" (ZEE Jaipur Literature Festival 2019).

Living abroad – whether under the aegis of diaspora, exile, or some hyphenated designation – is not new. Working in a university context is not new either. South Asian and Latin American authors have been doing both, often together, for decades. But writing in English is new, at least for authors from Latin America. As more join them, as likely they will, what will that mean for the conceptual formation of Latin American literature? What will it mean for the emergent formulation of Anglophone literature? This is a question that comparative scholarship between these two regions will find it necessary to answer.

Illuminated with Another Light

In 2019, the New Delhi World Book Fair hosted a poster exposition marking the fifty-year anniversary of Octavio Paz's tenure in India. Hosted by the Embassy of Mexico in India and titled "Re-Imagining Octavio Paz," the exposition featured colorful designs that invoked Paz's writing about the subcontinent ("Re-Imagining Octavio Paz" 2019). These include the photo exhibit discussed in Chapter 2, in which Indian citizens pose with lines of Paz's poetry in the landscape that inspired it. The curators of the show seemed to realize that South Asian audiences are in a unique position to recognize the sly literalism of Paz's Indian poetry – the same quality that appealed to his friends among the Indian poets and artists of the 1960s and 1970s.

Introducing the show was the Bengali poet Subro Bandopadhyay. Though Paz was the formal impetus for the talk, the actual bent of Bandopadhyay's argument was trying to bring the Indian audience up to speed on contemporary Mexican poetry, bringing them past the hurdle of the "boom" in the same way that Mahajan seems to do in his turn to Bolaño. Exactly the same way, in fact, since Bolaño's most famous novel, *Los detectives salvajes* (*The Savage Detectives*) (1998), concerns a group of upstart young poets fighting Paz's dominance in the poetry scene in Mexico during the 1970s (Bolaño 1998; Boullosa 2007). Ironic, then, that Bolaño has succeeded him as the very symbol of Latin American literature as an institutionalized, world-circulating force.

A few days after his talk, I sat with Bandopadhyay at the Instituto Cervantes in New Delhi, where he is the only South Asian Spanish teacher. Bandopadhyay knows something about contemporary poetry in Spanish – he also writes it. Winner of the Antonio Machado international fellowship and the distinction "Poeta de Otros Mundos" ("Poet from Other Worlds"), Bandopadhyay made the transition from writing only in Bangla to writing in Spanish a few years ago (Bandopadhyay 2018). He is also the author of a Bangla-language biography of Neruda. He knows that he would circulate better if he would just write in English. This is not just a matter of publications – because who really reads poetry nowadays, no matter the language? But, at least writing in English he would be competitive for the kind of paid MFA and teaching positions through which authors support themselves – the same types of fellowships that bring together writers like Mahajan and Ruíz Camacho at Texas (Subro Bandopadhyay, personal communication, January 6, 2019).

Just as, event by event, he brings contemporary Hispanophone poetry into the awareness of Indian readers, in the Institute's small library Bandopadhyay has more or less single-handedly built a bookshelf of Latin American literature translated into Indian languages. There I found a copy of a three-year literary experiment, a joint venture between the Indian government and the embassies of Spain, Portugal, and several countries in Latin America. Ostentatiously large, the book's gorgeous ruby and onyx two-color printing recalls the lines from that icon of multilingual literary friendship between India and Latin America, "Al pintor Swaminathan":

>   Springs the Mexican red
>   Turns black
>   The Indian red springs
>   Turns black
>
>   (Paz 1966)

It was named *Vislumbres*, named for Paz's last book about India, the memoir *Vislumbres de la India* (*In Light of India*) (1995). In one last gesture of Latin American affiliation, Agha Shahid Ali, a lifelong reader of Paz, reviewed the book for the *Los Angeles Times*. In his review, Ali emphasized Paz's qualifications to write about India, reauthorizing them through his own connection to the subcontinent:

> As a Third Worlder, Paz does not identify with what one might loosely call a monolithic First World attitude, as does E. M. Forster or even V. S. Naipaul, a writer of Indian extraction who identifies more with Great Britain than his native Trinidad, or for that matter, India. "To a certain extent," he writes, "I can understand what it means to be Indian because I am Mexican." (Paz quoted in Ali 1997)

Here Ali uses Paz as he did in "Return to Harmony 3," as part of a reading practice that can counter the authority of an Anglophone tradition that "identifies more with Great Britain" than the Global South. "With a light touch," he writes, "Paz offers us India, knowing that modern India could be illuminated 'with another light, crueler but more real'" (Ali 1997).

The full title of Paz's memoir literally means "glimpses of India," or "glimmers of India." In it, Paz imagines India as a shining object partially obscured by the writer's self-confessed ignorance, revealing "realities perceived between light and shadow" (Paz 1998, 33). But the title of the English translation, the one Ali reviewed, is not *Glimmers of India* but *In Light of India*. Here India remains a shining object, but one that illuminates something beyond itself. This is, in a literal sense, a mistake. Obviously intentional on the part of the translator, this mistake acts a bit like Columbus', in that it suggests a new dimension to the reading of the text. Paz, as an outsider, will never be able to tell us as much about India as he will about the sense of a Mexican poet of himself and his own place in the world. India illuminates this, otherwise. This is implicit in the text; the mistranslation makes it explicit. Like the fantasies that often engender them, "misunderstandings" of this type do something tremendously productive. In this book, the gaze is turned back. It is South Asia's encounter with Latin America, which illuminates something different, I hope, about the conundrum of Anglophone writing in the present.

"In a Pool of Sunlight"

Later that year, I found myself in conversation with the Pakistan-born, USA-based historian Taymiya Zaman. She was explaining to me why she had used her recent sabbatical to move to Mexico and learn Spanish. It was not the usual story about fantasy and affiliation but the confrontation with unassimilable difference that drove Zaman from California. She began to read pre-Columbian history and found herself frustrated by an utter inability to separate her historian self from the judgments she made as a lay reader (Taymiya Zaman, personal communication, May 6, 2019). Like Ghose, Anita Desai, Agha Shahid Ali, and Sunny Singh before her, she needed to go south to reframe her own positionality in US academia.

The result of that journey was her methodological essay, "Cities, Time, and the Backward Glance" (2018). Zaman uses Latin America not as a historical analogue but as a formal model for epistemological decolonization in her essay. She does this by invoking stylistically the short stories of Jorge Luis Borges and, to a lesser extent, Julio Cortázar. Although she mentions them only in footnotes, their non-European worldliness operates in much the same way it is for all of the South Asian authors in this book. Moreover, Borges and Cortázar hold the space for "creative writing" as such – that is, writing outside of, supplementary to, and free from the constraints of the evidentiary requirements of the academy. For Zaman, the shortness of the short story – especially the extreme brevity perfected by generations of Argentine writers – fit within the requirements of an academic article.

Zaman's essay explores the splitting of the self, accomplished by a convent-school, English-medium education and American graduate training, making one half of her a Pakistani woman and the other half "a European man from the Renaissance" (Zaman 2018, 699). Her training, then, echoes the kind of deforming educational influence imagined by the Macaulay Minute's most infamous phrase. As with all of the other writers in this book, the turn to a Latin American countershelf has the potential to heal this rift.

Zaman's Pakistani consciousness inheres in the image of a sleeping man "in a pool of sunlight" in the middle of a Mughal ruin, while she herself is trapped in the perspective of the American academic who watches him (Zaman 2018, 699). She writes: "In sleep, there would be no difference between him and me. Awake, we inhabit worlds separated by class, language, and gender, and most importantly, by understandings of time and space" (Zaman 2018, 699). The image of the mutually constitutive dreaming of two figures and their location in a ruined mosque clearly evoke Borges' "Las ruinas circulares" ("Circular Ruins") (1940). The central conundrum of a muted Pakistani consciousness also evokes Cortázar's "Axolotl" (1967), about a man who finds himself doubled into the object of his observation, an amphibian native to Mexico after which the story is titled. This doubling dooms the narrator to a version of "shut-in" syndrome in which he is fully aware but unable to communicate. The axolotl position is akin to her own Pakistani-ness, an affective relation to the Mughal past that she can speak about only as an outsider and inhabit only mutely.

At the end of the essay, Zaman works through the same tension between her Pakistani and academic selves through an homage to Borges' "Borges y yo" ("Borges and I") (1960):

> THE OTHER ONE, THE HISTORIAN, is the one who goes to monuments in search of the past. I walk into the mosque to listen to the timeless hum of prayer, to watch bars of light alternate with bars of shadow across the floor in perfect symmetry. She pulls out her camera and scribbles things in a book. I am wary of her pen. I like cats, cushions, the nastaliq script, the smell of jasmine, and the story of Shaykh San'an in Attar's The Conference of the Birds; she likes these things, too, but above all else, she likes language. I exist so she can write about me and capture me as she does everything else, and in giving me over to language, she will erase me. (Zaman 2018, 703)

Zaman doubles – or, perhaps more accurately, quadruples – Borges' experience of the painful splitting of an author into person and persona. Agency slips between the doubles moment by moment, phrase by phrase, until, at some point beyond the text's horizon, the written double will totally overtake its human counterpart.

Borges and Cortázar are most evidently formal exemplars, literary containers. Zaman's writing slips occasionally into theirs, and they clarify its interpretive shape. They are somewhat secondarily the purveyors of a motif – the double – through which Zaman gives body and heft to the problems of epistemology in her field. Only in the deep, but not quite invisible, background do these authors and texts register as Latin American, in the way that idea operates for other authors in this book: a comparable location of colonized experience. Zaman's project is an explicitly decolonial one, demanding the unknotting of the web of colonized knowledges that persists long after colonialism itself becomes an object of her discipline, history. By calling up Borges and Cortázar as her countershelf, she names them the formal models that can counter Eurocentric ways of writing, and knowing, history.

A Hollow Sphere among the Stars

Like the doubles of Zaman's story, the ending of this book forces a splitting – a doubling. I end with two fables about the way that South

Asian Anglophone literature circulates in the absolute contemporary: the pessimist's ending and the optimist's ending. The technology of printing forces me to explore them consecutively, but I want you to think, as you read them, about how they sit together in the same space, drawing on the same delirious fantasies, referencing the same frank realities, without resolving either way. Both must be reckoned with in an assessment of the literary present. The last element that makes the journeys of South Asian Anglophone literature "unexpected" is this: that you, reader, will have to choose where it ends.

The Pessimist's Ending

The Indian novelist Tanuj Solanki names Bolaño as one of the two biggest influences on his countershelf. His passion for contemporary fiction was ignited at the same moment in the 2000s when Bolaño's *2666* (2004) was translated into English: "What I write is very connected to the kind of stuff I like reading, and I loved [Bolaño] more than anybody else" (Solanki quoted in Anasuya 2018).

Solanki's short story "The Geometry of the Gaze" (2013) explores his attachment to Bolaño, alternating between a description of his quotidian activities in contemporary Mumbai and a series of literary fantasies experienced as dreams. In the dreams, two peripatetic realist writers, Bolaño and Saadat Hasan Manto, the self-proclaimed greatest storyteller in Urdu, come together on a park bench in the afterlife. For South Asian Anglophone authors, Urdu writing often holds a space of fantasized authenticity similar to that of Spanish. Manto, in particular, is often raised as an iconoclastic literary persona in the vein of Pablo Neruda. Both authors are part of "a hollow sphere made of a hard wood called The Third World. Inside it an abyss, an abyss both created and protected by The Third World" (Solanki 2013). Solanki imagines Manto as a termite, desperately trying to bore into this sphere and, through it, into global literary significance.

After expressing surprise that they both died of liver cirrhosis – "I always wanted to die of the lung ... because of Kafka" – Manto and Bolaño get down to a discussion of their respective art (Solanki 2013). They reenact the fantasy of perfect understanding, of multilingual equality that has always informed South Asian visions of Latin America.

On the park bench of the afterlife, where time and space disappear, the fantasy is heightened further. "'I cried when I read Khol Do,' Bolaño says" – suggesting an unlikely but not entirely impossible circulation for Manto's most famous story (Solanki 2013). Still, the potential realism of his statement is undercut by Bolaño's citation of the story in Urdu. "'Frankly I haven't understood you yet,' Manto says" – responding with a temporal paradox of reading Bolaño fifty years after his own death (Solanki 2013). Only in this completely fantasized space can absolute reciprocity exist between short story writers who lived half a world and died half a century apart.

Together, they consider what it means to be authors seemingly trapped outside the wooden sphere. "'I tried to enter, you know, I tried to bore through,' Manto says. 'But it was tough for me.' 'I know,' Bolaño says. 'The Third World requires the work of previous ones'" (Solanki 2013). When Manto asks him how contemporary authors have fared in their fight for relevance, Bolaño demurs. He concludes with a kind of pessimism that echoes so much of what we read about globally circulating literature:

> "It's not that important you know," [Bolaño] says.
> "What? What is not important?"
> "Boring through. Reaching the abyss. For what?"
> "For literature."
> "But it's not important."
> "What is not important?"
> "Literature. Literature's not important."
>
> (Solanki 2013)

The dream of egalitarian, multilingual, unexpected circulation has finally been achieved. But compared to the realities of its global circulation under capitalism, literary dreams just don't matter. "It vanishes, the dream," Solanki concludes (Solanki 2013). "All that exists is the absence of a dream" (Solanki 2013). Perhaps this is where we end, as well: in a hollow sphere, where a dream once lived and now leaves no trace.

The Optimist's Ending

Mohsin Hamid's novel, *Exit West* (2017), reapproaches magical realism in a new way. This form that just a decade ago seemed both politically overdetermined and stylistically moribund has shown some recent signs of life. But the conditions have changed. Gone is the verbal playfulness or postmodernist self-awareness that once seemed indissolubly associated with the form. Hamid's language is powerful in its simplicity; his narrative is strikingly straightforward in both time and action.

Yet a connection to Latin America remains – though not in the clear-cut way that the pilgrim writers discussed in Chapter 4

A Hollow Sphere among the Stars 187

understood magical realism as a specifically Latin American narrative form.[1] Rather, in style and content the novel feels more aligned with the quietly declarative, almost fable-like quality of Borges' short stories than García Márquez's recondite prose. Like Zaman's recapitulation of "Borges y yo," Hamid underscores the Argentinian's stylistic impact by referencing pet themes like the double:

> Once as Nadia sat on the steps of a building reading the news on her phone across the street from a detachment of troops and a tank she thought she saw online a photograph of herself sitting on the steps of the building reading the news on her phone across the street from a detachment of troops and a tank ... and she almost felt that if she got up and walked home at this moment there would be two Nadias, that she would split into two Nadias, and one would stay on the steps reading and one would walk home, and two different lives would unfold for these two different selves. (Hamid 2017, 157)

But for the most part, Hamid gives us a straightforward realist novel with one major magical conceit: portals have opened up all over the world, facilitating mass migration on an unprecedented scale. The utter randomness of where they are located and where they go cuts short the logic of traditional migration patterns based on dyadic movement between historically connected heres and theres. It inaugurates instead a form of movement that is unprecedentedly unpredictable.

Despite the magically mediated randomness of the portals in Hamid's novel, Nadia and Saeed's "realist" trajectory from a vaguely anonymized Pakistan to Europe and ultimately the United States closely tracks existing patterns of global capital. Yet, Hamid argues, the same portals may also open the way for a new, unexpected type of movement, one based not on realities of displacement but on fantasies of connection. As I recounted in the Introduction, long before they are forced from their home country Nadia and Saeed briefly dream of a different kind of mobility, voluntary journeys to Cuba and Chile.

Jumping fifty years into the future, Hamid projects a moment where portals are no longer only one-way funnels of desperate escape but hold out the possibility of unexpected connections. It is the same imaginary "tinged with wonder" that brought the two estranged lovers together all those years ago – and that beckons still. Hamid writes:

> Nadia asked if Saeed had been to the deserts of Chile and seen the stars and was it all he imagined it would be. He nodded and said if she had an evening free he would take her, it was a sight worth seeing in this life, and she shut her eyes and said she would like that very much, and they rose and

embraced and parted and did not know, then, if that evening would ever come. (Hamid 2017, 230–231)

Hamid ends his book here, with these lines of open-ended wondering and hesitant optimism about the world. Perhaps this is where we end, as well: in a moment of connection where, in spite of everything, a dream lives on. There may not be portals in this world. But there are books that can take you from the cafes of Lahore to the deserts of Chile, if only you make room on the shelf.

Notes

Introduction

1. The consistent imaginary of transparent, "perfect understanding" despite linguistic difference seems to offer an echo of Walter Benjamin's image in "The Task of the Translator" (1921), where various versions of the same text fit together side-by-side to recreate a complete, mystic utterance, without ever instantiating hierarchies implied by the common translational metaphor of layering (Benjamin 1968). This meditation recalls an idea of a universal language before the tower of Babel – one not particularly operative for most of the South Asian authors in this study. It also recalls anthropological fantasies of perfectly intelligible forms of speech among small, isolated communities, in which "perfect understanding" implied perfect social harmony – a fantasy critiqued by Jacques Derrida (Derrida 1980). On the other hand, Madhumita Lahiri suggests that these scenes of untranslated literary listening "invoke the two-way gaze known as *darshan* ... both a devotional and political form of reciprocal vision" (Lahiri 2020, 53).
2. Several scholars have recently argued that South Asia is thus the ideal location through which to theorize some of the knottiest problems in world literature. Francesca Orsini, for example, exploring the same internal multilingualism that drew Sontag, argues that an alternative concept of world literature might be developed in relation to the circulation of multiple literary traditions in a relatively circumscribed space (Orsini 2015; SOAS MULOSIGE 2017). Sheldon Pollock argues that the recent domination of English and its potential threats to language diversity can be historicized in relation to the spread of Sanskrit from the subcontinent and its historic battles with other Asian vernaculars (Pollock 1998). Aamir Mufti takes the opposite tack, arguing that the colonial-era definition of South Asian languages as "vernaculars" was an Orientalist project revealing the fundamental Eurocentric underpinnings of the project of multilingual world literature as such (Mufti 2016). As his title *Forget English!* suggests, this argument is also centrally about the negotiation between English and its others. So while many other locations are equally suitable for telling the story of either world literature or

Global Anglophone literature, South Asia is supremely appropriate for exploring the nexus between them.

3. Karoline Watroba offers a lovely compilation that is worth citing at length, in which writers who circulate like the South Asian Anglophone authors in this study are accused of creating "'new globally directed works all too *easy* to understand'; 'works produced primarily for foreign consumption'; airport novels or 'romans de gare'; that is, mass-market paperbacks sold to travelers at airport or train station newsstands; 'global babble'; testament to the 'Disneyfication' or 'McDonaldization of the globe'; 'market realism'; and 'contemporary world literature [that] isn't worth the effort it doesn't require'" (Damrosch, Abu-Lughod, Culler, and Ali quoted in Watroba 2018, 55, emphasis original). It is notable that the major authors used to substantiate the "World-Lite" argument in *n+1* – Rushdie, Arundhati Roy, Mohsin Hamid, and even Rohinton Mistry – are actually all South Asian Anglophone authors who rose to prominence during the South Asian "boom" (Kantor 2018). The same unacknowledged conflation of "boom" authors with much broader global collectives also occurs in Graham Huggan's *The Postcolonial Exotic* (2001). What Huggan described in 2001 as a "postcolonial" trend around the Man Booker Prize shortlists and awards is, upon closer examination, very marked, and indeed increased, preference for South Asian authors from the 1980s to the 2000s: Anita Desai and Rushdie in the 1980s, Mistry, Michael Ondaatje, and Roy in the 1990s, and no fewer than ten authors between 2000 and 2008, with prizes to Kiran Desai for *The Inheritance of Loss* (2006) and Aravind Adiga for *The White Tiger* (2008) (Huggan 2001). In hindsight, these awards seem to speak to discrete, geographically bounded phenomenon emerging from South Asia.

4. Caliban was later brought to his current, "resistant" usage in the writing of George Lamming and Aimé Césaire as well as the literary theory of Roberto Fernández Retamar (Fernández Retamar 1989; Lamming 1992; Césaire 1997).

5. This is, of course, Rebecca Walkowitz's clever coinage, but the idea had been in currency for quite a while before her 2015 book of the same name. It is perhaps most clearly articulated in *Postcolonial Translation: Theory and Practice* (1999), edited by Susan Bassnett and Harish Trivedi. Both Trivedi's contribution to the editors' introduction and G. J. V. Prasad's chapter in that same volume depart from the already standard assumption that all Indian writing in English writing is effectively translated (Bassnett and Trivedi 1999; Prasad 1999). Lest we be in doubt, Trivedi explicitly argues that such "translation" reflects "more acutely than ever before the asymmetrical power relationship between the various local 'vernaculars' (i.e. the languages of the slaves, etymologically speaking) and the one master-language of our post-colonial world, English" (Bassnett and Trivedi 1999, 13). These critical uses of translation, which depend

on "analytical categories such as major and minor, national and ethnic, or mainstream and marginal," as Yu-ting Huang argues, "implicitly privilege a binary or dualistic consideration of translational relationship" (Huang 2019, 486). They are therefore poorly suited to the literary analysis of more complex power relations, especially those between groups in the Global South.

6. I use the term "South Asian Anglophone" to describe literature written by authors of South Asian origin who write in English. I do not include other writing in English composed from or about South Asia – say, the popular nineteenth-century Orientalist writing by authors like Rudyard Kipling. The reception history of those texts is strikingly different, despite the efforts of scholars such as Graham Huggan, who conflates the two lines in his concept of "Raj Nostalgia" (Huggan 2001).

7. Ranasinha's writing parallels Carlo Coppola's earlier work on Anand's associate Ahmed Ali and brings it into larger conversations on Black British and Commonwealth authors in the same period (Coppola 2018). All of these narratives share something of the more traditional approach to postcolonial cosmopolitanism as a "third space" hybridity between colonizer and colonized (Bhabha 1984).

8. In fact, as we shall see, quite a lot was happening in those decades. Literary journals of the era were chock-a-block with the early work of major writers including Trivedi and the Pakistani critic Aijaz Ahmad, both of whom were, at that time, famous for writing and translating verse. Their presence reminds us, in passing, that a shorthand division between "authors" and "scholars" can be a dubious one and is sometimes undercut by the realities of participation in this field.

9. This concept is indebted to ideas of the Indian public sphere and its counterpublics, as articulated by Francesca Orsini and Laura Brueck (Orsini 2002; Brueck 2014). But those studies emphasize relationships among various religious, sociological, and linguistic groups within India, while the present work considers a group of authors explicitly focused on how their writing might circulate globally.

10. The Global South is a contested but useful term to describe the connections in this book. Although its history is equally bound up with Cold War geopolitics, the term's adherents tend to distinguish it from other categories like Third World and postcolonial through an emphasis on willful affiliation. As Anne Garland Mahler suggests, it encodes a turn away from "trait based or circumstantial conditions" and toward a shared "ideological frame" (Mahler 2018, 244). Lahiri celebrates its "elasticity" in marking out shared conditions between formerly colonized countries and oppressed communities in powerful countries, marking W. E. B. Du Bois as the godfather of the concept (Lahiri 2020, 123). Leah Feldman gives an extensive history of the

term, noting that it "emerges as a comparative mode of reading decoloniality through structures of feeling that crossed the Cold War divide, which crucially exposes nodes of difference in forms of decolonial literature and attendant conceptions of race and ethnicity that they produced" (Feldman 2020, 203).

11. Following Damrosch, a significant trend in world literature studies has been to assess the circulation of a single author or text in a receiving tradition (Damrosch 2003). In themselves, these are valuable contributions to our understanding of how and why literature circulates. But a core argument of this book is that something distinct happens when books and authors are not received singly, through the idiosyncrasies of global taste-making, nor in bulk, through the violences of colonial pedagogy, but consciously through an understanding (however flawed) of both taking in and producing a tradition.

12. Ignacio Sánchez Prado's *Strategic Occidentalism* (2018) offers perhaps the most direct intervention into the difference between the way Latin American literature is read in its contexts of origin and its exoticist reception in the Global North (Sánchez Prado 2018). The titular concept describes how contemporary authors manage those expectations from abroad – cannily drawing on two of the most impactful concepts in postcolonial criticism, Orientalism and strategic essentialism (Said 1978; Spivak 2009). A similar underlying tension informs Héctor Hoyos' *Beyond Bolaño* (2015), which demands that the worldliness of Latin American literature be understood not only in its reception abroad but through the concepts that authors themselves raise within their fictions (Hoyos 2015). Yet this group of South Asian readers occupies a distinct location from that of the readers Sánchez Prado, Hoyos, and others address. And the project they have used Latin American literature to undertake, regardless of its historical accuracy, merits examination.

13. However, it would be a mistake to follow Yogita Goyal's avowal of in the transparency of the Anglophone as an apolitical analytic category (or, indeed, her equally credulous faith in the transparently "good" politics inherent in the name "postcolonial") (Goyal 2019). Instead, most scholarship that embraces the Global Anglophone as its organizing term has done an admirable job of historicizing its meaning. Daniel DeWispelare and Rita Raley both take their cues from the renewed focus on language and accent promised by the "Anglophone," tying the term to the new forms of English and its imagined teleologies that emerged in the era of colonial expansion in the eighteenth and early nineteenth centuries (DeWispelare 2017; Raley 2000). From the late nineteenth and early twentieth centuries, Madhumita Lahiri and Marina Bilbija both tie the Anglophone productively to a type of white supremacy specific to the British colonial project and its aftermaths (Lahiri 2020; Bilbija

2019). While Bilbija raises this connection as a warning, however, Lahiri is hopeful that a reassessment of early Anglophone writing can wrest the term away from these anxieties and allow scholars to embrace its "elasticity" (Lahiri 2020, 23).
14. "Is par 'mukarrar' aur 'vah vah' ka shor buland hota hai. Yaha~n ghaḍı-ghaḍı aur qadam-qadam par aise hı aʿjube milte hai~n."

1 Transmigrant

1. "[M]ere paon ke sab rishte ek duje se jud jate hain / mere lafz daraxton ke gambad meñ kabūtar ban ke gaṭalne lagte hain / main apne sirhane bethe Neruda se kuch baten puchta hun."
2. So well-known is this tendency that it inspired the first serious book-length treatment of Neruda's writing – Amado Alonso's *Poesía y estilo de Pablo Neruda* (*The Poetry and Style of Pablo Neruda*) (1946) – as well as a novelty pamphlet by Francisco Velasco, *Diccionario Neruda: a través de sus metáforas* (*Neruda Dictionary: Through His Metaphors*) (1984) (Alonso 1979; Velasco 1984).
3. Indeed, having begun a project of tracing Neruda's reception among Hindi-medium poets, Vibha Maurya goes so far as to call him "the poet laureate of India" (Maurya 2016; Vibha Maurya, personal communication, January 29, 2019).
4. "[S]umhāre Pablo, kāvi Pablo . . . ." "Neruda ke nām par."
5. "[S]iyāsat aur ishq ke imtahān mein."
6. "Mutua y profunda correspondencia . . . entre el Yo y el no-yo."
7. Notice the echo of "delirious fantasy and frank realism" in the evocative Hindi title of the Vishnu Khare's edited collection, of which Satyarthi's memories of the poet's later visit are recorded: *Swapna Aur Yathārth Ka Srijan Sikhar Pablo Neruda* (*Dream and Reality of the Pinnacle of Creativity: Pablo Neruda*).
8. "Contadme todo, cadena a cadena, / eslabón a eslabón, y paso a paso."
9. Gabriel had published intermittently in the little magazines discussed in Chapter 2 and had also published a chapbook of poetry through the Calcutta Writers Workshop in 1968, also coediting a book of short stories the same year. She was discussed as part of a rising generation of Indian Anglophone poets in P. Lal's pathbreaking *Modern Indians Poetry in English: An Anthology & A Credo* (1971) yet subsequently all but disappeared. Her book *Thirteen Months of Sunshine* (1979) about Ethiopia suggests an ongoing engagement with South–South internationalism.
10. "[I] stirred my tea with English, / drank India down with a faint British accent, / . . . / Divided between two cultures, I spoke a language foreign even to my ears; / I diluted it in a glass of Scotch" (Ali n.d.).

11. The idea of poetic witness had long-standing personal significance to Ali. Many of his poems invoke his middle name "Shāhid." In his *ghazal*s, it functions as a *takhallus* – a kind of pen name that operates as an internal signature within oral poetry in South Asia. "They ask me to tell them what Shahid means: Listen, listen: / it means 'The Belovéd' in Persian, 'witness' in Arabic." As Ali's own political project as a speaker for Kashmir came into focus in the later 1990s, "beloved witness" crystalized as an epithet for him. It lives on as the title of one of his poetry collections, a forthcoming book of critical essays, and the name of his online archive (Ali 2009, 226).
12. Harleen Singh provides a critical description of this tendency. The 2012 film adaptation of the novel reinforces a 9/11-centric reading in part by relocating the Chilean publishing episode to Istanbul (Singh 2012). It is also worth noting that Hamid famously added the reference to 9/11 in a rewrite undertaken after having already finished the majority of the novel in 2001.
13. "Artefactos," "cosas."
14. In an interview, the archivists at La Chascona discussed the museum's strategies for placing artifacts in Neruda's houses. Javier Ormeño Bustos said that the curators have something of a "horror vacui" regarding these rooms. They want to fill them up in the "Neruda" style, either by shuffling around existing stuff or even by purchasing new things à la Neruda. He explained that although the museums are meant to evoke Neruda, as if he were living there, in reality the way he lived was very messy with things everywhere, while a museum needs to give people access and ability to move around freely (Javier Ormeño Bustos and Dario Oses Moya, personal communication, July 29, 2013).
15. "Verdaderamente evoque la presencia del Poeta en Valparaíso."
16. "Conocida es la fascinación que tuvo Neruda por coleccionar todo tipo de cosas."
17. "Este libro de fotografías está centrado en la relación mágica entre los objetos escogidos por el Nobel y los espacios que creó para ellos en cada una de sus casas-museo."
18. This absence of archival evidence has had a very clear impact on one specific area of Neruda scholarship: writings about his purported Burmese lover, Josie Bliss (Kantor 2014). Aside from the several poems she inspired, there is no other evidence that Bliss ever existed. Although Neruda called her any number of things, from "the most beautiful in Mandalay" ("la más bella de Mandalay") to "the evil one" ["maligna"], no one knows her real name (Neruda 2004, 62, 84). There are no photos of her, either. In an extension of the object-logic of the *casa-museos*, a 2013 retrospective of the Residencia period at his Santiago residence used a black and white photograph of Javanese mask – from Neruda's lost 1930s collection, naturally – to represent her face (Kantor 2014).

19. "Puede considerarse una gestación provocada por particulares experiencias personales, por la enajenadora estada en Oriente."
20. "El poeta no encuentra asideros, ni culturales ni sociales ni históricos, ninguna significación positivo para cubrir el vacío."
21. "Su poesía en Oriente no refleja otra cosa que la soledad."
22. In the interview, the archivists reflected on the museum's strategies for navigating the known and the unknown – how they know about certain objects and books but not necessarily about their context. Burma is a big hole, Dario Oses Moya agreed, although he recalled that we know Neruda had a woman ("mujer") there and she was a nightmare ("pesadilla"). Still, there is almost no correspondence. He suggested that there may be some held by Chile's Ministry of Foreign Relations (Ministerio de Relaciones Exteriores de Chile). He said that Neruda biographers Hernán Loyola and Edmundo Olivares Briones used these sources and noted that Loyola found other testimony about Burma during the time Neruda was there from other diplomats. It took me a moment to realize that he was referring to Loyola's use of George Orwell (Javier Ormeño Bustos and Dario Oses Moya, personal communication, July 29, 2013).
23. Thus, in Loyola's reading, the poem "Colección nocturna" ("Nocturnal Collection") is a reiteration of the French exoticist Pierre Loti's novel *Mon Frère Yves* (*My Brother Yves*) (1883) (Loyola 2006, 306). Loyola also draws heavily on Orwell's novel *Burmese Days* (1934), citing it at least a dozen times, including extended comparisons that run for three or four pages at a stretch (Loyola 2006, 329–332, 336–340, 342, 349, 352, 363). In the same vein, Feinstein understands Neruda's flight from Chile and subsequent "hellish" experience in Rangoon in terms of Arthur Rimbaud's poetry (Feinstein 2004, 52, 64). In Feinstein's and Loyola's accounts, Neruda's impressions of life in Ceylon follow the contours of Leonard Woolf's *The Village in the Jungle* (1913), a novel written during the latter's time as a colonial administrator for the British government (Feinstein 2004, 68; Loyola 2006, 391–394). If the cosmology of *Residencia I* seems to echo Buddhist thought, it is because Neruda was reading Arthur Schopenhauer or T. S. Eliot, not the fact that he was living in countries where Buddhism was the religion of the majority (Loyola 2006, 429).
24. "He leído en algunos ensayos sobre mi poesía que mi permanencia en Extremo Oriente influye en determinados aspectos de mi obra, especialmente en Residencia en la tierra … . Digo que me parece equivocado eso de la influencia."
25. "Aventureros occidentales, sin faltar americanos del Norte y del Sur … esa gente se llenaba la boca con el Dharma y el Yoga."

26. "Una grande y desventurada familia humana, sin destinar sitio en mi conciencia para sus ritos ni para sus dioses."
27. "Empapados de un pesimismo y angustia atroces."
28. "Algo muy uniforme, como una sola cosa comenzada y recomenzada, como eternamente ensayada sin exito."
29. "Extraño Budha hambriento, después de aquellos inútiles seis años de privación."
30. "Un violento vuelo comenzado desde hace muchos días y meses y siglos."
31. "Ay, que lo que soy siga existiendo y cesando de existir, / Y que mi obediencia se ordene con tales condiciones de hierro / Que el temblor de las muertes y de los nacimientos no conmueva / El profundo sitio que quiero reservar para mí eternamente. / Sea, pues, lo que soy, en alguna parte y en todo tiempo, / Establecido y asegurado y ardiente testigo, / Cuidadosamente destruyéndose y preservándose incesantemente, / Evidentemente empeñado en su deber original."
32. Poppies (*amapolas*), having appeared only once in all of Neruda's early poetry, crop up seemingly everywhere in the *Residencia* series. In one of the first book-length analyses of Neruda's poetry, Amado Alonso paid special attention to the symbolism of this potent flower, especially in its role as a representative of sleep. "This symbol is frequently associated with night or with dusk, suggesting the reign of sleep" ("Es frecuente asociar este símbolo con la noche o con el crepúsculo, sugiriendo ... el reinado del sueño") (Alonso 1979, 261). This is no accident, of course, since, as Alonso reminds us, the poppy is also known as the flower of sleep ("flor de adormidera") for its role as the base crop of opium. In 1927, when Neruda served there, Burma was one of the largest opium producers in the world (it remains so today).
33. "Cada uno dentro de un sueño diferente, como dentro de un vestido."
34. "Los negros de la Martinica," "los arabes," "los chinos," "los hindúes."
35. "Un vestido."
36. "No volví a los fumadores."
37. "Pablo duerme, se tira una caña de opio y despierta justamente para cumplir sus deberes oficiales."
38. "Ángel del sueño," "es el viento que agita los meses," "perfumado de frutos agudos." "un vino de color confuse," "un paso de polvoriento de vacas bramando."
39. "Extrañamente repulsivo y poderoso," the color of its smoke "caliginoso" and "lechoso."
40. "Sustancia" "alimento profético," "frutos blandos del cielo."
41. "Canasto negro."
42. "Uvas negras, inmensas, repletas."
43. "Galopa en la respiración y su paso es de beso."

Notes to Pages 53–62 197

44. "Guerreros."
45. "Reconozco a menudo sus guerreros, / sus piezas corroídas por el aire, sus diemensiones, / y su necesidad de espacio es tan violenta / que baja hasta mi corazón a buscarlo: / ... Yo oigo el sueño de viejos compañeros y mujeres amadas, / sueños cuyos latidos me quebrantan: / su material de alformbra piso en silencio, / su luze de amapola muerdo con delirio."
46. "Preguntaréis: ¿Y dónde están las lilas? / ¿Y la metafísica cubierta de amapolas?"
47. "Preguntaréis ¿por qué su poesía / no nos habla del sueño ... ?"
48. "¡Venid a ver la sangre por las calles!"
49. The trope of Neruda's "translation" or "plagiarism" of Tagore is raised frequently, and with good reason, among Indian writers. I discuss Tagore's early-twentieth-century circulation in Latin America in Chapter 4. Here it is sufficient to note that Neruda's engagement with Tagore, like his travel to India, is taken as a signal of reciprocity by Indian writers, a desire I discuss in Chapter 2.

2 Stranger

1. "Mi experiencia de india ha sido ... la extrañeza total. No la hostilidad (eso es español y mexicano) ni tampoco la indiferencia (a la sajona) sino ... no sé como decirlo. La coexistencia – la promiscuidad, el sentirte rodeado de una vegetación humana que no te conoce y a la que no conocerás nunca" (Paz 2008, 26). The translation of the abstract noun "extrañeza total" (total estrangement) into the more concrete "total stranger" is a bit of poetic license here.
2. "Un lugar paradisíaco y, en aquella época, solitario. Cuál no sería mi sopresa cuando, un año después, me enteré de que Pablo Neruda había vivido en ese lugar trienta años antes y de que, según le cuenta un amigo en una carta, lo había encontrado abominable" (Paz 1995, 29).
3. "En el caso de mis tres libros los dos significados se mezclan: fueron escritos en los caminos de la India, los de la geografía y los de la historia, los del arte y los del pensamiento."
4. Paz later claims that all of *Vislumbres de la India*, his 1995 memoir and the most frequently cited and studied of his meditations on India, is but a footnote to *Ladera este*, which is probably the least studied of these texts. "What I lived and felt during the six years I spent in India is in my book of poems *Ladera este*, and in a short prose book, *El mono gramático*. A book of poems is a sort of diary in which the author tries to preserve certain exceptional moments, whether joyful or unfortunate. In that sense, this book is nothing more than a long footnote to the poems of Eastern slope. It is their context – not vital, but intellectual" (Paz 1998, 32, emphasis added). Notice here the invocation of the "diary" as a generic marker for *Ladera este*. "Diario" (diary) or "bitácora" (ship's log/daily record) appears in the titles of several other

Latin American texts about South Asia, including Agusto d'Halmar's *Nirvana: (cuaderno de bitácora) viajes por occidente, oriente y extremo oriente* (*Nirvana: (Ship's Log) Travels in the West, Middle East, and Far East*) (1935); Severo Sarduy's "Diario Indio" ("Indian Diary") section of *Cobra* (1972); and Cantú Zegers's *Bitácora* (*Ship's Log*) (1990).

5. "Estoy aquí / no sé es dónde / No la tierra / el tiempo / en sus manos vacías me sostiene ... Lejanías / *pasos de un peregrino son errante.*" While the meaning of "errante" here is primarily physical, errantry has to do, etymologically, with error and the mental wandering mind that produces misunderstanding. This idea of wandering as potentially leading to error resonates with the connection made by many writers in both India and the Americas about the enduring psychic connection established by Columbus' original disorientation, that of having mistaken the Caribbean for India.

6. Ayesha Ramachandran explores the relationship between the baroque conception of conquest and the current globalized world, including Luís de Camões's *Os Lusíadas* (*The Lusiads: Or, The Discovery of India: an Epic Poem*) (1572). *Os Lusíadas* is a major intertext for *Las soledades* (Ramachandran 2015). Eric Hayot's book about literary worlds also offers a chapter on the age of exploration, though he arguably neglects the important and well-circulated Iberian contributions to these discourses (Hayot 2016). Like Hayot, Lisa Lowe consistently places the origin of maritime planetarity and the continental "intimacies" of colonialism significantly later, which allows British, and not Iberian, colonialism to be the foundational form (Lowe 2015). In particular, Lowe manages a slippage where the two American continents exist in an uneasy intimacy as her single "fourth" continent, former Iberian holdings slipping in and out of focus as it suits a historical argument that centers the Anglophone world (Lowe 2015).

7. These literary experiments have tended to be classed as "Orientalist." Indeed, "Latin American Orientalism" has been the only avenue through which India becomes a legible place in the study of Hispanophone literature (Kushigan 1991; Tinajero 2004; Taboada 2006; Vilches 2008; López-Calvo 2010; Siskind 2014). While these representations are indeed problematic, the exclusive focus on Orientalism tends to dismiss or subordinate the other political projects inherent in Paz's writing. In place of this kind of symptomatic reading, I follow Paz's explicit investment in the surface, in literalism, to show surprising solidarities lurking within otherwise questionable representational strategies. These politics manifest in Paz's formalist experimentation, especially baroque ekphrasis and concrete poetry, and it is precisely these potentially exoticist qualities of "estrangement" that most appeal to the Indian poets who read him.

8. "Un sistema de espejos que poco a poco han ido revelando otro texto."

9. "Un tejido de presencias que no esconden ningún secreto. Exterioridad sin más."

10. "Las pirámides escalones de Mesoamérica y a la de ciertos templos de India."

11. "Al debate de las avispas / la dialéctica de los monos / gorjeos de las estadísticas opone / (alta llama rosa / hecha de piedra y aire y pájaros / tiempo en reposo sobre el agua) / la arquitectura del silencio." The lines of the poem in the photograph are from a different translation of the text.
12. "Hijo de Babur, el conquistador de la India, el emperador Humayún fue el padre del gran Akbar. La familia decendía de Timur o Tamerlán, el Tamburlaine de Marlowe, el Tamurbeque de Clavijo. En las cercanías del mausoleo de Humayún se encuentra, o se encontraba, uno de esos centros de estudio de lo que llaman los economistas y los sociólogos el 'desarrollo,' muy concurrido por funcionarios indios y 'expertos' extranjeros."
13. "Como en algunos pasajes aparecen palabras y alusiones a personas, ideas y cosas que podrían extrañar al lector no familiarizado con esa región del mundo, varios amigos me aconsejaron incluir unas cuantas notas que aclarasen esas obscuridades."
14. "[Tengo] el temor (¿la esperanza?) de que estas notas, lejos de disiparlos, aumenten los enigmas."
15. This affiliation was reflected in the older, more established and ideologically uniform character of its South Asian contributors. Even Faiz, a writer for *Lotus* and ultimately its editor, complained that the journal did not publish contemporary writing and that the standard between original and republished works was uneven (Faiz 1970, 134). A close consideration of the style promoted by *Lotus* reveals a politically motivated rejection of the kind of experimental writing favored by the *sathottari*s.
16. The Hungryalists group was another faction of iconoclastic poets in the 1960s. To an extent, the group's own writing has been overshadowed by their association with Allen Ginsberg, who became their aesthetic and, later, legal champion in the West (Singh 2020). Displaying some of its characteristic irreverence, Thayil claims that the collective's name is actually rendered incorrectly: it was meant to be the "Hung Realists" (Thayil 2017).
17. Swaminathan's translation of "To the Painter Swaminathan" also appeared in *Dialogue India* in 1973 (Paz 1973b).
18. The publisher of the *Aldebaran Review*, Noh Directions Press, also published writing by Mehrotra, suggesting that it circulated at least a little among Indian audiences.
19. "La limpidez / (Quizá valga la pena / Escribirlo sobre la limpieza. De esta hoja) / No es límpida: / [. . .] / (Los empleados / Municipales lavan la sangre / En la plaza de los sacrificios.) / Mira ahora, / Manchada / Antes de haber dicho algo / Que valga la pena, / La limpidez."

3 Displacee

1. Indeed, the disproportionate interest that South Asian Muslim authors have shown to the Latin American countershelf may emerge, in part, from this existing habit of affiliation, or even from their frequent failure to adequately differentiate between Hispanophone literature from Latin America and its counterpart on the Iberian peninsula.
2. In the same letter, Jusawalla bemoans the state of Latin American literature: "Didn't you find the latest [García] Márquez disappointing? I think he's played the same trick once too often" (Jussawalla 1995).
3. Thanks to Marci Kwon for helping me read the formal register of this image.
4. The common notion of an idealized al-Andalus was brought into prominence in the Western, English-speaking world by Washington Irving's *Tales from Alambra* (1832). Maria Rosa Menocal provides an overview that promulgates the legend of *convivencia*, a term pioneered by Americo Castro in 1948 (Menocal 2002; Castro cited in Wolf 2009). Darío Fernández-Morera paints a much more negative picture of the religious and political harmony of the period (Fernández-Morera 2016). And Atef Laouyene makes a very pointed critique of Andalusian nostalgia among contemporary Arab Muslims as a justification for terrorist violence in the present (Laouyene 2007).
5. He also mentions, but does not analyze, Tariq Ali's *Shadows of the Pomegranate Tree*, which I discuss later in this chapter.
6. While only Minoli Salgado makes the palimpsest the explicit topic of her study of *The Moor's Last Sigh*, the meaning of layering and allegory are a leitmotif for scholarship on the novel (Salgado 2007). Nicole Thiara, for example, writes insightfully that "the palimpsest is the defining image" through which Rushdie construes secularism as a spatial and temporal layer papering over the Indian nation's deeper commitment to Hindu majoritarianism (Thiara 2007, 27). This relationship between secularism and layering is also noted by Caroline Herbert and Jill Didur, while for Paul Cantor the palimpsest is a metaphor for the much more general idea of "culture" (Cantor 1997; Didur 2004; Herbert 2012). While most of the analyses in this line praise Rushdie's purportedly unique symbolic innovation in the turn to medieval Spain, there is a significant subset of highly critical readings of the same gesture. Ironically, these denunciations equally rely on the idea that the turn to al-Andalus is historically unprecedented within South Asia, tying it instead to a set of European representations that are both ideologically and aesthetically distinct. Thus, Laouyene denounces *The Moor's Last Sigh* as openly and exclusively appealing to a Western reader's romantic nostalgia (Laouyene 2007). Similarly, in her eagerness to identify the cover design of *The Moor's Last Sigh* as Orientalist exotica (which it no doubt is), Ursula Kluwick misses the very obvious way in which the layering of

the Arab Rider over the mysterious face of an Indian woman precisely invokes the palimpsestic painting produced by Aurora in the middle of the novel and deconstructed by her son, the protagonist, in its final pages (Kluwick 2011).
7. "Arabī shah savār."
8. "Hukūmat," "zulmat-e Yūrup."
9. "Kisi aur zamāne ke khawāb."
10. "Jin kī lahū kī tufail āj bhī hain andalusī / khush-dil-o-garm-ikhtalāt, sādah-o-raushan-jabīn / āj bhi us des men ām hai chasm-e gazāl / aur nigāhon ke tīr āj bhi hain dil nashīn."
11. "Khūn-e Musalman ka amīn."
12. "Azād tarjuma." Shadab Zeest Hashmi replicates this countershelf gesture to the deep Muslim past in *The Baker of Tarifa* (2010) (Hashmi 2010).
13. "Pardes mein nā-sabūr."
14. "Momin ke jahān ki had nahin hai / momin ka maqām har kahin hai."
15. It is no coincidence that Sharar's story revolves around the appropriate locus of patriarchal control for an ethnically mixed woman. British accusations of decadence directly attacked Muslim masculinity – part of a larger project of construing India as feminized and, in the immortal words of Gayatri Spivak, "white men saving brown women from brown men" (Spivak 1988, 297). Unsurprisingly, responses to these accusations were also deeply bound up with patriarchal power. As Zaman reminded me, this is but one area in which we might examine the investment in Latin America and its literature as also playing off fantasies of masculine power for a corpus of predominantly male authors (Taymiya R. Zaman, personal communication, May 6, 2019).
16. "Wazir, āp hut jaiye. Malka Victoria tashrīf lā rahi hai!"
17. "Mezquitas."
18. This seems to echo the later use of "Indian" as the portable allegory for colonialism's vision of its others. Gayatri Gopinath cites Jodi Byrd describing the recapitulation of the category of "Indians" in the United States as a way of reimporting logics where Indians are infinitely displaceable peoples encountered everywhere colonists wish to make the frontier conquerable (Gopinath 2018, 18).
19. In 1965, Paz writes to his American translator, Lysander Kemp, that he is considering a lecture series on baroque México, including on the nun Sor Juana, with the caveat, "I doubt it would be of interest" ("dudo que interese") (Paz 1965).
20. "No sea exagerado ver en la conquista y evangelización de América una empresa en la que el temple musulmán no fue menos determinante que la fé católica. Cualquiera que haya vivido en la India percibe inmediatamente la semejanzas y las diferencias entre la dominación islámica, la portuguesa, y la inglesa.

Musulmanes y portugueses destruyeron los templos hindúes con la misma furia con que Cortés derribó los ídolos del Gran Teocalli; sobre esas ruinas y a veces con las mismas piedras, levantaron soberbias mezquitas y catedrales" (Paz 1983, 47).

21. There are slightly, tellingly distinct phrasings between Paz's original and Margaret Sayers Penden's translation: Paz's original – "cualquiera que haya vivido en la India percibe inmediatamente" – is best rendered as "anyone who has [ever] lived in India," which suggests Paz's positionality much more precisely than "anyone who lives in India" (Paz 1983, 47; Paz 1990, 28).
22. Ali wrote the introduction for the reissued book in 1993, shortly before his death.
23. Although outside the ambit of this argument, this question of historiography also extends to narrations of each field. If names like Gayatri Spivak and Edward Said ring loud in John Beverley's 1999 study of Latin American cultural production, *Subalternity and Representation*, they are deafening in their absence from Nelson Maldonato-Torres' field-assessment "Thinking through the Decolonial Turn" just over a decade later in 2011 (Beverley 1999; Maldonato-Torres 2011).
24. "¿De qué manera se relacionó o se debió relacionar el subalterno latinoamericano con el sudasiático? ¿Por que los subalternistas sudasiáticos ignoran, en general, olímpicamente a sus pares latinoamericanos?"

4 Pilgrim

1. "Inesperada," "inhabitual," "inadvertida."
2. The debates between social realism and nonrealist modes echo the predominant polemic in Latin American letters immediately prior to the emergence of the "nueva novela latinoamericana" ("New Latin American Novel") of the 1960s "boom" – indeed, precisely what made that *novela* so "new."
3. Thus, among South Asian audiences, the adoption of magical realism was perceived to distinguish "globally" oriented – and thus politically suspect – South Asian authors from those who wrote in English but were read primarily within the subcontinent. Two writers of the latter type, Vijay and Kavery Nambisan, lamented that "if the books we write don't suit that stereotype, that fixed notion, they don't get published in the West" (Nambisan and Nambisan 2005).
4. Brennan actually inverts the meaning of this episode. "Inevitably and by a sleight-of-hand, untruth in a more unthreatening literary sense gradually comes to the fore: namely, 'Latin America as the home of anti-realism,' a feature it is supposed to share with India (according to one of the book's

anecdotes) through the agency of Rabindranath Tagore" (Brennan 1989, 65). It is clear that this is a basic misreading of the scene, in line with the overall casual and instrumentalist use of the travelogue in Brennan's argument. But further misunderstanding emerges from an apparent unfamiliarity with the distinct kinds of world-literary relationships and values that Tagore would have stood for in India, in Latin America, and globally through the Nobel Prize.

5. Ghose wrote to Berger in 1990: "My own news is worse than ever. I finished the Triple Mirror novel last March and sent it to my agents in London and New York. The former was too busy to read it for two months and the latter did not even acknowledge it, and then, three months after I'd delivered the book, both of them wrote to say they thought it unreadable and that they could not represent it. After having had my previous novel rejected by twenty or more publishers I found myself in the novel situation of being rejected by my agent" (Ghose 1990b).

6. Ghose later wrote of the Nobel: "I was delighted to see that for a change the Nobel Prize has gone to a good writer, the wonderful Octavio Paz. As usual, there's a political element to the award. A few days before it was announced I'd said to Helena that since it had been given in recent years to writers in Africa and Europe, it was now likely to be given to a Latin American and that among them I thought Paz was the best candidate. And so it was" (Ghose 1990c).

7. "Quieto / no en la rama / en el aire / no en el aire / en el instante / el colibrí."

8. "Al ver de nuevo las esculturas del periodo Pallava ... me pareció evidente un parentesco con las obras mayas. No se trata, por supuesto, de influencias ni de contactos históricos ..., sino de una misma concepción del espacio y de la forma, una visión estética que se nutre en las mismas fuentes ... dos fotos de unos gemelos, cada uno en un paisaje distinto y vestido de manera diferente."

9. Several analyses of Rushdie's *Grimus* (1975) suggest a certain canniness on Rushdie's part where the transition toward magical realism in *Midnight's Children* is merely a saleable veneer on top of a more juvenile or overtly commercial interest in Fantasy or Sci-Fi writing (Brennan 1989; Bahri 2003; Brouillette 2007).

5 Revenant

1. "La novela lleva a su punto extremo un principio que había sido apuntado en los Cien años de soledad ... : el de un tiempo cíclico que encadena un fin con un comienzo anterior."

2. "El primer capítulo ... parte de la muerte del patriarca en el palacio semidestruido y devorado por las vacas y los gallinazos, para proceder a la reconstrucción de un ciclo ya transcurrido de su existencia."

3. "Pertenece a su estirpe."

4. William Maxwell coins the term "ghostreaders" to describe FBI surveillance of Black writers and underscore their impact on writerly style (Maxwell 2015).
5. Even more than *Midnight's Children*, *Shame* is a direct descendent from *Cien años de soledad*. To take just a brief sampling, the novel begins and ends within the labyrinthine ancestral house of the main character, Omar Khayam. Nishapur echoes earlier gothic residences including the Buendía ranch and Sutpen's Hundred. So, too, its character types. This is most obvious in the intellectually simple but supernaturally powerful beauty: Sofia Zenobia in *Shame* is clearly indebted to Remedios the Beauty in *Cién años de soledad*. However, *Shame* also includes the growing and shrinking bon vivant Omar Khayyam Shakil who echoes the similarly shape-shifting Aureliano Segundo. The ice-queen Bilquís, wife of Zia-stand-in Hyder and mother of Sophia Zenobia, closely tracks with Aureliano Segundo's wife Fernanda, while, in her obsession with sewing her own shroud, sometimes also appearing as the virgin aunt, Amaranta. These latter female characters, in their injured dignity, chilly chastity, and obstinate endurance, also take something from Judith Sutpen and Miss Rosa in the earliest generation. An equally long but totally distinct list of comparisons between the two novels appears in Timothy Brennan's *Salman Rushdie and the Third World* (1989), but its sole purpose is to underscore Rushdie's inappropriate and cynical attachment to literary fantasy (Brennan 1989, 66).
6. In fact, the tension between Shigri's privileged background and his crass masculine bravado trace what Laura Brueck identifies as transitions in the vernacular detective fiction traditions of South Asia – the shift from asexual gentleman detectives of the early independence period to the uniformed anti-heroes closer to the present (Brueck 2020). When it is revealed, late in the novel, that Shigri and Obaid are both led toward their respective attempts on Zia's life in part because of a romance between them, Hanif can be seen to be playing with detective tropes in which the protagonist is drawn toward a life of crime because of his involvement with a femme fatale (Brueck 2020).

Epilogue

1. "My reading interests stretched out in my late teens to encompass Hemingway and Tolstoy and [García] Márquez" (Hamid 2015, 103).

References

Aboul-Ela, Hosam M. 2020. "William Faulkner and the World Literature Debate: Is the Radical in Radical Form the Radical in Radical Politics?" In *A Companion to World Literature*, edited by Ken Seigneurie et al., pp. 1–10. New York: Wiley.
Adiga, Aravind. 2008. *The White Tiger*. New York: Simon & Shuster.
Agosín, Marjorie. 1986. *Pablo Neruda*. Translated by Lorraine Roses. Boston, MA: Twayne.
Ahmad, Aijaz. 1987. "Jameson's Rhetoric of Otherness and the 'National Allegory.'" *Social Text* (17): 3–25. https://doi.org/10.2307/466475.
———. 1992. *In Theory: Classes, Nations, Literatures*. London: Verso.
Ali, Agha Shahid. n.d. "The Editor Revisited." http://sundeepdougal.tripod.com/ali.html.
———. 1997. "*In Light of India*. By Octavio Paz. Translated from the Spanish by Eliot Weinberger. Harcourt Brace: 210 Pp., $22." *Los Angeles Times*, March 30, 1997. www.latimes.com/archives/la-xpm-1997-03-30-bk-43411-story.html.
———. 2000. *The Country Without a Post Office: Poems 1991–1995*. Delhi: Orient Blackswan.
———. 2009. *The Veiled Suite: The Collected Poems*. New York: W. W. Norton & Co.
Ali, Ahmed. 1994. *Twilight in Delhi: A Novel*. New York: New Directions.
Ali, Tariq. 1992. *Shadows of the Pomegranate Tree*. London: Chatto & Windus.
———. 2007. *The Leopard and the Fox: A Pakistani Tragedy*. London: Seagull Books.
Alonso, Amado. 1979. *Poesía y estilo de Pablo Neruda* [*The Poetry and Style of Pablo Neruda*]. Barcelona: EDHASA.
Alter, Robert. 1999. "*Midnight's Children* and *Tristram Shandy*." In *Rushdie's Midnight's Children: A Book of Readings*, edited by Meenakshi Mukherjee, pp. 112–115. Delhi: Pencraft International.
Anam, Nasia. 2019. "Introduction: Forms of the Global Anglophone." *Post45*, February 22, 2019. http://post45.research.yale.edu/2019/02/introduction-forms-of-the-global-anglophone/.
Anasuya, Shreya Ila. 2018. "Writing Is a Solitary Business, but It Doesn't Have to Be an Exercise in Loneliness." *The Wire*, April 24, 2018. https://thewire.in/books/tanuj-solanki-interview.
Anjaria, Ulka. 2012. *Realism in the Twentieth-Century Indian Novel: Colonial Difference and Literary Form*. Cambridge: Cambridge University Press.

2015. "Madness and Discontent: The Realist Imaginary in South Asian Literature." *THAAP Journal* 4 (1): 20–30.

2019. *Reading India Now: Contemporary Formations in Literature and Popular Culture*. Philadelphia, PA: Temple University Press.

Apter, Emily S. 2013. *Against World Literature: On the Politics of Untranslatability*. London: Verso.

Arellano, Jerónimo. 2010. "Minor Affects and New Realisms in Latin America." *Journal of Iberian and Latin American Studies* 16 (2–3): 91–106. https://doi.org/10.1080/14701847.2010.535652.

Armenti, Peter. 2015. "How the Library of Congress Helped Get Pablo Neruda's Poetry Translated into English." *From the Catbird Seat: Poetry & Literature at the Library of Congress*, July 31, 2015. https://blogs.loc.gov/catbird/2015/07/how-the-library-of-congress-helped-get-pablo-nerudas-poetry-translated-into-english/.

Armillas-Tiseyra, Magalí. 2019. *The Dictator Novel: Writers and Politics in the Global South*. Evanston, IL: Northwestern University Press.

Ashcroft, Bill, Gareth Griffiths, and Helen Tiffin. 2002. *The Empire Writes Back: Theory and Practice in Post-Colonial Literatures*. 2nd ed. London: Routledge.

Asif, Manan Ahmed. 2016. *A Book of Conquest: The Chachnama and Muslim Origins in South Asia*. Cambridge, MA: Harvard University Press.

Aubry, Timothy. 2018. *Guilty Aesthetic Pleasures*. Cambridge, MA: Harvard University Press.

Avelar, Idelber. 1999. *The Untimely Present: Postdictatorial Latin American Fiction and the Task of Mourning*. Durham, NC: Duke University Press.

Azeb, Sophia. 2019. "Crossing the Saharan Boundary: Lotus and the Legibility of Africanness." *Research in African Literatures* 50 (3): 91–115.

Bahri, Deepika. 2003. *Native Intelligence: Aesthetics, Politics, and Postcolonial Literature*. Minneapolis: University of Minnesota Press.

2017. *Postcolonial Biology: Psyche and Flesh after Empire*. Minneapolis: University of Minnesota Press.

Bal, Mieke. 2006. *A Mieke Bal Reader*. Chicago, IL: University of Chicago Press.

Bandopadhyay, Subhro. 2018. *Sumar Sal*. Translated by Subhro Bandopadhyay. Madrid: El Sastre de Apollinaire.

Bassnett, Susan, and Harish Trivedi. 1999. "Introduction: Of Colonies, Cannibals, and Vernaculars." In *Post-Colonial Translation: Theory and Practice*, edited by Susan Bassnett and Harish Trivedi, pp. 1–18. London: Routledge.

Batty, Nancy E. 1985. "The Art of Suspense: Rushdie's 1001 (Mid-)Nights." *ARIEL: A Review of International English Literature* 18 (3): 49–65.

Bell, Michael. 2010. "García Márquez, Magical Realism and World Literature." In *The Cambridge Companion to Gabriel García Márquez*, edited by Philip Swanson, pp. 179–195. New York: Cambridge University Press.

Benjamin, Walter. 1968. "Unpacking My Library." In *Illuminations: Essays and Reflections*, edited by Hannah Arendt, translated by Harry Zohn, pp. 59–67. New York: Shocken Books.

2009. *The Origin of German Tragic Drama*. Translated by John Osborne. Reprint ed. London: Verso.
Betts, Reginald Dwayne. 2017. "Borrowed Words: The Use of Quotations and Italics in the Ghazals of Agha Shahid Ali." In *Mad Heart Be Brave: Essays on the Poetry of Agha Shahid Ali*, edited by Kazim Ali, pp. 163–169. Ann Arbor: University of Michigan Press.
Beverley, John. 1999. *Subalternity and Representation: Arguments in Cultural Theory*. Durham, NC: Duke University Press.
2008. *Essays on the Literary Baroque in Spain and Spanish America*. Woodbridge, UK: Tamesis.
Bhabha, Homi K. 1984. "Of Mimicry and Man: The Ambivalence of Colonial Discourse." *October* 28: 125–33. https://doi.org/10.2307/778467.
Bhagat-Kennedy, Monika. n.d. "Seeking Indian Interpreters to the West: Hindu Heroism in Sarath Kumar Ghosh's *Indian Nights' Entertainments: The Trials of Narayan Lal*."
Bilbija, Marina. 2019. "What's in a Name? The Global Anglophone, the Anglosphere, and the English-Speaking Peoples." *Post45*, February 22, 2019. https://post45.org/2019/02/whats-in-a-name-the-global-anglophone-the-anglosphere-and-the-english-speaking-peoples/.
Bolaño, Roberto. 1998. *Los Detectives Salvajes*. Barcelona: Editorial Anagrama.
Borges, Jorge Luis. 1993. *Ficciones* [*Fictions*]. Translated by John Sturrock. New York: A. A. Knopf.
Boullosa, Carmen. 2007. "Bolaño in Mexico." *The Nation*, April 5, 2007. www.thenation.com/article/bolantildeo-mexico/.
Braz, Albert. 2015. "9/11, 9/11: Chile and Mohsin Hamid's The Reluctant Fundamentalist." *Canadian Review of Comparative Literature/Revue Canadienne de Littérature Comparée* 42 (3): 241–256.
Brennan, Timothy. 1989. *Salman Rushdie and the Third World: Myths of the Nation*. New York: St. Martin's Press.
Bronstein, Michaela. 2018. *Out of Context: The Uses of Modernist Fiction*. New York: Oxford University Press.
Brouillette, Sarah. 2007. *Postcolonial Writers in the Global Literary Marketplace*. Basingstoke, UK: Palgrave Macmillan.
Brueck, Laura. 2014. *Writing Resistance: The Rhetorical Imagination of Hindi Dalit Literature*. New York: Columbia University Press.
2020. "Bhais Behaving Badly: Vernacular Masculinities in Hindi Detective Novels." *South Asian Popular Culture* 18 (1): 29–46. https://doi.org/10.1080/14746689.2020.1733810.
Bulson, Eric. 2016. *Little Magazine, World Form*. New York: Columbia University Press.
Cantor, Paul S. 1997. "Tales of the Alhambra: Rushdie's Use of Spanish History in The Moor's Last Sigh." *Studies in the Novel* 29 (3): 323–41.
Cardone, Inés María. 2003. *Los Amores de Neruda*. Santiago: Plaza & Janés.
Carpentier, Alejo. 1995a. "On the Marvelous Real in America." In *Magical Realism: Theory, History, Community*, edited by Lois Parkinson Zamora

and Wendy B. Faris, translated by Tanya Huntington and Lois Parkinson Zamora, pp. 75–88. Durham,NC: Duke University Press.
   1995b. "The Baroque and the Marvelous Real." In *Magical Realism: Theory, History, Community*, edited by Lois Parkinson Zamora and Wendy B. Faris, translated by Tanya Huntington and Lois Parkinson Zamora, pp. 89–108. Durham, NC: Duke University Press.
Casanova, Pascale. 2004. *The World Republic of Letters*. Translated by Malcolm DeBevoise. Cambridge, MA: Harvard University Press.
Césaire, Aimé. 1997. *Une Tempête [A Tempest]*. Paris: Points French.
Chakravorty, Mrinalini. 2014. *In Stereotype: South Asia in the Global Literary Imaginary*. New York: Columbia University Press.
   2017. "No Future for South Asia: Tagore's Universality and the Refusal of Geopolitics." *South Asian Review* 38 (3): 79–89. https://doi.org/10.1080/02759527.2017.12023350.
Chaudhuri, Amit. 2005. "Introduction." In Arun Kolatakar, *Jejuri*. New York: New York Review of Books.
Chaudhury, Malay Roy. 1965. "Letter." *El Corno Emplumado 14*, April 1965. Open Door Archive.
Cheah, Pheng. 2016. *What Is a World? On Postcolonial Literature as World Literature*. Durham, NC: Duke University Press.
Chitre, Dilip Parameshwar. 1970. "Correspondence." *Quest*.
Cohn, Deborah N. 1997. "'He Was One of Us': The Reception of William Faulkner and the U.S. South by Latin American Authors." *Comparative Literature Studies* 34 (2): 149–169.
   2006. "A Tale of Two Translation Programs: Politics, the Market, and Rockefeller Funding for Latin American Literature in the United States during the 1960s and 1970s." *Latin American Research Review* 41 (2): 139–164.
   2012. *The Latin American Literary Boom and U.S. Nationalism during the Cold War*. Nashville, TN: Vanderbilt University Press.
Coleman, Alexander. 1972. "Two Latin American Poets and an Antipoet." *New York Times*, May 7, 1972. www.nytimes.com/1972/05/07/archives/selected-poems-by-pablo-neruda-edited-by-nathaniel-tarn-translated.html.
Connell, Liam. 1998. "Discarding Magic Realism: Modernism, Anthropology, and Critical Practice." *ARIEL: A Review of International English Literature* 29 (2): 95–110.
"CONTRA'66." 1967, June. Asia Art Archive. https://aaa.org.hk/en/collection/search/archive/gulammohammed-sheikh-archive-contra66/object/contra66-number-5-6.
Coppola, Carlo. 2018. *Urdu Poetry, 1935–1970: The Progressive Episode*. Karachi: Oxford University Press.
Coronil, Fernando. 2008. "Elephants in the Americas? Latin American Postcolonial Studies and Global Decolonization." In *Coloniality at Large: Latin America and the Postcolonial Debate*, edited by Mabel Moraña, Enrique D. Dussel, and Carlos A. Jáuregui, pp. 396–416. Durham, NC: Duke University Press.

Cortés, Hernán. 2012. *Segunda Carta de Relación y Otros Textos*. Buenos Aires: Corregidor.
Costa, René de. 1979. *The Poetry of Pablo Neruda*. Cambridge: Harvard University Press.
Cronin, Richard. 1987. "The Indian English Novel: Kim and Midnight's Children." *MFS Modern Fiction Studies* 33 (2): 201–213. https://doi.org/10.1353/mfs.0.1331.
Damrosch, David. 2003. *What Is World Literature?* Princeton, NJ: Princeton University Press.
Das, Sisir Kumar. 2001. *Indian Ode to the West Wind: Studies in Literary Encounters*. Delhi: Pencraft International.
Deb, Siddhartha. 2015. "Foreward: On Robert Bolaño." In *Roberto Bolaño, a Less Distant Star: Critical Essays*, edited by Ignacio López-Calvo, pp. ix–xxi. New York: Palgrave Macmillan.
Derrida, Jacques. 1980. *Of Grammatology*. Translated by Gayatri Chakravorty Spivak. Baltimore, MD: Johns Hopkins University Press.
Desai, Anita. 1978. "Correspondence." *Indian Literary Review*, October 1978. British Library.
   2000. *Diamond Dust: Stories*. Boston, MA: Mariner Books.
Desai, Gaurav. 2011. "Between Indigeneity and Diaspora: Questions from a Scholar Tourist." *Interventions* 13 (1): 53–66. https://doi.org/10.1080/1369801X.2011.545577.
DeWispelare, Daniel. 2017. *Multilingual Subjects: On Standard English, Its Speakers, and Others in the Long Eighteenth Century*. Philadelphia: University of Pennsylvania Press.
Didur, Jill. 2004. "Secularism beyond the East/West Divide: Literary Reading, Ethics, and The Moor's Last Sigh." *Textual Practice* 18 (4): 541–562. https://doi.org/10.1080/0950236042000287426.
Djagalov, Rossen. 2020. *From Internationalism to Postcolonialism: Literature and Cinema between the Second and the Third Worlds*. Montreal, QC: McGill-Queen's University Press.
dougald, david. 1969a. "A Page from 'Mexico City Sutras' by David-Dougald." *Tornado*. British Library.
   1969b. "From Mexico City Sutras." Aldebaran Review. University of California, Berkeley Bancroft Archive.
Dussel, Enrique D. 1992. *1492: El Encubrimiento Del Otro: Hacia El Origen Del "Mito de La Modernidad": Conferencias de Frankfurt, Octubre de 1992* [*1492: The Concealment of the Other: Towards the Origin of the "Myth of the Other": Frankfurt Conferences, October 1992*]. Santafé de Bogotá: Ediciones Antropos.
Eaton, Natasha. 2013. *Mimesis across Empires: Artworks and Networks in India, 1765–1860*. Durham, NC: Duke University Press.
Echenique Guzman, Juan. 1990a. "Letter to Jose Cruz Covarrubias," October 4, 1990. Fundación Pablo Neruda.
   1990b. "Letter to Jose Cruz Covarrubias," November 29, 1990. Fundación Pablo Neruda.

Elam, J. Daniel. 2020. *World Literature for the Wretched of the Earth: Anticolonial Aesthetics, Postcolonial Politics*. New York: Fordham University Press.
FACT: Fertilizers And Chemicals, Travancore, Ltd. 1967. "If Leaves of Grass Grow Pale." *Poetry India*.
Faiz, Faiz Ahmad. 1970. "On Some Poems." *Lotus: Afro-Asian Writings*, October 1970.
  1973. *Safarnāmāh-e Kyūbā [A Cuban Travelogue]*. Lahore: National Publishing House.
Faris, Wendy B. 1995. "Scheherazade's Children: Magical Realism and Postmodern Fiction." In *Magical Realism: Theory, History, Community*, edited by Lois Parkinson Zamora and Wendy B. Faris, pp. 163–190. Durham, NC: Duke University Press.
Feinstein, Adam. 2004. *Pablo Neruda: A Passion for Life*. New York: Bloomsbury.
Feldman, Leah. 2020. "Global Souths: Toward a Materialist Poetics of Alignment." *Boundary 2* 47 (2): 199–225. https://doi.org/10.1215/01903659-8193326.
Fernández-Morera, Darío. 2016. *The Myth of the Andalusian Paradise: Muslims, Christians, and Jews under Islamic Rule in Medieval Spain*. Wilmington, DE: ISI Books.
Fernández Retamar, Roberto. 1989. *Caliban and Other Essays*. Minneapolis: University of Minnesota Press.
Finlayson, Clarence. 1969. *Antología [de] Clarence Finlayson [Clarence Finlayson Anthology]*. Santiago: Editorial Andrés Bello.
Fisher, Philip. 1998. *Wonder, the Rainbow, and the Aesthetics of Rare Experiences*. Cambridge, MA: Harvard University Press.
Fisk, Gloria. 2008. "Putting Tragedy to Work for the Polis: The Rhetoric of Pity and Terror, before and after Modernity." *New Literary History* 39 (4): 891–902.
  2018. *Orhan Pamuk and the Good of World Literature*. New York: Columbia University Press.
Fraser, Nancy. 1990. "Rethinking the Public Sphere: A Contribution to the Critique of Actually Existing Democracy." *Social Text* (25/26): 56–80. https://doi.org/10.2307/466240.
Friedman, Susan Stanford. 2015. *Planetary Modernisms: Provocations on Modernity across Time*. New York: Columbia University Press.
Fuchs, Barbara. 2011. *Exotic Nation*. Philadelphia: University of Pennsylvania Press.
Gabriel, M. C. 1973. "Pablo Neruda." *Vrishchik* 4 (3): n.p.
Gamal, Ahmed. 2013. "The Global and the Postcolonial in Post-Migratory Literature." *Journal of Postcolonial Writing* 49 (5): 596–608.
Gandhi, Leela. 2006. *Affective Communities: Anticolonial Thought and the Politics of Friendship*. New Delhi: Permanent Black.
Ganguly, Debjani. 2016. *This Thing Called the World: The Contemporary Novel as Global Form*. Durham, NC: Duke University Press.
García Márquez, Gabriel. 2003. *Chronicle of a Death Foretold*. Translated by Gregory Rabassa. Reprint ed. New York: Vintage.

2006. *One Hundred Years of Solitude.* Translated by Gregory Rabassa. New York: Harper.

Ghose, Zulfikar. 1981. "Letter to Thomas Berger," August 20, 1981. Box 2 Folder 1. Harry Ransom Center. https://norman.hrc.utexas.edu/fasearch/findingAid.cfm?eadid=00322.

1982a. "Letter to Thomas Berger," August 31, 1982. Box 2 Folder 1. Harry Ransom Center. https://norman.hrc.utexas.edu/fasearch/findingAid.cfm?eadid=00322.

1982b. "Letter to Thomas Berger," October 7, 1982. Box 2 Folder 1. Harry Ransom Center. https://norman.hrc.utexas.edu/fasearch/findingAid.cfm?eadid=00322.

1984. "Letter to Thomas Berger," July 30, 1984. Box 2 Folder 2. Harry Ransom Center. https://norman.hrc.utexas.edu/fasearch/findingAid.cfm?eadid=00322.

1985a. "Letter to Thomas Berger," January 17, 1985. Box 2 Folder 2. Harry Ransom Center. https://norman.hrc.utexas.edu/fasearch/findingAid.cfm?eadid=00322.

1985b. "Letter to Thomas Berger," February 26, 1985. Box 2 Folder 2. Harry Ransom Center. https://norman.hrc.utexas.edu/fasearch/findingAid.cfm?eadid=00322.

1990a. "Letter to Thomas Berger," January 2, 1990. Box 2 Folder 5. Harry Ransom Center. https://norman.hrc.utexas.edu/fasearch/findingAid.cfm?eadid=00322.

1990b. "Letter to Thomas Berger," June 27, 1990. Box 2 Folder 5. Harry Ransom Center. https://norman.hrc.utexas.edu/fasearch/findingAid.cfm?eadid=00322.

1990c. "Letter to Thomas Berger," October 13, 1990. Box 2 Folder 5. Harry Ransom Center. https://norman.hrc.utexas.edu/fasearch/findingAid.cfm?eadid=00322.

1992. *The Triple Mirror of the Self.* London: Bloomsbury.

1998. *Veronica and the Góngora Passion: Stories, Fictions, Tales and One Fable.* Toronto, ON: Tsar.

Ghosh, Amitav. 1998. "The Testimony of My Grandfather's Bookcase." www.amitavghosh.com/essays/bookcase.html.

Gikandi, Simon. 2014. "Editor's Column – Provincializing English." *PMLA* 129 (1): 7–17. https://doi.org/10.1632/pmla.2014.129.1.7.

Goffman, Erving. 1981. *Forms of Talk.* Philadelphia: University of Pennsylvania Press.

González Echevarría, Roberto. 1990. *Myth and Archive: A Theory of Latin American Narrative.* Cambridge: Cambridge University Press.

González, Lucea. 1985. "Letter to Paucho," March 13, 1985. Fundación Pablo Neruda.

González, Octavio R. 2020. *Misfit Modernism: Queer Forms of Double Exile in the Twentieth-Century Novel.* University Park: Penn State University Press.

Gopinath, Gayatri. 2018. *Unruly Visions: The Aesthetic Practices of Queer Diaspora.* Durham, NC: Duke University Press.

Goyal, Yogita. 2019. "Postcolonial, Still." *Post45*, February 22, 2019. http://post45.research.yale.edu/2019/02/postcolonial-still/.

Granara, William. 2005. "Nostalgia, Arab Nationalism, and the Andalusian Chronotope in the Evolution of the Modern Arabic Novel." *Journal of Arabic Literature* 36 (1): 57–73.

Greenblatt, Stephen Jay. 1991. *Marvelous Possessions: The Wonder of the New World*. Chicago, IL: University of Chicago Press.

Grosfoguel, Ramón. 2011. "Decolonizing Post-Colonial Studies and Paradigms of Political-Economy: Transmodernity, Decolonial Thinking, and Global Coloniality." *Transmodernity: Journal of Peripheral Cultural Production of the Luso-Hispanic World* 1 (1): n.p.

Hadid, Diaa. 2020. "Pakistani Author Comes under Fire For Satirical Novel after Urdu Edition Is Published." *NPR*, January 10, 2020. www.npr.org/2020/01/10/794538415/pakistani-author-comes-under-fire-for-satirical-novel-after-urdu-edition-is-publ.

Halim, Hala. 2017. "Afro-Asian Third-Worldism into Global South: The Case of Lotus Journal." *Global South Studies: A Collective Publication with The Global South*, November 22, 2017. https://globalsouthstudies.as.virginia.edu/key-moments/afro-asian-third-worldism-global-south-case-lotus-journal.

Hall, Stuart. 1996. "When Was the Postcolonial? Thinking at the Limit." In *The Postcolonial Question: Common Skies, Divided Horizons*, edited by Iain Chambers and Lidia Curti, pp. 242–260. New York: Routledge.

Hamid, Mohsin. 2008. "The (Former) General in His Labyrinth." Penguin: We Tell Stories. https://web.archive.org/web/20120211110831/http://wetellstories.co.uk/stories/week6/.

———. 2010. "The (Former) General in His Labyrinth." *South Asian Review* 31 (3): 320–322. https://doi.org/10.1080/02759527.2010.11932801.

———. 2013. *The Reluctant Fundamentalist*. London: Hamish Hamilton.

———. 2015. *Discontent and Its Civilizations: Dispatches from Lahore, New York, and London*. New York: Riverhead Books.

———. 2017a. *Exit West*. New York: Riverhead Books.

———. 2017b. "'Writing Fiction Is a Form of Travel' – Mohsin Hamid." *Five Dials*, November 27, 2017. https://fivedials.com/fiction/writing-fiction-is-a-form-of-travel-mohsin-hamid-exit-west/.

Hanif, Mohammed. 1991. "The General in His Labyrinth." *Newsline*, January 1991.

———. 1992. "Viva Havana!" *Newsline*, February 1992.

———. 2009. *A Case of Exploding Mangoes*. New York: Vintage Books.

———. 2011. "Seven Places in My Heart." *Newsline*, January 2011.

———. 2019. "Explaining a Novel to Pakistani Intelligence." *Columbia Journalism Review* (blog). Summer 2019. www.cjr.org/special_report/explaining-a-novel-to-pakistani-intelligence.php/.

Harlow, Barbara, Sarah Brouillette, David Thomas, Maria Elisa Cevasco, Joshua Clover, and David Damrosch. 2016. "First Responses to the Warwick Collective." *Comparative Literature Studies* 53 (3): 505–534.

Hashmi, Salima, Mozeena Hashmi, and Murtaza Razvi. 2011. "Faiz the Father." *Dawn*, February 14, 2011. www.dawn.com/news/606166/920938.

Hashmi, Shadab Zeest. 2010. *Baker of Tarifa*. Madera: Poetic Matrix Press.
　2016. "Bread and the Secret Musk of Books." *Journal of Postcolonial Writing* 52 (2): 211–217. https://doi.org/10.1080/17449855.2016.1164966.
Hayot, Eric. 2016. *On Literary Worlds*. Oxford: Oxford University Press.
Herbert, Caroline. 2012. "Spectrality and Secularism in Bombay Fiction: Salman Rushdie's The Moor's Last Sigh and Vikram Chandra's Sacred Games." *Textual Practice* 26 (5): 941–971. https://doi.org/10.1080/0950236X.2012.703227.
Hirschkind, Charles. 2016. "Granadan Reflections." *Material Religion* 12 (2): 209–232. https://doi.org/10.1080/17432200.2016.1172767.
Hodgson, Marshall G. S. 1977. *The Venture of Islam, Volume 1: The Classical Age of Islam*. Reprint ed. Chicago, IL: University of Chicago Press.
Hon, Adrian. 2008. "Creating 'The (Former) General.'" *Mssv* (blog). April 22, 2008. https://mssv.net/2008/04/22/creating-the-former-general/.
Horta, Paulo Lemos. 2019. "Distant Star: Roberto Bolaño and Print Culture of the Cold War." Conference talk. London.
　2020. "Taste, Without Distinction." *Interventions* 22 (3): 416–432. https://doi.org/10.1080/1369801X.2019.1659170.
Hoyos, Héctor. 2015. *Beyond Bolaño: The Global Latin American Novel*. New York: Columbia University Press.
Huang, Yu-ting. 2019. "Being Ethnic in a Bicultural Nation: Acts of Translation in Chinese New Zealand Fictions." *MFS Modern Fiction Studies* 65 (3): 482–510. https://doi.org/10.1353/mfs.2019.0031.
Huggan, Graham. 2001. *The Postcolonial Exotic Marketing the Margins*. London: Routledge.
Husain, Intizar. 2015. *The Sea Lies Ahead*. Translated by Rakhshanda Jalil. New Delhi: Harper Perennial.
Huyssen, Andreas. 1984. "Mapping the Postmodern." *New German Critique* (33): 5–52. https://doi.org/10.2307/488352.
Iber, Patrick. 2015. *Neither Peace nor Freedom: The Cultural Cold War in Latin America*. Cambridge, MA: Harvard University Press.
Iqbal, Mohammed. 1935a. "Haspania." Allama Iqbal Poetry. http://iqbalurdu.blogspot.com/2011/04/bal-e-jibril-127-haspania.html.
　1935b. "Masjid-e Qurtuba." Translated by Frances W. Pritchett. www.columbia.edu/itc/mealac/pritchett/00urdu/iqbal/masjid_index.html?#index.
Izcue, Maribel. 2008. "Interview with Anita Desai." *Vislumbres: India and Iberoamerica*, June 2008.
Jalil, Rakhshanda. 2016. "Burden of Memories, Reality of the Present." *The Hindu*, February 3, 2016. www.thehindu.com/opinion/columns/tribute-intizar-husain-burden-of-memories-reality-of-the-present/article8184741.ece.
Jameson, Fredric. 1986. "Third-World Literature in the Era of Multinational Capitalism." *Social Text* 15: 65–88.
Jani, Pranav. 2010. *Decentering Rushdie: Cosmopolitanism and the Indian Novel in English*. Columbus: Ohio State University Press.

Johnson, Christopher D. 2010. *Hyperboles: The Rhetoric of Excess in Baroque Literature and Thought*. Cambridge, MA: Harvard University Press.

Joshi, Priya. 2002. *In Another Country: Colonialism, Culture, and the English Novel in India*. New York: Columbia University Press.

Jussawalla, Adil. 1995. "Letter to Salman Rushdie," August 2, 1995. Box 1 Folder 24. Cornell University Bombay Poets Archive.

   2004. "Letter to the Week," October 22, 2004. Box 3 Folder 8. Cornell University Bombay Poets Archive. https://rmc.library.cornell.edu/EAD/ht mldocs/RMM08519.html#s2.

Kantor, Roanne L. 2014. "Chasing Your (Josie) Bliss: The Troubling Critical Afterlife of Pablo Neruda's Burmese Lover." *Transmodernity: A Journal of Peripheral Cultural Production of the Luso-Hispanic World* 3 (2): 60–82.

   2018. "A Case of Exploding Markets: Latin American and South Asian Literary 'Booms.'" *Comparative Literature* 70 (4): 466–486. https://doi.org/10.1215/0 0104124-7215506.

Kapur, Geeta. 1973. "In Quest of Identity: Art & Indigenism in Post-Colonial Culture with Special Reference to Contemporary Indian Painting." *Vrishchik*. Asia Art Archive. https://aaa.org.hk/en/collection/search/archive/ gulammohammed-sheikh-archive-vrishchik/object/in-quest-of-identity-art-indigenism-in-post-colonial-culture-with-special-reference-to-contempor ary-indian-painting.

Khair, Tabish, and Sébastien Doubinsky. 2015. "The Politics and Art of Indian Fantasy Fiction." In *A History of the Indian Novel in English*, edited by Ulka Anjaria, pp. 337–347. Cambridge: Cambridge University Press.

Khakhar, Bhupen. 1995. "Salman Rushdie ('The Moor')." Oil on linen. National Portrait Gallery. www.npg.org.uk/collections/search/portrait/mw09598/Sal man-Rushdie-The-Moor.

Khan, Faiza S. 2010. "A Fictional Boom." *The Open Magazine*, January 7, 2010. www.openthemagazine.com/article/voices/a-fictional-boom.

Khullar, Sonal. 2015. *Worldly Affiliations: Artistic Practice, National Identity, and Modernism in India, 1930–1990*. Berkeley: University of California Press.

Kirsch, Adam. 2017. *The Global Novel: Writing the World in the 21st Century*. New York: Columbia Global Reports.

Klein, Lauren. 2018. "Distant Reading After Moretti." *ARCADE*. https://arcade .stanford.edu/blogs/distant-reading-after-moretti.

Kluwick, Ursula. 2011. *Exploring Magic Realism in Salman Rushdie's Fiction*. New York: Routledge.

Kristal, Efrain. 2002. "Considering Coldly ... " *New Left Review*, June 2002. https:// newleftreview.org/issues/II15/articles/efrain-kristal-considering-coldly.

Kumar, Ravish, and Akhil Katyal. 2018. *A City Happens in Love [Ishq Mein Shahar Hona]*. New Delhi: Speaking Tiger Books.

Kushigian, Julia. 1991. *Orientalism in the Hispanic Literary Tradition: In Dialogue with Borges, Paz, and Sarduy*. Albuquerque: University of New Mexico Press.

Laachir, Karima, Sara Marzagora, and Francesca Orsini. 2018. "Significant Geographies: In Lieu of World Literature." *Journal of World Literature* 3 (3): 290–310. https://doi.org/10.1163/24056480-00303005.
Lahiri, Madhumita. 2020. *Imperfect Solidarities: Tagore, Gandhi, Du Bois, and the Global Anglophone*. Evanston, IL: Northwestern University Press.
Lamming, George. 1992. *The Pleasures of Exile*. Ann Arbor: University of Michigan Press.
Laouyene, Atef. 2007. "Andalusian Poetics: Rushdie's The Moor's Last Sigh and the Limits of Hybridity." *ARIEL: A Review of International English Literature* 38 (4): 143–165.
Larsen, Neil. 2011. "'Boom' Novel and the Cold War in Latin America." In *Global Cold War Literatures Western, Eastern and Postcolonial Perspectives*, edited by Andrew Hammond, pp. 100–112. Hoboken, NJ: Taylor & Francis.
Lawrence, Jeffrey. 2018. *Anxieties of Experience: The Literatures of the Americas from Whitman to Bolaño*. New York: Oxford University Press.
Lazarus, Neil. 2011. *The Postcolonial Unconscious*. Cambridge: Cambridge University Press.
Loomba, Ania. 1998. *Colonialism/Postcolonialism*. London: Routledge.
López-Calvo, Ignacio, ed. 2010. *One World Periphery Reads the Other: Knowing the "Oriental" in the Americas and the Iberian Peninsula*. Newcastle upon Tyne: Cambridge Scholars Publishing.
Lowe, Lisa. 2015. *The Intimacies of Four Continents*. Durham, NC: Duke University Press.
Loyola, Hernán. 2006. *Neruda: La Biografía Literaria 1 La Formación de Un Poeta: 1904–1932* [*Neruda: A Literary Biography Part 1, The Formation of a Poet: 1904–1932*]. Santiago: Ed. Planeta.
Macaulay, T. B. 1835. "Minute on Indian Education." http://home.iitk.ac.in/~hcverma/Article/Macaulay-Minutes.pdf.
Mahajan, Karan. 2015. "The Rumpus Interview with Antonio Ruiz-Camacho." *The Rumpus*, May 8, 2015. https://therumpus.net/2015/05/the-rumpus-interview-with-antonio-ruiz-camacho/.
Mahler, Anne Garland. 2018. *From the Tricontinental to the Global South: Race, Radicalism, and Transnational Solidarity*. Durham, NC: Duke University Press.
Majumdar, Megha. 2016. "Karan Mahajan on the Inner Lives of Terrorists & Victims in Today's India." *Electric Literature*, March 22, 2016. https://electricliterature.com/karan-mahajan-on-the-inner-lives-of-terrorists-victims-in-todays-india/.
Maldonado-Torres, Nelson, guest ed. 2011. "Thinking through the Decolonial Turn: Post-Continental Interventions in Theory, Philosophy, and Critique – An Introduction." *TRANSMODERNITY: Journal of Peripheral Cultural Production of the Luso-Hispanic World* 1 (2): 2–15.
Mani, B. Venkat. 2017. *Recoding World Literature: Libraries, Print Culture, and Germany's Pact with Books*. New York: Fordham University Press.

Martin, Gerald. 1989. *Journeys through the Labyrinth: Latin American Fiction in the Twentieth Century*. London: Verso.
Marvel, Ishan. 2016. "'Academia in India Is Not Something about Which You Can Have Any Illusions': An Interview with Arvind Krishna Mehrotra." *The Caravan*, January 12, 2016. https://caravanmagazine.in/vantage/interview-with-arvind-krishna-mehrotra.
Maurya, Vibha. 2016. "Cruces Revolucionarios: La Recepción de La Poesía de Pablo Neruda En India." In *Sur/South: Poetics and Politics of Thinking Latin America/India*, edited by Susanne Klengel and Alexandra Ortiz Wallner, pp. 17–26. Madrid: Iberoamericana.
Maxwell, William J. 2015. *F. B. Eyes: How J. Edgar Hoover's Ghostreaders Framed African American Literature*. Princeton, NJ: Princeton University Press.
McGrath, Laura B. 2019. "Comping White." *Los Angeles Review of Books*, January 21, 2019. https://lareviewofbooks.org/article/comping-white/.
McHale, Brian. 1987. *Postmodernist Fiction*. New York: Methuen.
McLain, Karline. 2001. "The Fantastic as Frontier: Realism, the Fantastic, and Transgression in Mid-Twentieth Century Urdu Fiction." *Annual of Urdu Studies* 16: 139–165.
Mehrotra, Arvind Krishna. 1968. "Editor's Note." *Ezra*, 1968.
  1969. "Note to Adil Jussawalla," n.d. (likely 1969). Box 3 Folder 7. Cornell University Bombay Poets Archive. https://rmc.library.cornell.edu/EAD/htmldocs/RMM08519.html#s2.
  1971. "Pomes Poems Poemas." *Vrishchik*. Asia Art Archive. https://aaa.org.hk/en/collection/search/archive/gulammohammed-sheikh-archive-vrishchik/object/vrishchik-year-2-no-6-7.
  1998. "Borges." In *The Transfiguring Places*, p. 3. New Delhi: Ravi Dayal.
  2014. *Partial Recall: Essays on Literature and Literary History*. New Delhi: Permanent Black.
Mehrotra, Arvind Krishna, and Alok Rai. 1965. "Copyright Statement." *Damn You*, 1965.
Melas, Natalie. 2007. *All the Difference in the World: Postcoloniality and the Ends of Comparison*. Stanford, CA: Stanford University Press.
Menocal, Maria Rosa. 2002. *The Ornament of the World: How Muslims, Jews, and Christians Created a Culture of Tolerance in Medieval Spain*. Boston, MA: Little, Brown.
Meyer-Minnemann, Klaus. 1992. "Octavio Paz: Topoemas Elementos Para Una Lectura." *Nueva Revista de Filogía Hispánica* 40 (2): 1113–1134.
Mignolo, Walter D. 1994. "Signs and Their Transmission: The Question of the Book in the New World." In *Writing Without Words: Alternative Literacies in Mesoamerica and the Andes*, edited by Elizabeth Hill Boone and Walter D. Mignolo, pp. 220–270. Durham, NC: Duke University Press.
  2011. *The Darker Side of Western Modernity: Global Futures, Decolonial Options*. Durham, NC: Duke University Press.
Mikhail, Alan. 2020. *God's Shadow: The Ottoman Sultan Who Shaped the Modern World*. London: Faber & Faber.

Mondragón, Sergio. 1969. "Opening." *Mundus Artium: Journal of International Literature and the Arts* (Winter).
Moretti, Franco. 2000. "Conjectures on World Literature." *New Left Review* (1): 54–68.
Morey, Peter. 2007. "Rushdie and the English Tradition." In *The Cambridge Companion to Salman Rushdie*, edited by Abdulrazak Gurnah, pp. 29–43. Cambridge: Cambridge University Press.
Moscaliuc, Mihaela. 2017. "Palimpsestic Intertextualities in 'A Lost Memory of Delhi' and 'The Last Saffron.'" In *Mad Heart Be Brave: Essays on the Poetry of Agha Shahid Ali*, edited by Kazim Ali, pp. 156–62. Ann Arbor: University of Michigan Press.
Mufti, Aamir. 1991. "Reading the Rushdie Affair: An Essay on Islam and Politics." *Social Text* (29): 95–116. https://doi.org/10.2307/466301.
    2007. *Enlightenment in the Colony: The Jewish Question and the Crisis of Postcolonial Culture*. Princeton, NJ: Princeton University Press.
    2016. *Forget English! Orientalisms and World Literatures*. Cambridge, MA: Harvard University Press.
Mukherjee, Meenakshi. 1966. "Review of Confessions of a Native Alien by Zulfikar Ghose." *Poetry India*.
    2000. *The Perishable Empire: Essays on Indian Writing in English*. New Delhi: Oxford University Press.
    ed. 2002. *Early Novels in India*. New Delhi: Sahitya Akademi.
Nadiminti, Kalyan. 2018. "The Global Program Era: Contemporary International Fiction in the American Creative Economy." *Novel* 51 (3): 375–398. https://doi.org/10.1215/00295132-7086426.
Naipaul, V. S. 1981. *Among the Believers: An Islamic Journey*. New York: Vintage Books.
Nambisan, Vijay, and Kavery Nambisan. 2005. "A Dialogue on Sincerity in Writing." Vijay Nambisan Papers Box 1. Cornell University Bombay Poets Archive.
Nandy, Pritish. 1975. *Riding the Midnight River: Selected Poems of Pritish Nandy*. New Delhi: Arnold Heinemann Publishers.
Narayanan, Pavithra. 2012. *What Are You Reading? The World Market and Indian Literary Production*. New Delhi: Routledge.
Nerlekar, Anjali. 2016. *Bombay Modern: Arun Kolatkar and Bilingual Literary Culture*. Evanston, IL: Northwestern University Press.
Neruda, Pablo. n.d. "Official Diplomatic Records for Pablo Neruda." Vol. 1108, No. 95–99. Archivo Histórico del Ministerio de Relaciones Exteriores.
    1978. *Cartas a Laura* [*Letter to Laura*]. Madrid: Ediciones Cultura Hispánica del Centro Iberoamericano de Cooperación.
    1999. *Obras Completas* [*Complete Works*]. Buenos Aires: Editorial Losada.
    2000. *Confieso Que He Vivido: Memorias* [*The Complete Memoirs*]. Buenos Aires: Seix Barral.
    2004. *Residencia En La Tierra/Residence on Earth*. Translated by Donald Walsh. New York: New Directions.

2008. *Itinerario de Una Amistad: Pablo Neruda, Héctor Eandi: Epistolario 1927–1943* [*Itinerary of a Friendship: Pablo Neruda in Correspondence with Héctor Eandi: 1927–1943*]. Buenos Aires: Corregidor.
Noorani, Yaseen. 1999. "The Lost Garden of Al-Andalus: Islamic Spain and the Poetic Inversion of Colonialism." *International Journal of Middle East Studies* 31 (2): 237–254.
North, Michael. 2019. "The Afterlife of Modernism." *New Literary History* 50 (1): 91–112. https://doi.org/10.1353/nlh.2019.0005.
Orsini, Francesca. 2002. *The Hindi Public Sphere 1920–1940: Language and Literature in the Age of Nationalism*. New York: Oxford University Press.
  2015. "The Multilingual Local in World Literature." *Comparative Literature* 67 (4): 345–374. https://doi.org/10.1215/00104124-3327481.
Parameswaran, Uma. 1983. "Handcuffed to History: Salman Rushdie's Art." *ARIEL: A Review of International English Literature* 14 (4): 34–45.
Patel, Vinod Ray. 1971. "Linocut." *Vrishchik*, November 1971. Asia Art Archive. https://aaa.org.hk/en/collection/search/archive/gulammohammed-sheikh-archive-vrishchik/object/vrishchik-year-2-3-no-12-1.
Patke, Rajeev S. 2013. *Modernist Literature and Postcolonial Studies*. Edinburgh: Edinburgh University Press.
Paz, Octavio. 1963. "Surrounded by Infinity." In *Group 1890 Catalogue*, 4. https://aaa.org.hk/en/collection/search/library/group-1890.
  1965. "Letter to Lysander Kemp," April 1965. Lysender Kemp Papers Box 1 Folders 1.5–1.6. Harry Ransom Center.
  1966. "Al Pintor Swaminathan/To the Painter Swaminathan." Translated by Jagdish Swaminathan and Octavio Paz. *El Corno Emplumado*, 1966. Open Door Archive.
  1969. "México: Olimpiada de 1968/Mexico: The XIX Olimpiad." Translated by Mark Strand. *El Corno Emplumado*, 1969. Open Door Archive. https://opendoor.northwestern.edu/archive/items/show/64.
  1970. *Ladera Este: Ladera Este, Hacia El Comienzo, Blanco* [*East Slope: East Slope, Toward the Beginning, and Blanco*]. México, D.F.: Joaquín Mortiz.
  1973a. *Alternating Current*. Translated by Helen R. Lane. New York: Viking Press.
  1973b. "To the Painter Swaminathan." Translated by Jagdish Swaminathan. *Dialogue India*, [1966] 1973.
  1983. *Sor Juana Inés de La Cruz, o, Las Trampas de La Fe* [*Sor Juana, or, The Traps of Faith*]. Translated by Margaret Sayers Peden. 3rd ed. México, D.F.: Fondo de Cultura Económica.
  1990. *Sor Juana, or, The Traps of Faith*. Translated by Margaret Sayers Peden. Cambridge: Belknap Press.
  1995. *Vislumbres de La India* [*In the Light of India*]. Barcelona: Seix Barral.
  1996. *Ladera Este: Seguido de Hacia El Comienzo y Blanco, 1962–1968* [*East Slope: Followed by Toward the Beginning and Blanco, 1962–1968*]. Barcelona: Círculo de Lectores.
  1998. *In Light of India*. Translated by Eliot Weinberger. New York: Mariner Books.

2008. "Nueva Delhi Noviembre 1965–Nueva Delhi Agosto 1968 [New Delhi November 1965–New Delhi August 1968]" In *Cartas a Tomás Segovia (1957–1985)* [*Letters to Tómas Segovia (1957–1985)*], pp. 37–167. México, D.F.: Fondo de Cultura Económica.
Pollock, Sheldon. 1998. "The Cosmopolitan Vernacular." *Journal of Asian Studies* 57 (1): 6–37. https://doi.org/10.2307/2659022.
Prasad, G. J. V. 1999. "Writing Translation: The Strange Case of the Indian English Novel." In *Post-Colonial Translation: Theory and Practice*, edited by Susan Bassnett and Harish Trivedi, pp. 41–57. London: Routledge.
Pratt, Mary Louise. 1992. *Imperial Eyes: Travel Writing and Transculturation*. London: Routledge.
Pravinchandra, Shital. 2018. "Short Story and Peripheral Production." In *The Cambridge Companion to World Literature*, edited by Ben Etherington and Jarad Zimbler, 197–210. Cambridge: Cambridge University Press.
Premachand. 2007. *Shatranj Ke Khiladi* [*The Chess Players*]. Delhi: Gyan Ganga.
Pritchett, Frances W. 1994. *Nets of Awareness: Urdu Poetry and Its Critics*. Berkeley: University of California Press.
Quayson, Ato. 2012. "Periods versus Concepts: Space Making and the Question of Postcolonial Literary History." *PMLA* 127 (2): 342–348. https://doi.org/10.1632/pmla.2012.127.2.342.
Quijano, Aníbal. 2000. "Coloniality of Power and Eurocentrism in Latin America." *International Sociology* 15 (2): 215–232. https://doi.org/10.1177/0268580900015002005.
Quintero-Herencia, Juan Carlos. 2002. *Fulguración Del Espacio: Letras e Imaginario Institucional de La Revolución Cubana, 1960–1971* [*Solar Flare: Literature and Institutional Imaginary of the Cuban Revolution, 1960–1971*]. Roasario: B. Viterbo.
Rabassa, Gregory. 2005. *If This Be Treason: Translation and Its Discontents: A Memoir*. New York: New Directions Book.
Radhakrishnan, R. 2009. "Why Compare?" *New Literary History* 40 (3): 453–471.
Raley, Rita. 2000. "A Teleology of Letters; or, From a 'Common Source' to a Common Language." *Romantic Circles*. https://romantic-circles.org/praxis/containment/raley/raley.html.
Rama, Ángel. 1976. *Los Dictadores Latinoamericanos* [*Latin American Dictators*]. México, D.F.: Fondo de Cultura Económica.
2005. "El Boom En Perspectiva [The Boom in Perspective]." *Signos Literarios* 1 (January–June): 161–208.
Ramachandran, Ayesha. 2015. *The Worldmakers: Global Imagining in Early Modern Europe*. Chicago, IL: University of Chicago Press.
Ramazani, Jahan. 2009. *A Transnational Poetics*. Chicago, IL: University of Chicago Press.
2020. *Poetry in a Global Age*. Chicago, IL: University of Chicago Press.
Ranasinha, Ruvani. 2007. *South Asian Writers in Twentieth-Century Britain: Culture in Translation*. Oxford: Oxford University Press.
Randall, Margaret. 2008. "El Corno Emplumado 1," March 6, 2008. www.margaretrandall.org/El-Corno-Emplumado-1.

Ray, Satyajit. 1977. *Shatranj Ke Khilari /The Plumed Horn*. Mexico City: anaxagoras.
   2019. "Re-Imagining Octavio Paz." Presented at the Embassy of Mexico in India, New Delhi. https://medium.com/@embamexindia/remembering-octavio-paz-20-years-after-d7efb2e900c9.
Rockwell, Daisy. 2003. "The Shape of a Place: Translation and Cultural Marking in South Asian Fictions." *Modern Philology* 100 (4): 596–618. https://doi.org/10.1086/379985.
Rodó, José Enrique. [1900] 1988. *Ariel*. Translated by Margaret Sayers Peden. Austin: University of Texas Press.
Rodríguez Monegal, Emir. 1988. *Neruda, El Viajero Inmóvil* [*Neruda, the Unmoving Traveler*]. Barcelona: Editorial Laia.
Roy, Parama. 1998. *Indian Traffic: Identities in Question in Colonial and Postcolonial India*. Berkeley: University of California Press.
Rubenstein, Mary-Jane. 2008. *Strange Wonder: The Closure of Metaphysics and the Opening of Awe*. New York: Columbia University Press.
Rushdie, Salman. 1983. *Shame*. New York: Picador.
   1992. *Imaginary Homelands: Essays and Criticism 1981–1991*. London: Granta Books.
   1995. *The Moor's Last Sigh*. New York: Pantheon Books.
   2006. *Midnight's Children*. New York: Random House.
   2008. *The Jaguar Smile: A Nicaraguan Journey*. New York: Random House Trade Paperbacks.
   2012. *Joseph Anton: A Memoir*. New York: Random House.
Russell, Ralph. 1992. *The Pursuit of Urdu Literature: A Select History*. London: Zed Books.
Sadana, Rashmi. 2012. *English Heart, Hindi Heartland: The Political Life of Literature in India*. Berkeley: University of California Press.
Sahni, Bhishm, ed. 1974. *Dedicated to the Memory of Pablo Neruda*. Delhi: The Indian National Committee of Afro-Asian Writers.
Said, Edward. 1978. *Orientalism*. New York: Vintage Books.
   1993. *Culture and Imperialism*. New York: Knopf.
   2000. *Reflections on Exile and Other Essays*. Cambridge, MA: Harvard University Press.
Salgado, Minoli. 2007. "The Politics of the Palimpsest in *The Moor's Last Sigh*." In *The Cambridge Companion to Salman Rushdie*, edited by Abdulrazak Gurnah, pp. 153–168. Cambridge: Cambridge University Press.
Sánchez Prado, Ignacio M. 2018. *Strategic Occidentalism: On Mexican Fiction, the Neoliberal Book Market, and the Question of World Literature*. Evanston, IL: Northwestern University Press.
Sangari, Kumkum. 1987. "The Politics of the Possible." *Cultural Critique* (7): 157–186. https://doi.org/10.2307/1354154.
Santí, Enrico. 1982. *Pablo Neruda, the Poetics of Prophecy*. Ithaca, NY: Cornell University Press.
Satyarthi, Devendra. 2006. "Pablo Neruda Se Bhenṭ [A Visit with Pablo Neruda]." In *Swapna Aur Yatharth Ka Srijan Sikhar Pablo Neruda: Bhartiya Sandarbh*

[*Pablo Neruda, the Creative Apex of Dream and Realism: The Indian Context*], edited by Vishnu Khare, pp. 17–26. Delhi: Udbhavana.
Schwartz, Lawrence H. 1988. *Creating Faulkner's Reputation: The Politics of Modern Literary Criticism*. Knoxville: University of Tennessee Press.
Sedgwick, Eve. 2003. *Touching Feeling: Affect, Pedagogy, Performativity*. Durham, NC: Duke University Press.
Shamsie, Muneeza. 2016. "Introduction: The Enduring Legacy of al-Andalus." *Journal of Postcolonial Writing* 52 (2): 127–135. https://doi.org/10.1080/17449 855.2016.1164969.
Shankar, Subramanian. 2012. *Flesh and Fish Blood: Postcolonialism, Translation, and the Vernacular*. Berkeley: University of California Press.
Shklovsky, Viktor. 1990. *Theory of Prose*. Translated by Benjamin Sher. Elmwood Park, IL: Dalkey Archive Press.
Singh, Akanksha. 2020. "The Beats, the Hungryalists, and the Call of the East." *Los Angeles Review of Books*, February 19, 2020. https://lareviewofbooks.org /article/the-beats-the-hungryalists-and-the-call-of-the-east/.
Singh, Harleen. 2012. "Insurgent Metaphors: Decentering 9/11 in Mohsin Hamid's The Reluctant Fundamentalist and Kamila Shamsie's Burnt Shadows." *ARIEL: A Review of International English Literature* 43 (1): 23–44.
Singh, Sunny. 2000. *Nani's Book of Suicides*. New Delhi: HarperCollins Publishers India.
  2001. "Twin in the Mirror: India and Mexico." In *Indian Writings on Latin American Literature*, edited by Susnigdha Dey, Om Gupta, and Anil Dhingra, pp. 48–53. Delhi: Sahitya Akademi.
Siskind, Mariano. 2012. "Magical Realism." In *The Cambridge History of Postcolonial Literature*, edited by Ato Quayson, pp. 833–868. Cambridge: Cambridge University Press.
  2014. *Cosmopolitan Desires: Global Modernity and World Literature in Latin America*. Evanston, IL: Northwestern University Press.
SOAS MULOSIGE. 2017. "About." http://mulosige.soas.ac.uk/about/.
Solanki, Tanuj. 2013. "The Geometry of the Gaze." *Litro*, July 2013. www .litro.co.uk/2013/07/the-geometry-of-the-gaze/.
Sontag, Susan. 2007. "The World as India." Susan Sontag Foundation. 2007. www .susansontag.com/prize/onTranslation.shtml.
Sorensen, Eli Park. 2010. *Postcolonial Studies and the Literary: Theory, Interpretation and the Novel*. Basingstoke: Palgrave Macmillan.
Spindler, William. 1993. "Magic Realism: A Typology." *Forum for Modern Language Studies XXIX* (1): 75–85. https://doi.org/10.1093/fmls/XXIX.1.75.
Spivak, Gayatri Chakravorty. 1988. "Can the Subaltern Speak?" In *Marxism and the Interpretation of Culture*, edited by Cary Nelson and Lawrence Grossberg, pp. 271–313. Urbana: University of Illinois Press.
  1999. *A Critique of Postcolonial Reason*. Cambridge, MA: Harvard University Press.
  2005. *Death of a Discipline*. New York: Columbia University Press.

2009. *Outside in the Teaching Machine*. New York: Routledge.
Squires, Claire. 2007. *Marketing Literature: The Making of Contemporary Writing in Britain*. Basingstoke: Palgrave Macmillan.
Srinivasan, Ragini Tharoor. 2018a. "Call Center Agents and Expatriate Writers: Twin Subjects of New Indian Capital." *ARIEL: A Review of International English Literature* 49 (4): 77–107. https://doi.org/10.1353/ari.2018.0030.
2018b. "Introduction: South Asia from Postcolonial to World Anglophone." *Interventions* 20 (3): 309–316. https://doi.org/10.1080/1369801X.2018.1446840.
Sundaram, Vivan. 1972. *The Heights of Macchu Picchu*. Asia Art Archive. https://aaa.org.hk/en/collection/search/archive/geeta-kapur-and-vivan-sundaram-archive-the-heights-of-macchu-picchu-1972.
Swaminathan, Jagdish. 1965. "Editor's Note." *CONTRA'66*, 1965. Asia Art Archive. https://aaa.org.hk/en/collection/search/archive/gulammohammed-sheikh-archive-contra66/object/contra66-number-1.
1971. "Letras Letrillas Letrones." *Plural*. Cambridge, MA: Harvard University.
Syed, Asghar Nadeem. n.d. "Shahr Badar." Rekhta. https://www.rekhta.org/nazms/shahr-badar-asghar-nadeem-sayed-nazms?lang=ur.
Taboada, Hernán. 2006. "Latin American Orientalism: From Margin to Margin." In *Paradoxical Citizenship: Edward Said*, edited by Silvia Nagy, pp. 121–128. Lanham, MD: Lexington Books.
Taneja, Anand Vivek. 2018. *Jinnealogy: Time, Islam, and Ecological Thought in the Medieval Ruins of Delhi*. Stanford: Stanford University Press.
Teitelboim, Volodia. 2004. *Neruda*. 4th ed. Buenos Aires: Sudamerica.
Teskey, Gordon. 1996. *Allegory and Violence*. Ithaca: Cornell University Press.
Thayil, Jeet. 2017. *The Book of Chocolate Saints*. New Delhi: Aleph Book Company.
Thiara, Nicole. 2007. "Salman Rushdie's The Moor's Last Sigh: Hindu Nationalism, Democracy, and the 'New God-and-Mammon India.'" *Journal of Commonwealth and Postcolonial Studies* 14 (2): 19–33.
Thornber, Karen Laura. 2009. *Empire of Texts in Motion: Chinese, Korean, and Taiwanese Transculturations of Japanese Literature*. Cambridge, MA: Harvard University Asia Center.
Ticktin, Miriam. 2017. "A World without Innocence." *American Ethnologist* 44 (4): 577–590. https://doi.org/10.1111/amet.12558.
Tietchen, Todd F. 2010. *The Cubalogues: Beat Writers in Revolutionary Havana*. Gainesville: University Press of Florida.
Tinajero, Araceli. 2004. *Orientalismo En El Modernismo Hispanoamericano [Orientalism in Latin American Mondernismo]*. West Lafayette, IN: Purdue University Press.
Tiwari, Bhavya. 2011. "Rabindranath Tagore's Comparative World Literature." In *The Routledge Companion to World Literature*, edited by Theo D'haen, David Damrosch, and Djelal Kadir, pp. 41–48. New York: Routledge.
Torres-Rodríguez, Laura J. 2015. "Orientalizing Mexico: Estudios Indostánicos and the Place of India in José Vasconcelos's La Raza Cósmica." *Revista Hispánica Moderna* 68 (1): 77–91.

Vadde, Aarthi. 2016. *Chimeras of Form: Modernist Internationalism Beyond Europe, 1914–2016*. New York: Columbia University Press.
Varas, José Miguel. 2003. *Neruda Clandestino* [*Clandestine Neruda*]. Santiago: Alfaguara.
Vargas Llosa, Mario. 2001. *The Feast of the Goat*. Translated by Edith Grossman. New York: Farrar, Straus, and Giroux.
Velasco, Francisco. 1984. *Diccionario Neruda, a Través de Sus Metáforas* [Neruda Dictionary, through His Metaphors]. Santiago: Ediciones Minga.
Verdesio, Gustavo. 2005. "Introduction: Latin American Subaltern Studies Revisited: Is There Life after the Demise of the Group." *Disppsitio/n* [*Dispositio*] 25 (52): 5–42.
Verma, Nirmal. 1971. "Of Being Somewhere Trapped: Borges in London." *Vrishchik*, November 1971. Asia Art Archive. https://aaa.org.hk/en/collection/search/archive/gulammohammed-sheikh-archive-vrishchik/object/vrishchik-year-2-3-no-12-1.
Vial, Aleka, and Cristina Alemparte. 2010. *Las casas y cosas de Pablo Neruda* [*Neruda's House and Belongings*]. México, D.F.: Baobab.
Vilches, Patrici. 2008. "'La Más Bella de Mandalay': Construcciones Orientalistas de La Feminidad En Dos Poemas de Neruda ['The Beauty of Mandalay': Orientalist Constructions of Femininity in Two Poems by Pablo Neruda]." In *Moros En La Costa: Orientalismo En Latinoamérica* [*Moors on the Coast: Orientalism in Latin America*], edited by Silvia Nagy, pp. 201–217. Madrid: Iberoamericana.
Viswanathan, Gauri. 1989. *Masks of Conquest: Literary Study and British Rule in India*. New York: Columbia University Press.
——— 2008. "The Literary Rushdie: An Interview with Gauri Viswanathan." In *Midnight's Diaspora: Critical Encounters with Salman Rushdie*, edited by Daniel Alan Herwitz and Ashutosh Varshney, pp. 23–42. Ann Arbor: University of Michigan Press.
Walkowitz, Rebecca L. 2006. *Cosmopolitan Style: Modernism Beyond the Nation*. New York: Columbia University Press.
——— 2015. *Born Translated: The Contemporary Novel in an Age of World Literature*. New York: Columbia University Press.
Wardrip-Fruin, Noah, and Nick Montfort, eds. 2003. *The New Media Reader*. Cambridge: MIT Press.
Warner, Michael. 2002. "Publics and Counterpublics." *Public Culture* 14 (1): 49–90.
Warnes, Christopher. 2005. "The Hermeneutics of Vagueness: Magical Realism in Current Literary Critical Discourse." *Journal of Postcolonial Writing* 41 (1): 1–13. https://doi.org/10.1080/17449850500062733.
Watroba, Karolina. 2018. "World Literature and Literary Value: Is 'Global' The New 'Lowbrow?'" *Cambridge Journal of Postcolonial Literary Inquiry* 5 (1): 53–68. https://doi.org/10.1017/pli.2017.41.
Wolf, Kenneth Baxter. 2009. "Convivencia in Medieval Spain: A Brief History of an Idea." *Religion Compass* 3 (1): 72–85. https://doi.org/10.1111/j.1749-8171.2008.00119.x.

n+1. 2013. "World Lite." *n+1* (blog). Fall 2013. https://nplusonemag.com/issue-17/the-intellectual-situation/world-lite/.
WReC (Warwick Research Collective) (Sharae Deckard, Nicholas Lawrence, Neil Lazarus, Graeme Macdonald, Upamanyu Pablo Mukherjee, Benita Parry, and Stephen A. Shapiro, eds.). 2015. *Combined and Uneven Development: Towards a New Theory of World-Literature*. Liverpool: Liverpool University Press.
Yaqin, Amina. 2016. "La Convivencia, La Mezquita and al-Andalus: An Iqbalian Vision." *Journal of Postcolonial Writing* 52 (2): 136–152. https://doi.org/10.1080/17449855.2016.1164972.
Yildiz, Yasemin. 2013. *Beyond the Mother Tongue: The Postmonolingual Condition*. New York: Modern Language Initiative.
Yoon, Duncan M. 2015. "'Our Forces Have Redoubled': World Literature, Postcolonialism, and the Afro-Asian Writers' Bureau." *Cambridge Journal of Postcolonial Literary Inquiry* 2 (2): 233–252. https://doi.org/10.1017/pli.2015.11.
Young, Robert J. C. 2016. *Postcolonialism: An Historical Introduction*. Anniversary ed. Malden, MA: Wiley Blackwell.
Yurkievich, Saul. 1971. *Fundadores de La Nueva Poesía Latinoamericana [Leaders in the New Poetry of Latin America]*. Barcelona: Ariel.
Zaman, Taymiya R. 2018. "Cities, Time, and the Backward Glance." *American Historical Review* 123 (3): 699–705. https://doi.org/10.1093/ahr/rhy010.
Zecchini, Laetitia. 2014. *Arun Kolatkar and Literary Modernism in India: Moving Lines*. London: Bloomsbury.
2017a. "'More than One World': An Interview with Gulammohammed Sheikh." *Journal of Postcolonial Writing* 53 (1–2): 69–82. https://doi.org/10.1080/17449855.2017.1294724.
2017b. "'We Were like Cartographers, Mapping the City': An Interview with Arvind Krishna Mehrotra." *Journal of Postcolonial Writing* 53 (1–2): 190–206. https://doi.org/10.1080/17449855.2017.1296631.
ZEE Jaipur Literature Festival. 2019. "About the Festival." https://jaipurliteraturefestival.org/about/.

Index

9/11, 25, 27, 43–45, 173

al-Andalus, 90–94, 96–98, 100, 101–102
Ali, Agha Shahid, 16, 40–43, 182
  "I See Chile in My Rearview Mirror," 42
  "The Previous Occupant," 40–42
Ali, Tariq
  "Chile: Lessons of the Coup, Which Way to Workers' Power?," 161
  Shadows of the Pomegranate Tree, 101–105
  The Leopard and the Fox: A Pakistani Tragedy, 161
Anglophone, 2
  Global, 21, 24, 27, 133, 140, 165, 172, 177, 178, 185, 186, 192
  Latin American, 180
  poetry, 61, 115
  South Asian, 6–10, 62, 70, 85, 108, 179, 191
archive, 58, 68, 86, 149, 150, 173
  sleuth, 151, 167, 169, 176

baroque, 58, 76, 89, 106, 121, 137
  citation, 84
  ekphrasis, 65, 72, 74, 89, 135
Benjamin, Walter, 14, 96, 189
Bhabha, Homi, 77, 107, 114
Bolaño, Roberto, 60, 178, 185
  Los detectives salvajes, 85, 181
Bombay/Mumbai, 17, 89, 141
  poets, 62, 80, 88
  riots 1992–1993, 91, 95, 104
boom, 2, 10
  Latin American, 26, 131, 138, 144, 150
  South Asian, 9–10, 141, 175, 190
Borges, Jorge Luis, 13, 17–18, 76, 79, 125, 132, 183
  "Borges y yo," 184, 187
  "El jardín de senderos que bifurcan," 158–161

Caribbean, 106, 109, 112, 163, 166, 176
Carpentier, Alejo, 119, 137, 149
  El recurso del método, 161

lo real maravilloso, 119–122
Los pasos perdidos, 129–130
Chile, 40, 187
Cold War, 22, 25, 82, 157, 173
colonial
  wonder, 125
colonialism, 96
  1857 Uprising, 95, 100, 108
  conquest, 22, 63, 103, 105
  decadence, 102, 103, 122, 201
  despotism, 94, 97
  epistemology, 119, 120, 122, 135
  wonder, 64, 125
Commonwealth, 2, 14, 24, 113
Cordoba, 96, 100
Cortázar, Julio, 125, 183
countershelf, 2, 3, 11–20, 32, 101
  circulated, 62, 68, 72, 75, 81–82, 85, 86, 131, 146, 167
  contested, 18, 33
  contrarian, 14, 78, 89, 113, 118, 179, 182
  counterpublic, 11, 61, 148, 173
  curated, 15, 40, 58, 70, 73
  encryption, 16, 41, 61, 64, 83, 85, 89, 96, 101, 112, 148, 162, 169, 170, 175
  good shelf, 5, 48, 80
  mirror, 21, 25, 41, 42, 45, 60, 65, 82, 91, 100, 117, 128, 139, 176
  write out, 69, 85
Cuba, 24–27, 124
  Cuban Revolution, 27, 109

Delhi, 59, 62, 66–67, 95, 100
Desai, Anita
  "Tepotzlán Tomorrow," 135
  The Zigzag Way, 133–137
detective fiction, 150, 168, 204
dictatorship
  Chilean coup, 42, 44, 124, 161
  Dominican Republic, 171, 176
  fiction, 147, 156–166, 172, 176

225

dictatorship (cont.)
  Pakistan, 147, 156–166
discovery
  New World, 25, 93, 110, 112
  rhetoric of, 64, 109, 121, 124, 135

El corno emplumado, 73, 81, 84

Faiz, Faiz Ahmed, 1, 70, 124
fantasy
  colonial, 123
  delirious, 12, 111
  genre, 140
Faulkner, William, 146, 147, 155, 157
  Absalom, Absalom!, 149–150

García Márquez, Gabriel, 17, 27, 116, 121, 125, 132–133
  Cien años de soledad, 150–153, 204
  Crónica de una muerte anunciada, 133, 144, 155–156, 167–169
  El general en su laberinto, 158
  El otoño del patriarca, 133, 148, 155, 161, 162
Ghose, Zulfikar, 70
  "Arrival in India," 111–112
  "Lila of the Butterflies and Her Chronicler," 132–133
  personal correspondence, 39, 115, 131, 134, 140, 141, 203
  The Triple Mirror of the Self, 39, 128–133, 141–142
Global South, 2, 11, 69, 81, 115, 147, 191
Góngora, Luis de, 63–64, 81, 111
Granada, 101, 104, 111

Hamid, Mohsin, 1
  Exit West, 25
  "The (Former) General in His Labyrinth," 157–161
  The Reluctant Fundamentalist, 1, 43–45
Hanif, Mohammed, 13
  A Case of Exploding Mangoes, 144, 166–174
  The General in His Labyrinth, 164–166
historical fiction, 102, 173
Husain, Intizar, 98–100

Ibn Rushd, 90, 111
indigeneity, 78, 94, 98, 99, 136, 152
influence, 174
  derivative, 19, 115
  genealogy, 147, 165
Iqbal, Muhammad, 70
  "Abdur Rehman Awwal Ka Boya Huwa Khajoor Ka Pehla Darakht," 98
  "Masjid-e Qurtubah," 96–97

Jussawalla, Adil, 81, 87, 89

Kapur, Geeta, 88, 114
  "In Quest of Identity," 78–79
Karachi, 13, 99
Khakhar, Bhupen, 76, 88
  The Moor, 89–90

literary market, 43, 85, 115, 164
  anti-commercial, 68, 72, 83, 116
  commercialism, 71, 115, 123, 125, 140–143, 175, 179
  little magazines, 60, 68–73
Lotus, 38, 69

Macaulay, Thomas Babington, 4, 19, 41, 79, 122, 183
magical realism, 113–124, 132–133, 137, 138, 145, 151–155, 163, 164, 168, 170, 186
Man Booker Prize, 9, 134, 190
Manto, Saadat Hasan, 185
Mehrotra, Arvind Krishna, 16, 17, 72
  "Pomes Poems Poemas," 80
Mexico, 78, 79, 133–137, 138–140, 179, 183
  Tenochtitlan, 105–108, 121
  Tlatelolco massacre 1968, 83
mirror, 3
modernism, 119, 145–146, 149–150
  politics of, 157, 158, 163, 172
mother tongue, 7

Naipaul, V. S., 106, 124
Neruda, Pablo, 1, 126, 181
  "Alturas de Macchu Picchu," 36, 43
  Canto general, 151
  casa-museo, 44–46
  "Colección nocturna," 51–54
  "El sueño de la tripulación," 52
  España en el corazón, 34, 54
  Memorias, 49, 52
  Residencia en la tierra, 31, 155
  "Significa sombras," 50
Nobel Prize, 15, 35, 113, 118, 126, 131, 167, 203

One Thousand and One Nights, 114, 153, 158, 161

Partition, 98–100, 103–105, 166
Paz, Octavio, 1, 124, 135, 137
  "¿Qué Nombra La Poesía?," 81–82
  "Al pintor Swaminathan," 74, 181
  "El balcón," 62
  "El laberinto de la soledad," 78
  "El Mausoleo de Humayún," 66–67
  El mono gramático, 62, 65
  "Exclamación," 135

"México: Olimpiada de 1968," 84
Piedra de sol, 81, 151
Qué Nombra La Poesía, 64
Sor Juana Ines de la Cruz: o, las trampas de la fé, 106
Topoemas, 65
Vislumbres de la India, 180–182
Peru, 128, 132
poetry, 14, 59, 60
  concrete, 65, 80, 84
  Urdu, 26
postcolonial, 2, 10, 22–24, 79
  canon, 9, 113
  epistemology, 183
  historiography, 107, 108–111
  literature, 153
  magical realism, 114
  write back, 7, 23, 69, 80, 90, 109, 116, 133
Pound, Ezra, 69, 80
Premchand, Munshi
  Shatranj ki khiladi, 102
  The Nature and Purpose of Literature, 122
prolepsis, 144, 150, 155
  foretelling, 151, 152, 154, 156, 163, 165, 166, 168, 173
  nostalgia, 91, 100, 155
  prophecy, 149, 166

realism, 122, 126–128, 202
  cryptorealist, 119, 122, 131, 139, 152
ruin, 96, 97, 100, 106, 183
Rushdie, Salman, 9, 20, 61
  "Commonwealth Literature Does Not Exist," 3, 14
  Midnight's Children, 114, 153–154
  Rushdie affair, 90
  Shame, 162–164, 204
  The Jaguar Smile, 39, 124–128
  The Moor's Last Sigh, 88–92
  Two Years, Eight Months, and Twenty-Eight Nights, 90

Said, Edward, 202
  Orientalism, 17, 48, 80, 198
  Reflections on Exile, 92
  world literature, 23
Shakespeare
  Caliban, 7, 133
  Othello, 90
Sheikh, Gulammohammed, 59, 67, 88
  Vrishchik, 76
Singh, Sunny, 138–140
Solanki, Tanuj, 185–186
Spivak, Gayatri, 110, 202
  "Can the Subaltern Speak?," 201
  epistemic violence, 120
  strategic essentialism, 6
Sundaram, Vivan, 35
Swaminathan, Jagdish, 59, 71
  CONTRA'66, 73

Tagore, Rabindranath, 55, 80, 126–128
Third World, 3, 19, 22, 69, 182, 185
tradition, 12, 70, 92–93
translation, 14, 34, 55, 71, 74, 75, 76, 81, 121, 133, 165, 167, 168, 175, 178, 182, 189
  born translated, 8, 17, 81, 174, 190

Urdu, 98–100, 165, 174, 185

Vargas Llosa, Mario, 27, 130–132
  La fiesta del chivo, 166, 171–172
  Vrishchik, 76–82

wonder, 3, 26, 120–121, 135
  magical realism, 119
world literature, 2, 3–6, 59, 74, 81, 178, 183, 185
  genre, 158, 183
  history, 118
  Innocence, 6, 85–87, 116, 142
  poetry, 80
  World Lite, 6, 72, 175, 190

Yeats, William Butler, 80, 126, 153

For EU product safety concerns, contact us at Calle de José Abascal, 56–1°, 28003 Madrid, Spain or eugpsr@cambridge.org.

www.ingramcontent.com/pod-product-compliance
Lightning Source LLC
LaVergne TN
LVHW041628060526
838200LV00040B/1482